THE NEW DINOSAUR ENCYCLOPEDIA

Clare Hibbert, Ben Hubbard,
Claudia Martin, and Liz Miles

ARCTURUS

Picture Credits:
Every attempt has been made to clear copyright. Should there be any inadvertent omission, please apply to the publisher for rectification.
Key: b–bottom, t–top, c–center, l–left, r–right

Alamy Stock Photo: 10–11 (Sylvia Buchholz/Reuters), 12–13, 220–221, 220cl (Sergey Krasovskiy/Stocktrek Images), 72–73 (Elena Duvernay/Stocktrek Images), 191br (Universal Images Group North America LLC/DeAgostini); **Stefano Azzalin:** 3tr, 4tl, 20tr, 20cr, 27bl, 63t, 74–75, 79t, 88c, 89tr, 107tl, 114cr, 116–117, 122–123, 127t, 143bl, 144c, 151tl, 164b, 176–177, 206–207, 206cr, 212bl, 216c, 218–219, 218cl, 222l, 239c, 239b, 242tl, 244; **Martin Bustamente:** 5tl, 46br, 64c, 83t, 92–93, 102br, 104–105, 114–115, 116c, 154l, 170–171, 174bl, 192c, 202–203, 202l, 204–205, 204c, 227cr, 236cr, 252tr; **Juan Calle:** 1, 19t, 66c, 67r, 68c, 75br, 146–147, 154–155, 236cl; **Mat Edwards:** profile box icons, 5br, 16–17, 18–19, 23tr, 24bl, 35cl, 39cr, 45br, 46–47, 49cl, 62–63, 64–65, 76bl, 82–83, 95cr, 99tr, 100–101, 102–103, 112–113, 118–119, 121cr, 121bc, 124–125, 126–127, 130–131, 132–133, 134–135, 136–137, 138–139, 140–141, 142–143, 148–149, 150–151, 150c, 152–153, 158–159, 160–161, 162bl, 163b, 164–165, 169cr, 174–175, 178–179, 181cr, 184–185, 186–187, 192–193, 194–195, 210bl, 211c, 215cr, 216–217, 228c, 232bl, 233b, 234cl, 246tr; **Rudolf Farkas:** 231, 241cr; **Colin Howard:** 21tr, 26cr, 240b, 250br; **Stuart Jackson-Carter:** 229c, 240tl; **Kunal Kundu:** 110–111, 144–145, 166–167, 212–213; **Liberum Donum:** 85tc, 230cr, 238br, 242b, 243b; **Jerry Pyke:** 21tr, 43c, 93bl, 110tr, 166b, 241cl; **Science Photo Library:** 10c (Gary Hincks), 14c (John Sibbick), 30–31, 86–87, 224–225 (James Kuether), 38–39, 56–57 (Mark Garlick), 55cr (Millard H. Sharp/Science Source), 58–59, 190–191, 200cr (Jaime Chirinos), 180–181 (Masato Hattori), 200–201 (Walter Myers), 221cr (Mark P. Witton); **Shutterstock:** 3tl, 16cl (Marques), 3bl, 43cr (Roni Setiawan), 3br, 9cr, 21tr, 60c, 71c, 86br, 96cl, 97cr, 117r, 156bl, 232c, 249tr (Herschel Hoffmeyer), 4tr, 6–7, 7cr, 15c, 21tcl, 48bl, 54–55, 90cr, 94–95, 96–97, 108–109, 139br, 152l, 162–163, 172–173, 180bl, 196–197, 210–211, 235tl, 245tl (Warpaint), 4bl, 40b, 43bc, 56cr, 66–67, 80–81, 81c, 87cr, 98c, 136bl, 247bl (Elenarts), 4br, 157tr (Ton Bangkeaw), 5tr, 6br, 45cl, 51bl, 53cr, 105t, 149br, 168–169, 172cr, 188–189, 188bl, 196cl, 208–209, 208cl, 214–215, 225cr, 249br (Michael Rosskothen), 6cr, 8–9, 14–15, 24–25, 32–23, 32tl, 36br, 40–41, 41cr, 44–45, 48–49, 50–51, 52–53, 54cl, 58bl, 59cr, 68–69, 70–71, 78–79, 90–91, 98–99, 120–121, 128–129, 129cr, 156–157, 198–199, 226br, 247tc, 248bl, 251tr (Daniel Eskridge), 8b (miha de), 9cl, 18c, 22–23, 25cr, 26–27, 28–29, 31tr, 32c, 34–35, 34c, 43br, 72cl, 74cr, 76–77, 78cl, 94cl, 105bl, 109cr, 168cl, 190cl, 198bl, 219t, 226tl, 237cr (Catmando), 11cr (releon8211), 12cr, 36–37, 42ccr, 84–85, 85cr, 199cr (Dotted Yeti), 13tl, 246b (Nicolas Primola), 17ct (nld), 17cb, 146cr, 184c, 250tl (Valentyna Chukhlyebova), 20br, 43bl, 80b (YuRi Photolife), 21tl, 234cr (Bee_acg), 21crb, 43cl (Liliya Butenko), 23b, 247tr (Alex Coan), 28cl (Filippo Vanzo), 29cr, 91br (DM7), 30cl (gorosan), 36cl (frantic00), 38c (Lukasz Pawel Szczepanski), 42cl (Diego Barucco), 42ccl (Designua), 42bc (Blue Bee), 43tl (NoPainNoGain), 51br (Noiel), 52cl (dcwcreations), 57cr (Natursports), 60–61, 189bl (Andreas Meyer), 61r, 226c, 238tr (ChastityQ), 62cr (Didier Descouens), 69c (Akkharat Jarusilawong), 70br, 197bc (Evgeniy Mahnyov), 72br (topimages), 77cr (Ryan M Bolton), 88–89 (Kostiantyn Ivanyshen), 106cr, 160cl, 251bl (Ozja), 108cl (Wlad74), 113t, 125t, 178b (Linda Bucklin), 115t (watthanachai), 118cr (cjchiker), 128cl (Martina Badini), 131r (CTR Photos), 134tr (Adwo), 173br, 252bl (Love Lego), 201tc (AuntSpray), 209br (Reimar), 214bl (Eugen Thome), 224cl (Danny Ye), 230br (Matis75), 237cl (Vac1), 245br (Nikolayenko Yekaterina); **Parwinder Singh:** 142b, 186b, 227bl, 253br; **Val Walerczuk:** 106–107, 159bl, 194l, 222–223; **Wikimedia Commons:** 5bl, 203r (Smart Destinations/Harvard Museum of Natural History), 47bl (Ghedoghedo), 65tr (Didier Descouens/Peabody Museum of Natural History), 82b (Kevmin/Burke Museum/Museum of the Rockies), 92l (Funk Monk/Lindsay E Zanno), 103cr (Funk Monk/philosophygeek), 110c (Gastón Cuello/Museo Paleontológico Egidio Feruglio), 112c (CaptMondo/Royal Ontario Museum), 119cr (D Gordon and E Robertson/Royal Ontario Museum), 122c, 250tr (Carol Abraczinskas, Paul C Sereno/ZooKeys), 122br (Daderot/University of California Museum of Paleontology), 125bl (Joseph Smit/biodiversitylibrary.org), 127cr (Aimé Rutot), 132cr (FunkMonk), 134bl (William Diller Matthew), 138c (Conty and Ballista/Oxford University Museum), 140l (UNC Sea Grant College Program), 141t (Tim Evanson/Museum of the Rockies), 144bl (Daderot/Naturmuseum Senckenberg), 147br (Kumiko), 148bl (Christophe Hendrickx/American Museum of Natural History), 153 (Tim Evanson/Museum of the Rockies), 155t (American Museum of Natural History), 158l (Eduard Solà/Royal Belgian Institute of Natural Sciences), 160br (John R Horner and Mark B Goodwin), 164tr (Dmitry Bogdanov/FunkMonk), 167tr (Joseph Dinkel), 171t (Drow Male/Natural History Museum, London), 175br (H Zell/Natural History Museum, Berlin), 176cr (Mariana Ruiz Lady of Hats), 178cr (Ryan Somma), 182c (JT Csotonyi), 183tr (Eden, Janine, and Jim, NYC), 185t (Victoria M Arbour and Philip J Currie/American Museum of Natural History), 192br (Ra'ike/Museum am Löwentor, Stuttgart), 195br (Daderot/Royal Ontario Museum), 205c (Tai Kubo, Mark T Mitchell, and Donald M Henderson/Smokeybjb), 207br (Ghedoghedo/Royal Belgian Institute of Natural Sciences), 212tr (James Erxleben/British Museum), 217cl (Ghedoghedo/Museo di Storia Naturale di Verona), 223r (Régine Debatty). All additional profile box icons and design elements by Shutterstock.
Front cover: Shutterstock: c, cl, cr, tr, (Warpaint), tl (Daniel Eskridge), bl velociraptor (MattLPhotography).
Back cover: Shutterstock: cl (Michael Rosskothen), cr, c, bl, br (Mat Edwards). **All cover illustrations by Paul Oakley.**

In this book, one billion means one thousand million (1,000,000,000) and one trillion means one million million (1,000,000,000,000).

ARCTURUS

This edition published in 2023 by Arcturus Publishing Limited
26/27 Bickels Yard, 151–153 Bermondsey Street, London SE1 3HA

Copyright © Arcturus Holdings Limited

Authors: Clare Hibbert, Ben Hubbard, Claudia Martin, and Liz Miles
Design: Top Floor Design Ltd, Lorraine Inglis, and Amy McSimpson
Front cover design: Paul Oakley
Editors: Claudia Martin, Lydia Halliday
Managing Editor: Joe Harris

ISBN: 978-1-3988-9179-1
CH010985NT
Supplier 29, Date 0423, PI 00002673

Printed in Guangdong, China

1st printing

Contents

Introduction

Millions of years ago, reptiles called dinosaurs walked the Earth. Today's reptiles include lizards and crocodiles, but dinosaurs were larger, fiercer, or stranger than any reptile alive today. Find out about the amazing dinosaurs, from *Tyrannosaurus* to *Diplodocus*, as you read this book.

Meat-Eating Dinosaurs

Little meat-eating dinosaurs chased insects, lizards, or frogs. Big meat-eaters used sharp teeth and claws to kill other dinosaurs, fish, or mammals.

The Asian dinosaur *Ichthyovenator* ate fish and flying reptiles.

Acrocanthosaurus was a meat-eating dinosaur 11 m (36 ft) long.

Plant-Eating Dinosaurs

Plant-eaters fed on leaves, fruits, or nuts. Every plant-eater needed to escape the jaws of meat-eaters. Some ran away fast, while others were too big or spiky to be eaten.

Gigantspinosaurus had long spikes on its shoulders, which made it hard to capture.

Its upper jaw held 38 long, jagged-edged teeth suited to ripping through flesh.

Like all dinosaurs, *Acrocanthosaurus* had four limbs. Its back legs could be held directly underneath its body, unlike those of a lizard or crocodile.

Flying reptiles had wings up to 11 m (36 ft) wide.

Flying and Swimming Reptiles

While dinosaurs stomped or scampered across the land, other reptiles flew through the air on wide wings. In the oceans, swimming reptiles snapped up fish, squid, or each other.

Chapter 1

The Age of Dinosaurs

The first dinosaurs lived 233 million years ago. Over millions of years, around 1,000 species of dinosaurs walked our planet. A species is a group of animals that look very similar to each other. By approximately 66 million years ago, all the dinosaurs were gone.

The dinosaur *Altirhinus* lived between 107 and 100 million years ago.

Changing Earth

Earth's surface is made of giant plates of rock, known as tectonic plates, that move slowly on the melted rock that lies beneath them. On average, the plates move by 3 to 5 cm (1.2 to 2 in) a year. Yet, over many millions of years, these moving plates have changed the shape of the continents.

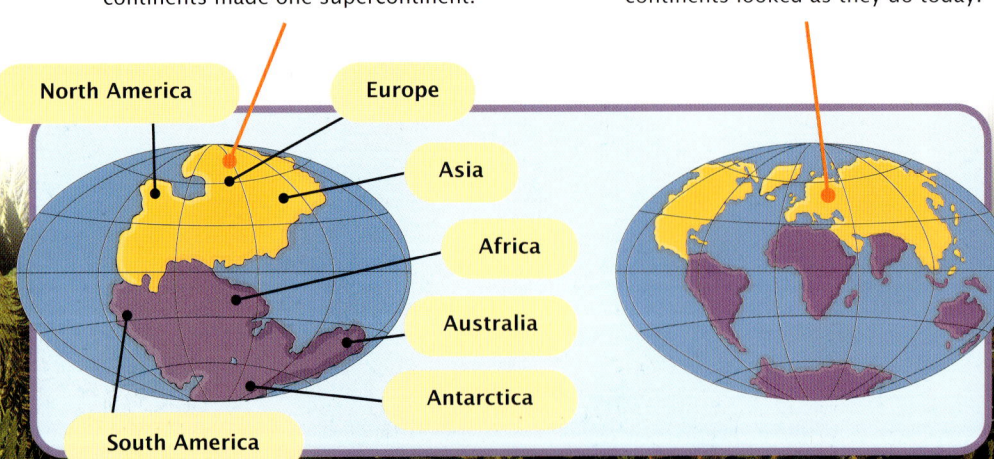

When the first dinosaurs were alive, all the continents made one supercontinent.

By 5 million years ago, Earth's continents looked as they do today.

North America

Europe

Asia

Africa

Australia

Antarctica

South America

Changing Dinosaurs

Over millions of years, all living things change, for example, growing bigger, smaller, toothier, or hairier. This slow change is called evolution. While new dinosaur species evolved, others died out. Evolution depends on the fact that parents can pass on their characteristics—such as tooth shape—to their babies. Useful characteristics, such as bigger teeth, give an individual a better chance of surviving long enough to reproduce. This means that useful characteristics stand a better chance of being passed on to the next generation, so they become more widespread.

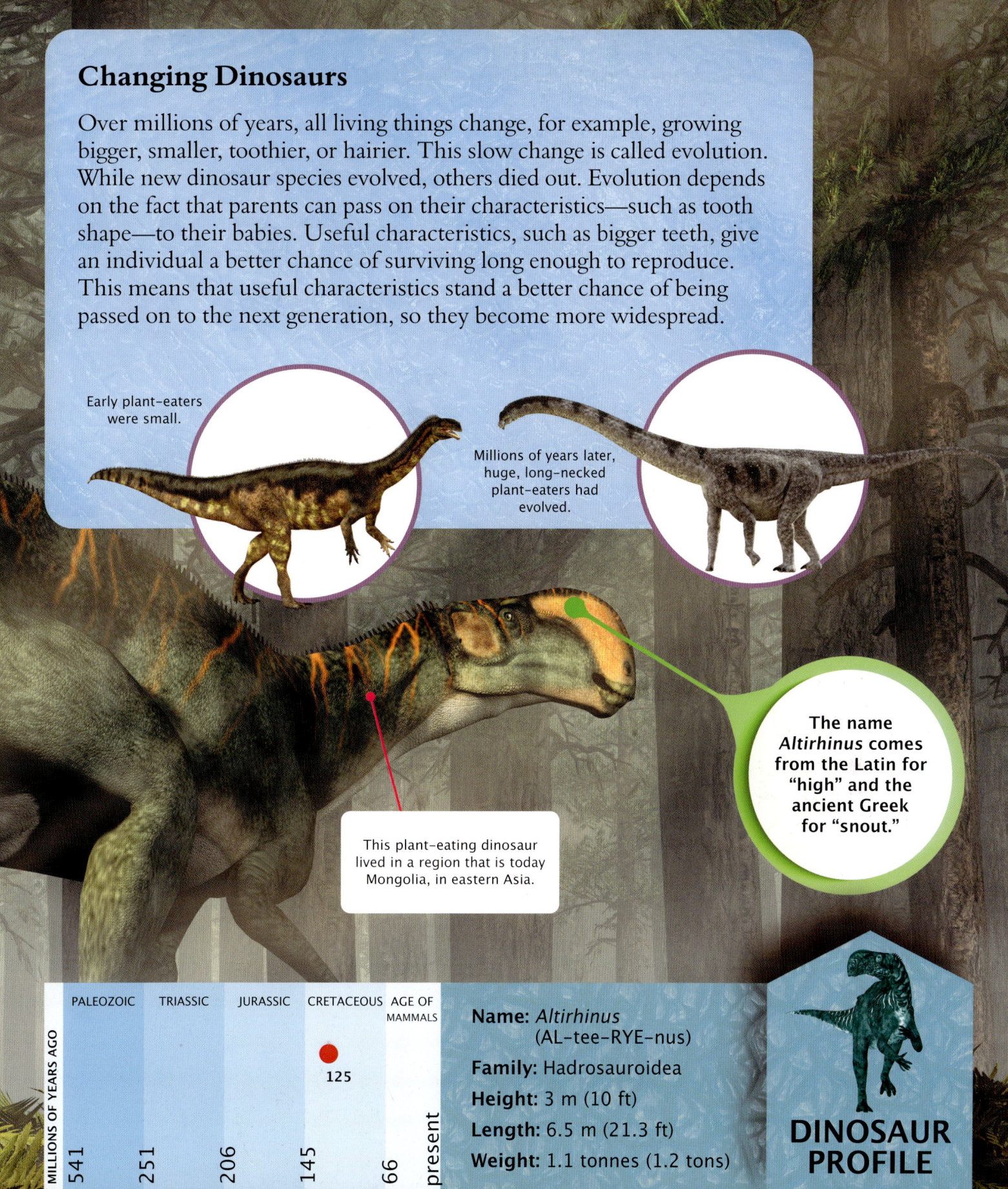

Early plant-eaters were small.

Millions of years later, huge, long-necked plant-eaters had evolved.

The name *Altirhinus* comes from the Latin for "high" and the ancient Greek for "snout."

This plant-eating dinosaur lived in a region that is today Mongolia, in eastern Asia.

	PALEOZOIC	TRIASSIC	JURASSIC	CRETACEOUS	AGE OF MAMMALS

MILLIONS OF YEARS AGO

541 251 206 145 66 present

125

Name: *Altirhinus* (AL-tee-RYE-nus)
Family: Hadrosauroidea
Height: 3 m (10 ft)
Length: 6.5 m (21.3 ft)
Weight: 1.1 tonnes (1.2 tons)

DINOSAUR PROFILE

DID YOU KNOW? *Altirhinus*'s large nose may have housed sensitive tissues that improved its sense of smell, helping it sense approaching predators.

Finding Fossils

We know about dinosaurs because of fossils. Fossils are the remains of animals and plants that died long ago. We can study a fossil to find out the size and shape of the animal. The place where we find a fossil tells us where the animal lived.

Making Fossils

When an animal dies, its body usually rots. However, a fossil can form if the body is quickly covered with sand or mud. Even then, the animal's soft parts, such as flesh, muscles, and feathers, usually rot, leaving behind the bones, teeth, and shells. Very slowly, the sand or mud around the skeleton hardens into rock. Water seeps into the bones, teeth, and shells, dissolving them. Yet minerals in the water fill the space left behind, creating a rock copy.

Scientists who study fossils, known as paleontologists, carefully uncover fossils, then piece together how a dinosaur may have looked.

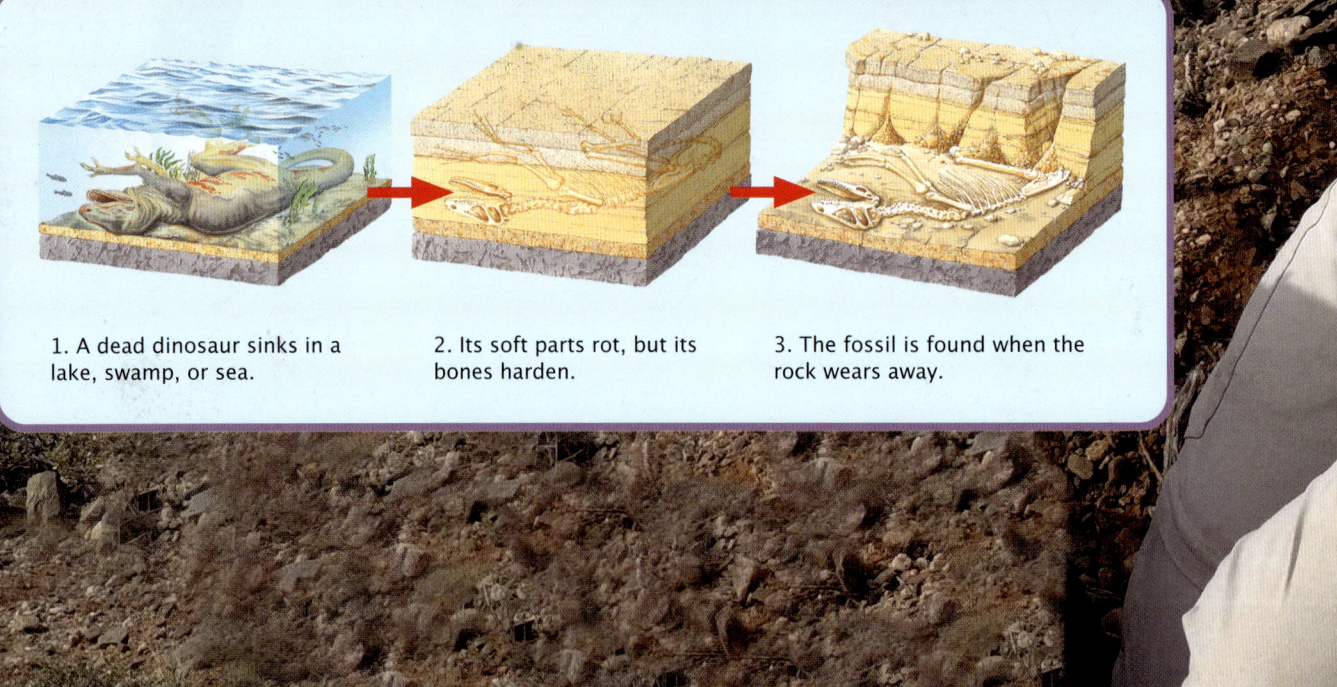

1. A dead dinosaur sinks in a lake, swamp, or sea.

2. Its soft parts rot, but its bones harden.

3. The fossil is found when the rock wears away.

DID YOU KNOW? *Ingentia's* full name, *Ingentia prima*, means "first huge one," as it was one of the very first large plant-eaters to evolve.

210

Name: *Ingentia* (In–JEN–tee–uh)
Family: Lessemsauridae
Height: 4.3 m (14 ft)
Length: 8.5 m (28 ft)
Weight: 10 tonnes (11 tons)

DINOSAUR PROFILE

The size and distance between a dinosaur's footprints tell us how big its feet and legs were.

Leaving Clues

Not all fossils are of bodies. Footprints and burrows can be fossilized if they are baked hard by the Sun, and then covered by sand and mud. We can also find dinosaurs' eggs, nests, and poop. These fossils are known as trace fossils because they are the trace of a long-dead animal, rather than the animal itself.

This fossil belongs to a meat–eating dinosaur named *Ingentia*.

By studying the layers of rock where a fossil is found, paleontologists can work out how long ago the dinosaur lived.

11

Life in Water

Our planet formed 4.5 billion years ago. For a long time, there was no life on Earth. Then, 3.5 billion years ago, tiny, simple living things appeared in the oceans. Every animal or plant that ever lived—from dinosaurs to humans and trees—evolved from those tiny things.

Earliest Animals

The earliest living things were not animals: They were tiny, basic life forms called microorganisms. The earliest known animals evolved around 665 million years ago. Animals can move, eat other living things, and need oxygen to survive. The earliest animals were soft bodied, without shells or backbones. They absorbed oxygen from the water.

By around 500 million years ago, there were many different animals in the oceans.

	PALEOZOIC	TRIASSIC	JURASSIC	CRETACEOUS	AGE OF MAMMALS	
MILLIONS OF YEARS AGO	306					present
	541	251	206	145	66	

Name: *Diplocaulus*
(Dip-loh-COWL-us)

Family: Diplocaulidae

Height: 0.3 m (1 ft)

Length: 1 m (3.3 ft)

Weight: 4.5 kg (10 lb)

AMPHIBIAN PROFILE

DID YOU KNOW? Around 540 million years ago, some animals started to grow shells, which may have been useful for protection.

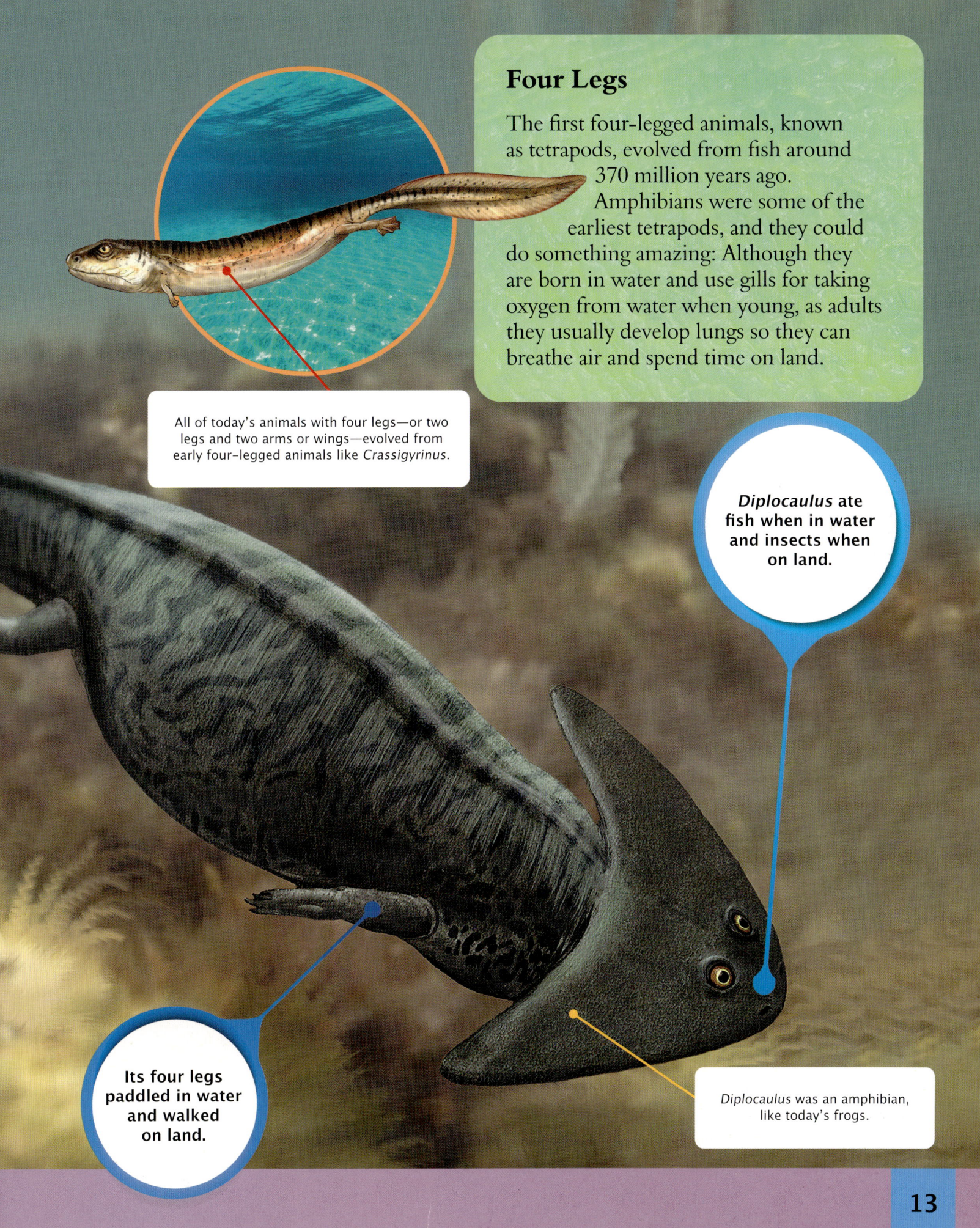

Four Legs

The first four-legged animals, known as tetrapods, evolved from fish around 370 million years ago. Amphibians were some of the earliest tetrapods, and they could do something amazing: Although they are born in water and use gills for taking oxygen from water when young, as adults they usually develop lungs so they can breathe air and spend time on land.

All of today's animals with four legs—or two legs and two arms or wings—evolved from early four-legged animals like *Crassigyrinus*.

Diplocaulus ate fish when in water and insects when on land.

Its four legs paddled in water and walked on land.

Diplocaulus was an amphibian, like today's frogs.

First Reptiles

Reptiles were the first four-legged animals to spend all their time on land. The earliest reptiles lived 312 million years ago. Over many millions of years, early reptiles evolved into dinosaurs, lizards, snakes, crocodiles, and turtles.

Suited to Land

Reptiles evolved from amphibians. Yet while amphibians needed to stay close to water, reptiles were suited to land. Amphibians had thin skin that had to be kept damp, but reptiles had scaly skin. Amphibians laid soft eggs in water, but reptiles laid eggs with shells that did not dry out on land.

Just 25 cm (10 in) long, *Hylonomus* was the earliest known reptile.

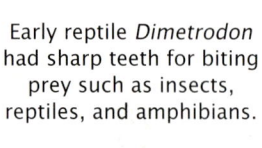

Early reptile *Dimetrodon* had sharp teeth for biting prey such as insects, reptiles, and amphibians.

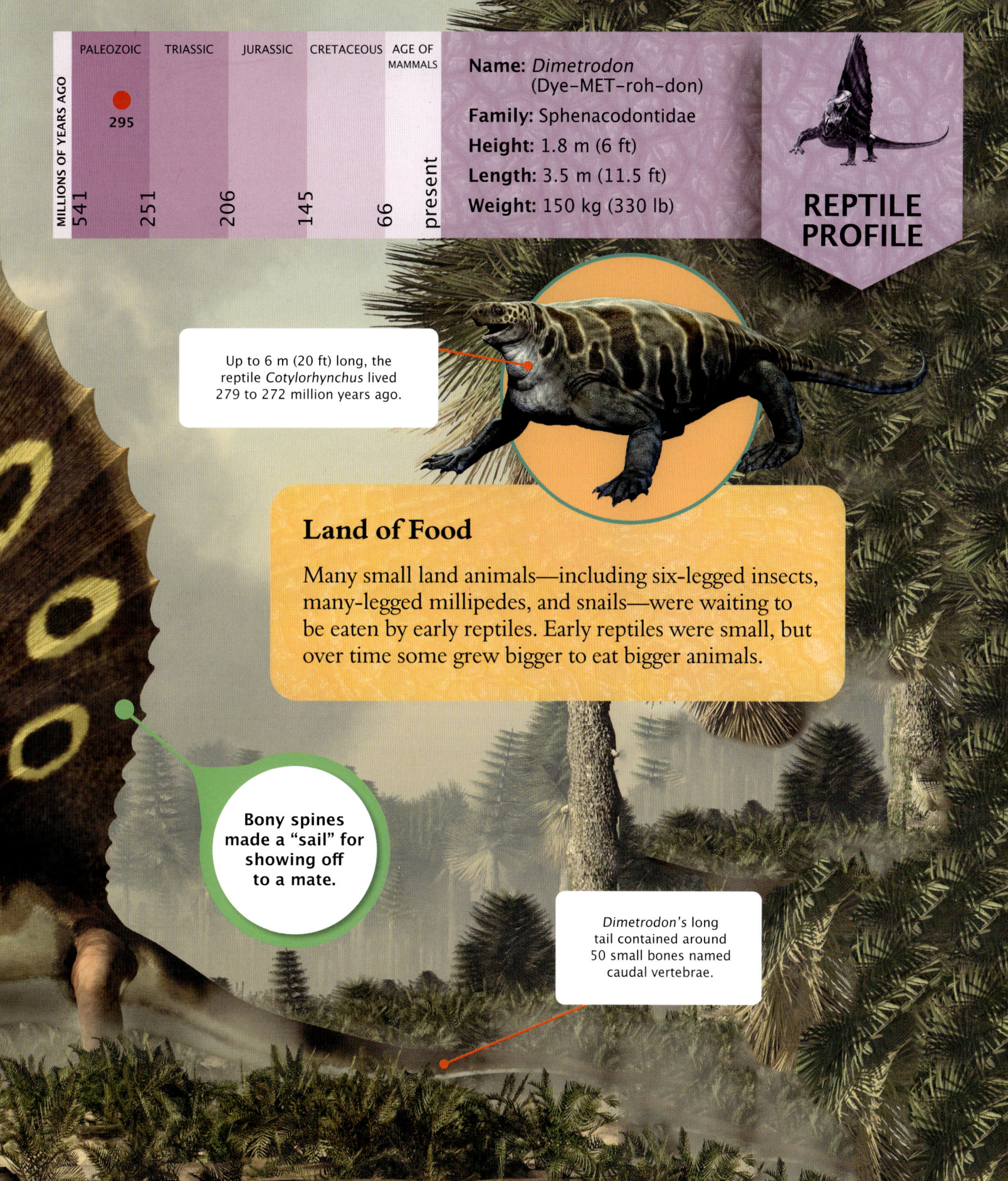

	PALEOZOIC	TRIASSIC	JURASSIC	CRETACEOUS	AGE OF MAMMALS	

MILLIONS OF YEARS AGO

295

541 251 206 145 66 present

Name: *Dimetrodon* (Dye–MET–roh–don)
Family: Sphenacodontidae
Height: 1.8 m (6 ft)
Length: 3.5 m (11.5 ft)
Weight: 150 kg (330 lb)

REPTILE PROFILE

Up to 6 m (20 ft) long, the reptile *Cotylorhynchus* lived 279 to 272 million years ago.

Land of Food

Many small land animals—including six-legged insects, many-legged millipedes, and snails—were waiting to be eaten by early reptiles. Early reptiles were small, but over time some grew bigger to eat bigger animals.

Bony spines made a "sail" for showing off to a mate.

Dimetrodon's long tail contained around 50 small bones named caudal vertebrae.

DID YOU KNOW? *Dimetrodon* may be more closely related to modern mammals than it is to modern reptiles.

15

Different Dinosaurs

Dinosaurs were a group of reptiles that evolved around 233 million years ago. Their skeletons had important differences from the bones of other reptiles. These differences gave dinosaurs advantages that made them very successful for millions of years.

Archosaur Advantages

Dinosaurs were a member of the archosaur, or "ruling reptiles," group of reptiles, which evolved around 250 million years ago. Archosaurs also included crocodiles and pterosaurs, which were flying reptiles. Archosaurs had an advantage over other reptiles: Their teeth were set deep into sockets, making them less likely to be torn out during feeding. They also had extraopenings in their skulls, making them even more lightweight.

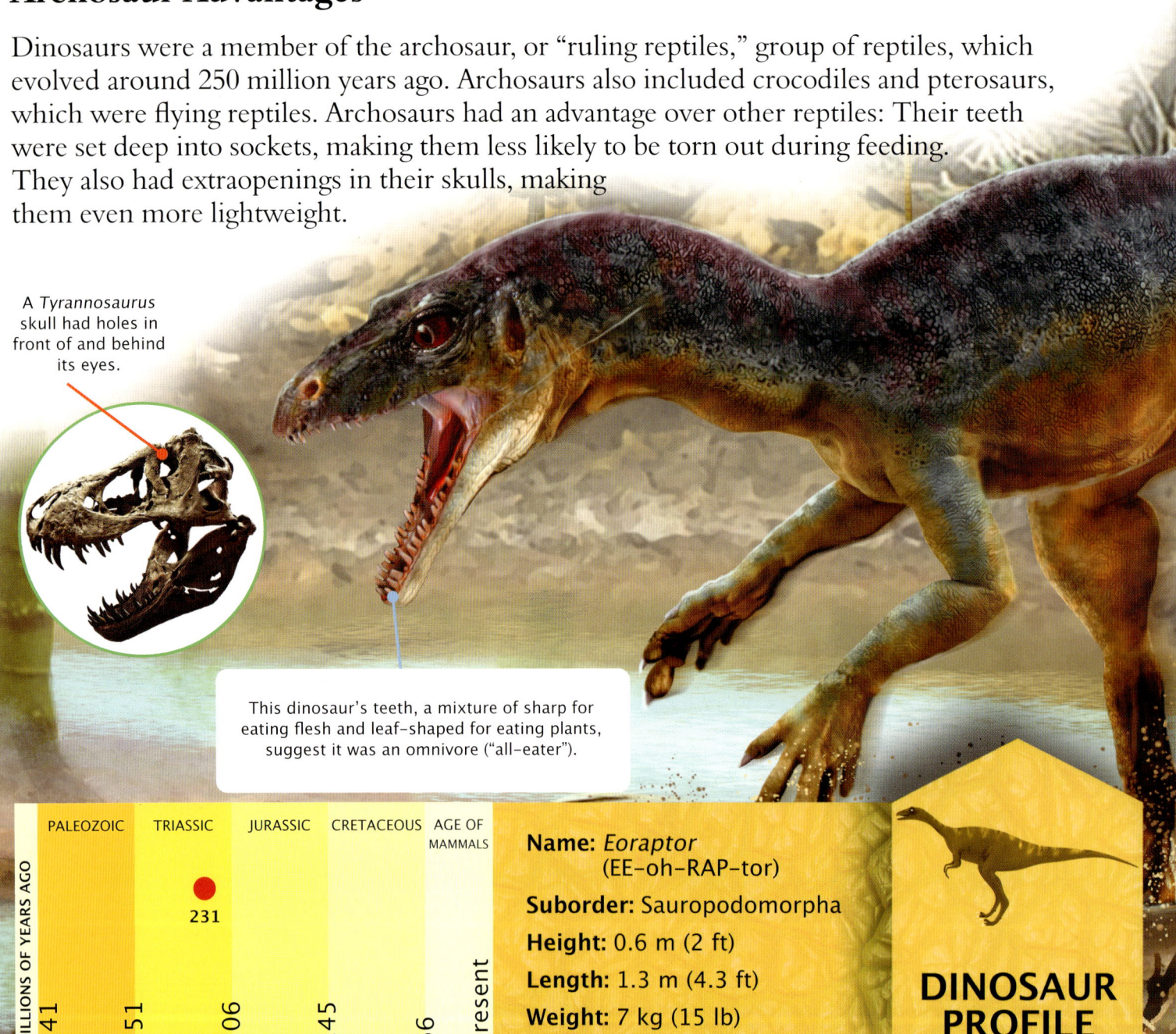

A *Tyrannosaurus* skull had holes in front of and behind its eyes.

This dinosaur's teeth, a mixture of sharp for eating flesh and leaf-shaped for eating plants, suggest it was an omnivore ("all-eater").

MILLIONS OF YEARS AGO	PALEOZOIC	TRIASSIC	JURASSIC	CRETACEOUS	AGE OF MAMMALS	
	541	251	206	145	66	present

231

Name: *Eoraptor*
(EE-oh-RAP-tor)

Suborder: Sauropodomorpha

Height: 0.6 m (2 ft)

Length: 1.3 m (4.3 ft)

Weight: 7 kg (15 lb)

DINOSAUR PROFILE

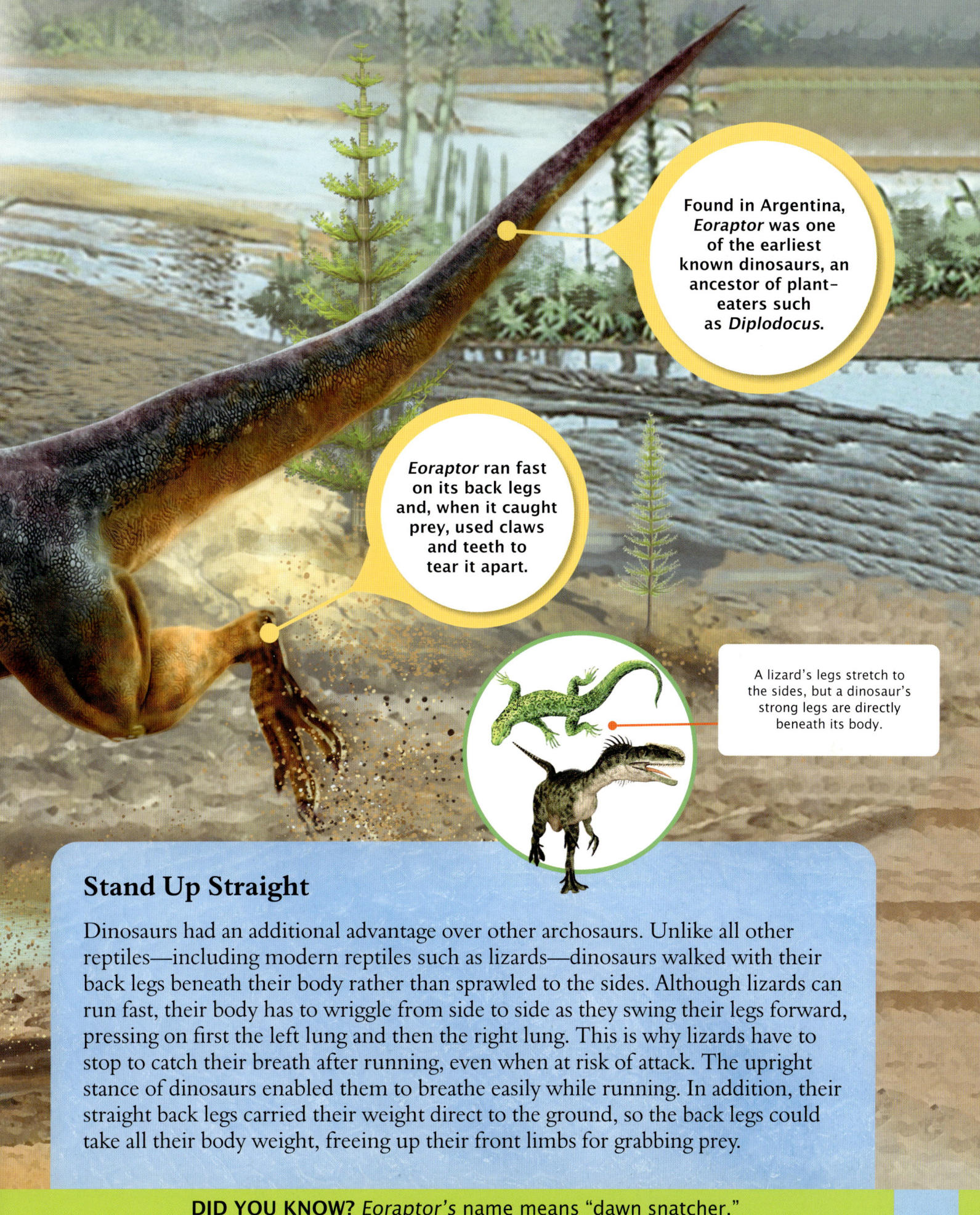

Found in Argentina, *Eoraptor* was one of the earliest known dinosaurs, an ancestor of plant-eaters such as *Diplodocus*.

Eoraptor ran fast on its back legs and, when it caught prey, used claws and teeth to tear it apart.

A lizard's legs stretch to the sides, but a dinosaur's strong legs are directly beneath its body.

Stand Up Straight

Dinosaurs had an additional advantage over other archosaurs. Unlike all other reptiles—including modern reptiles such as lizards—dinosaurs walked with their back legs beneath their body rather than sprawled to the sides. Although lizards can run fast, their body has to wriggle from side to side as they swing their legs forward, pressing on first the left lung and then the right lung. This is why lizards have to stop to catch their breath after running, even when at risk of attack. The upright stance of dinosaurs enabled them to breathe easily while running. In addition, their straight back legs carried their weight direct to the ground, so the back legs could take all their body weight, freeing up their front limbs for grabbing prey.

DID YOU KNOW? *Eoraptor's* name means "dawn snatcher," referring both to its early evolution and its sharp claws and teeth.

Dinosaur Times

The dinosaurs lived during the Mesozoic Era, which was broken into three shorter ages: the Triassic, Jurassic, and Cretaceous Periods. The dinosaurs appeared around 233 million years ago, during the Late Triassic Period. At the end of the Cretaceous Period, they became extinct.

Climate change led to the extinction of many groups of animals at the end of the Triassic Period, including the aetosaur reptiles, which were protected by bony plates.

Dividing Time

Scientists divide the history of Earth into periods of time called—from longest to shortest—eons (or aeons), eras, periods, and epochs. The beginnings and ends of these time periods are marked by major events, such as big steps forward in evolution, or catastrophes that caused widespread extinction. Scientists learned about such events by studying rocks and fossils.

During the warm Cretaceous Period, sea levels were high, so shallow seas covered much of the continents.

During the Cretaceous Period, a high number of volcanic eruptions released a lot of carbon dioxide gas, which traps the Sun's heat around Earth.

Three Periods

During the Age of Dinosaurs, the shapes of the continents, the climate, and the depths of the oceans went through constant, but extremely slow, changes:

During the **Triassic Period** (251–206 million years ago), Earth's continents were joined together in a large landmass called Pangea. Pangea had a hot, dry desert in the middle. Near the coastal regions, new animal life and the first forests appeared.

During the **Jurassic Period** (206–145 million years ago), Pangea divided into two huge continents. New oceans and waterways began to form, and there was more oxygen in the atmosphere. Many forms of plant and animal life evolved at this time.

In the **Cretaceous Period** (145–66 million years ago), the continents split into smaller continents, similar to those we have today. Flowering plants, such as daisies and fruit trees, appeared. Dinosaurs were the dominant land animals.

Plant–eaters such as *Kritosaurus* had evolved to be large to reach more food, while meat–eaters such as *Tyrannosaurus* had evolved to be even larger in order to prey on them.

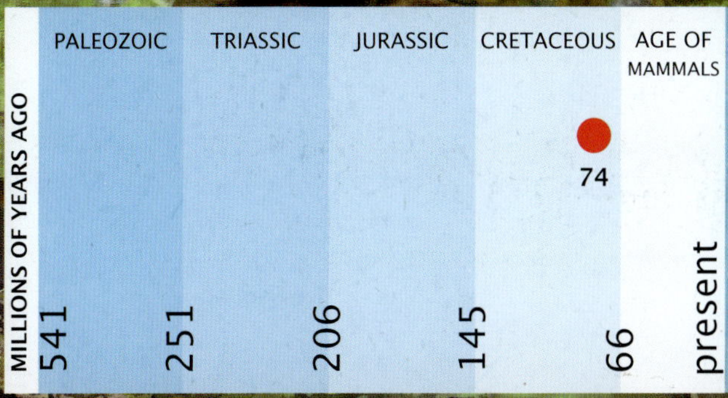

MILLIONS OF YEARS AGO	PALEOZOIC	TRIASSIC	JURASSIC	CRETACEOUS	AGE OF MAMMALS
	541	251	206	145	66 — present

74

Name: *Kritosaurus* (KRIT-oh-SAWR-us)

Family: Hadrosauridae

Height: 3 m (9.8 ft)

Length: 9 m (29.5 ft)

Weight: 4 tonnes (4.4 tons)

DINOSAUR PROFILE

DID YOU KNOW? During the Triassic Period, the Earth was spinning faster than it does today, so one day was only 23 hours long.

Dinosaur Groups

Paleontologists divide dinosaurs into groups based on similarities between their skeletons, teeth, and bony plates. Similar dinosaurs are placed in the same species. Where species share key characteristics, they are grouped into a family, and then larger groups such as classes. For example, *Tyrannosaurus* is a species in the Tyrannosauridae family of large meat-eaters, in the archosaur class.

Two Groups

Paleontologists often divide dinosaurs into two major groups, called orders, based on their hip types: ornithischians and saurischians. The ornithischians, or "bird-hipped" dinosaurs, were plant-eaters. They were named for their hips' similarity to those of birds, but ornithischians were not closely related to birds, which actually evolved from saurischian dinosaurs. The saurischians, or "lizard-hipped" dinosaurs, included both meat-eaters and plant-eaters.

Ceratopsians had horns as well as strong beaks for eating plants.

Ceratopsians

These winged reptiles had long, slim jaws.

Pterosaurs

The pubis bone pointed backward, below the ischium bone.

Ornithischian hips

The ischium formed the lower, back part of the hip bone.

Pseudosuchians had large skulls and long, narrow snouts.

Pseudosuchians

Saurischian hips

The pubis bone pointed away from the ischium bone.

Archosaur Family Tree

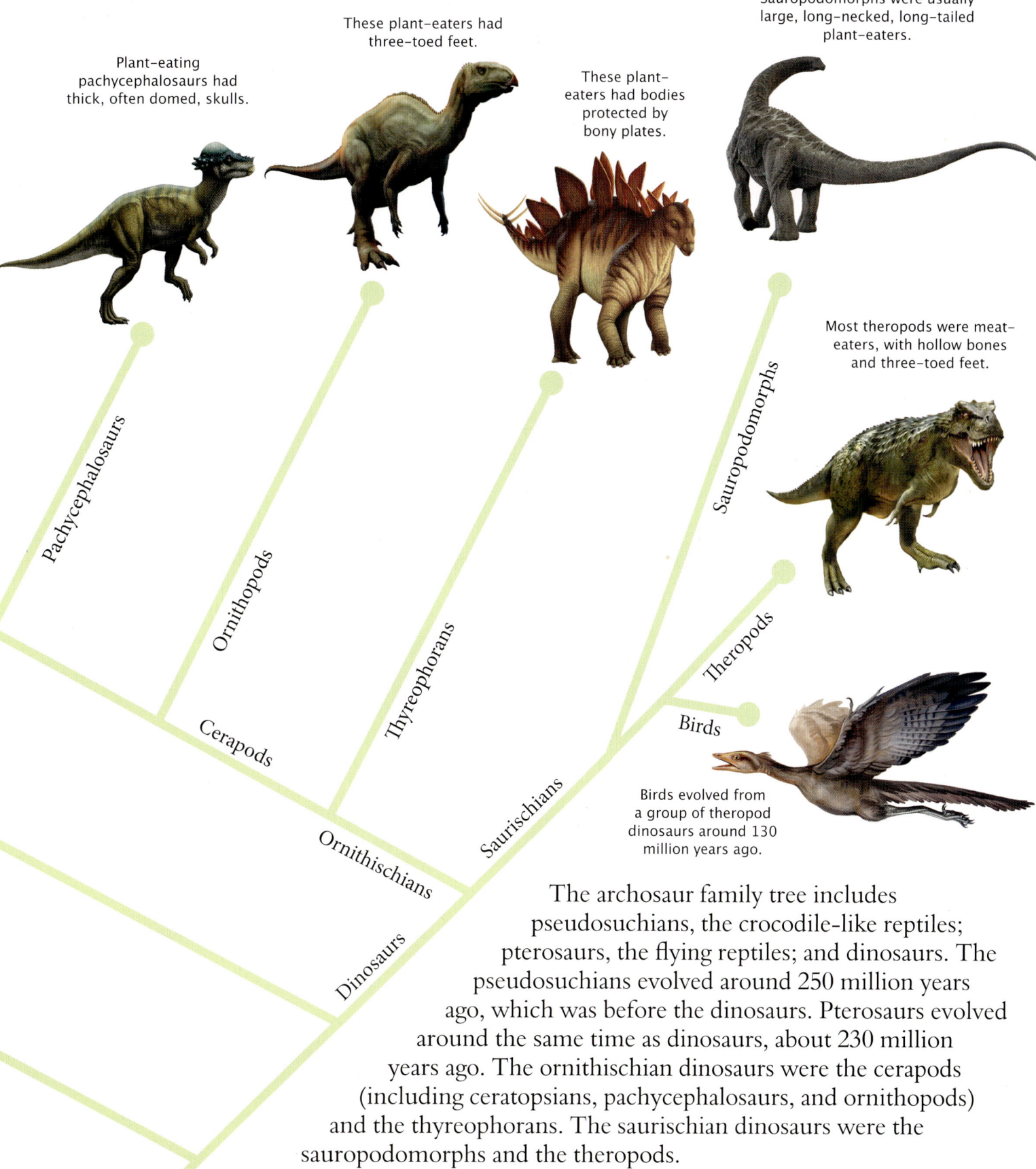

Plant-eating pachycephalosaurs had thick, often domed, skulls.

These plant-eaters had three-toed feet.

These plant-eaters had bodies protected by bony plates.

Sauropodomorphs were usually large, long-necked, long-tailed plant-eaters.

Most theropods were meat-eaters, with hollow bones and three-toed feet.

Birds evolved from a group of theropod dinosaurs around 130 million years ago.

Pachycephalosaurs

Ornithopods

Thyreophorans

Sauropodomorphs

Theropods

Birds

Cerapods

Ornithischians

Saurischians

Dinosaurs

The archosaur family tree includes pseudosuchians, the crocodile-like reptiles; pterosaurs, the flying reptiles; and dinosaurs. The pseudosuchians evolved around 250 million years ago, which was before the dinosaurs. Pterosaurs evolved around the same time as dinosaurs, about 230 million years ago. The ornithischian dinosaurs were the cerapods (including ceratopsians, pachycephalosaurs, and ornithopods) and the thyreophorans. The saurischian dinosaurs were the sauropodomorphs and the theropods.

DID YOU KNOW? Dinosaur classification began in 1842 when English paleontologist Richard Owen proposed a new "tribe or suborder" named Dinosauria ("terrible lizards").

Diets

The earliest dinosaurs were meat-eaters (carnivores), which ate all kinds of animals. Over millions of years, some dinosaurs became plant-eaters (herbivores) or ate whatever they found (omnivores). Around two-thirds of all dinosaurs were plant-eaters. Today, there are still fewer meat-eating animals than plant-eaters, as well as fewer plant-eaters than plants, so there is enough food to go around.

This dinosaur's robust skull and strong teeth suggest it ate coarser plant material than more slender-toothed herbivores.

Plant-eaters had larger stomachs than meat-eaters, as they had to eat lots of plants to get enough energy.

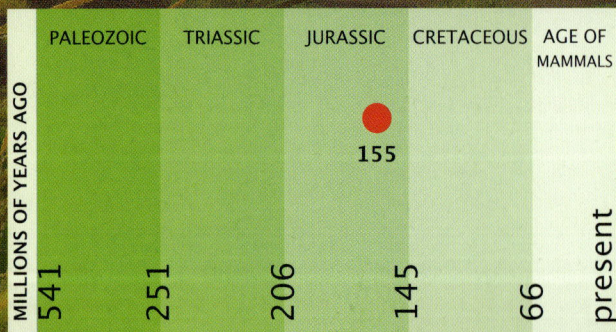

MILLIONS OF YEARS AGO	PALEOZOIC	TRIASSIC	JURASSIC	CRETACEOUS	AGE OF MAMMALS	present
	541	251	206	145	66	

155

Name: *Camarasaurus* (CAM-er-uh-SAWR-us)

Family: Camarasauridae

Height: 8.5 m (28 ft)

Length: 19 m (62 ft)

Weight: 20 tonnes (22 tons)

DINOSAUR PROFILE

DID YOU KNOW? Some plant-eaters swallowed stones, known as gastroliths, to help grind the tough food in their stomach.

Looking at Teeth

Paleontologists have compared dinosaur teeth and jaws with those of modern animals, such as meat-eating lions and plant-eating deer. They believe that animals with similar-shaped teeth have similar diets. Like lions, carnivorous dinosaurs had large, strong jaws and sharp teeth. Like modern plant-eaters, herbivorous dinosaurs had teeth suited to the particular plants they ate, whether they were soft-leaved or tough-stemmed. Some dinosaurs had no teeth, so they probably used their hard, beak-like jaws to crop plants or seize small animals.

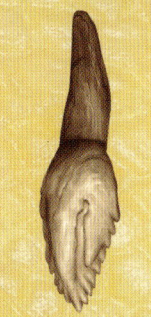

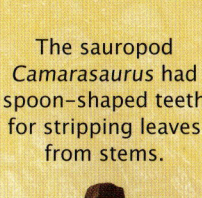

The sauropod *Camarasaurus* had spoon-shaped teeth for stripping leaves from stems.

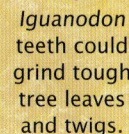

The sauropod *Rebbachisaurus* had leaf-shaped teeth for chewing soft plants such as ferns.

Iguanodon teeth could grind tough tree leaves and twigs.

Camarasaurus was a herbivorous dinosaur that lived in swampy lowlands of North America.

Studying Stomachs ... and Poop

A few fossilized dinosaur stomachs have been found. These can tell us exactly what a dinosaur ate, as well as whether it chewed its food or swallowed it whole. Fossilized poops, called coprolites, also contain fragments of what dinosaurs ate. It is not easy to match a coprolite to the dinosaur that created it, but coprolite size, shape, and location can give us clues.

Dinosaur coprolites may contain seeds, leaves, bark, or pieces of bone.

23

Scales and Feathers

The skin of early dinosaurs was covered by scales to protect it from damage. A few million years later, some meat-eating dinosaurs started to grow feathers. Scales and feathers are made of keratin, the same hard material that is in human hair and nails. Some dinosaurs had bigger, harder coverings called scutes.

Strong Scales and Scutes

Scales are small, hard, often overlapping plates that grow from the top layer of skin. Dinosaurs had smaller scales on body parts that needed to move easily, such as legs, and larger scales on areas, such as the soles of the feet, that got more wear. Scutes grow from deeper in the skin than scales. They are bony plates with keratin, also known as horn, over the surface of the skin. While most scutes lay flat on a dinosaur's body, others grew high or sharp so they stuck out as plates and spikes.

Small scales covered the skin where there were no scutes.

Bumpy scutes protected *Minotaurasaurus*'s snout.

We do not know the shade of *Citipati*'s feathers, but tests on other feathered dinosaur fossils suggest that, while some were brown, black, or green, others were brightly patterned.

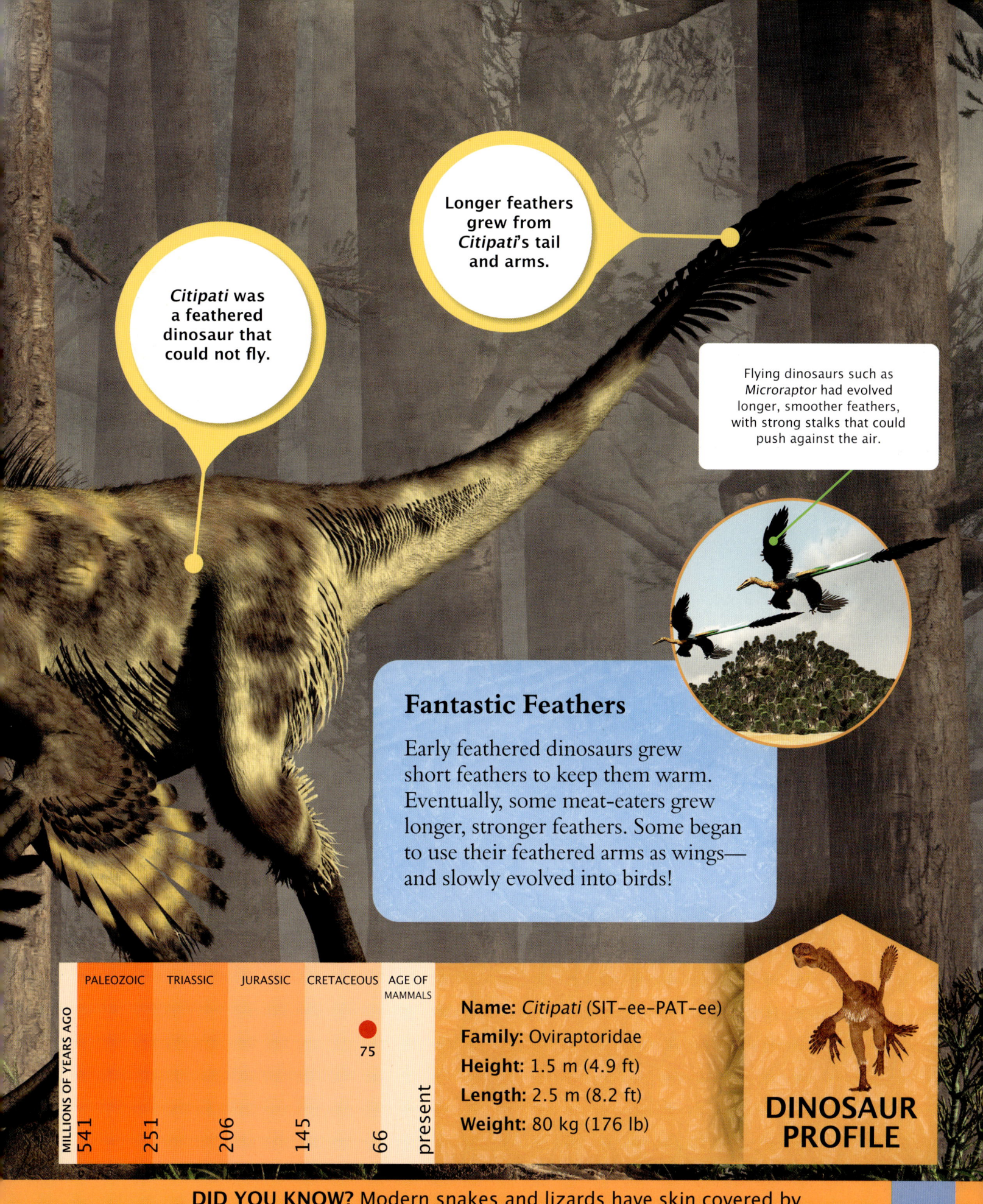

Citipati was a feathered dinosaur that could not fly.

Longer feathers grew from *Citipati*'s tail and arms.

Flying dinosaurs such as *Microraptor* had evolved longer, smoother feathers, with strong stalks that could push against the air.

Fantastic Feathers

Early feathered dinosaurs grew short feathers to keep them warm. Eventually, some meat-eaters grew longer, stronger feathers. Some began to use their feathered arms as wings— and slowly evolved into birds!

MILLIONS OF YEARS AGO	PALEOZOIC	TRIASSIC	JURASSIC	CRETACEOUS	AGE OF MAMMALS
	541	251	206	145	66 present

75

Name: *Citipati* (SIT-ee-PAT-ee)
Family: Oviraptoridae
Height: 1.5 m (4.9 ft)
Length: 2.5 m (8.2 ft)
Weight: 80 kg (176 lb)

DINOSAUR PROFILE

DID YOU KNOW? Modern snakes and lizards have skin covered by overlapping scales, while turtles and crocodiles also have scutes.

Senses

The senses of sight, smell, and hearing were important for dinosaurs, enabling them to find food, escape predators, and get a mate. Paleontologists can learn about these senses by studying the shape of dinosaurs' skull bones, such as the eye sockets. Less is known about dinosaurs' senses of taste and touch, because tongues and nerves have not been fossilized.

Dinosaurs had small ear holes that were probably not surrounded by fleshy outer ears like those of humans or dogs.

Carnivores vs. Herbivores

There were important differences between the senses of meat-eaters and plant-eaters. Meat-eaters had big, forward-facing eyes that helped them see prey. Having two forward-facing eyes enables the eyes to work together to judge how far away prey is, as well as how fast it is moving. In contrast, plant-eaters often had smaller eyes, which were positioned on the sides of their head, so they could watch all around for approaching predators. Some meat-eaters, including tyrannosaurs, also had better senses of smell than plant-eaters, so they could sniff out prey.

Like other meat-eaters, *Tyrannosaurus* had forward-facing eyes, which could probably see prey up to 6 km (3.7 miles) away.

	PALEOZOIC	TRIASSIC	JURASSIC	CRETACEOUS	AGE OF MAMMALS
MILLIONS OF YEARS AGO	541	251	206	145	66 present

75

Name: *Bistahieversor* (Bis-tah-HEE-ay-ver-suh)

Superfamily: Tyrannosauroidea

Height: 3 m (9.8 ft)

Length: 8 m (26.2 ft)

Weight: 2.5 tonnes (2.8 tons)

DINOSAUR PROFILE

DID YOU KNOW? *Tyrannosaurus*'s sense of smell was probably as powerful as that of a modern bloodhound dog.

A meat–eating theropod dinosaur, *Bistahieversor* had a large portion of its brain dedicated to processing smells.

Its tongue was simple, flat, and attached to the floor of the mouth, so *Bistahieversor* could not stick out its tongue like a lizard does.

Brain Size

Paleontologists have studied dinosaur skulls in order to work out the size and shape of their brains. Plant-eating dinosaurs had smaller brains than meat-eaters, with sauropodomorphs having the smallest brains of all. Meat-eaters needed bigger brains to track and catch moving prey. Meat-eaters' brains also had much larger front regions, where information from the eyes, nose, and ears is processed. This would have helped them to make good use of their senses.

The plant-eater *Stegosaurus*'s brain, about the size of a dog's, was suited to a slow-moving lifestyle.

Life in a Herd

The fossils of groups of dinosaurs are often found together, which probably means that some dinosaurs lived in herds. Plant-eating dinosaurs were safer in a herd. Some meat-eaters might also have hunted, slept, or nested together.

Together for Safety

Like a herd of today's deer, a herd of plant-eating dinosaurs could watch out for danger together. When attacked, the herd could claw and bite together—or could scatter in all directions, confusing the predator. There is plenty of fossil evidence that shows plant-eaters, such as sauropodomorphs and cerapods, lived in herds. Footprints show large numbers of dinosaurs walking together, with smaller, younger dinosaurs walking in the middle of the herd for safety.

Few predators could attempt to attack a fully grown *Sauroposeidon*, but young individuals were probably preyed on by the Gulf of Mexico region's apex predator, *Acrocanthosaurus*, and packs of the small dromaeosaur *Deinonychus*.

When the herd is attacked by *Gorgosaurus*, *Parasaurolophus* makes alarm calls to warn of danger.

Young dinosaurs were safer beside their parents.

28

Up to 18 m (59 ft) tall, *Sauroposeidon* was the tallest known dinosaur.

Hunting Together

Some meat-eaters may have lived together, hunting in packs to bring down large prey. In some cases, paleontologists cannot know for sure if the dinosaurs were a pack or whether they just happened to be together at a feeding or drinking spot when a sudden disaster, such as a landslide, struck. When the bodies of meat-eaters are found around the body of their prey, it may not be the case that the animals were working together. The meat-eaters may actually have been fighting over the body.

In North America, a pack of *Daspletosaurus* surrounds an outnumbered *Einiosaurus*.

	PALEOZOIC	TRIASSIC	JURASSIC	CRETACEOUS	AGE OF MAMMALS	
MILLIONS OF YEARS AGO	541	251	206	145	66	present

118

Name: *Sauroposeidon*
(SAWR-oh-puh-SY-don)

Clade: Somphospondyli

Height: 18 m (59 ft)

Length: 30 m (98.4 ft)

Weight: 50 tonnes (55 tons)

DINOSAUR PROFILE

DID YOU KNOW? *Sauroposeidon* was named after the Greek god of earthquakes, Poseidon, due to the way its heavy steps must have shaken the ground.

Laying Eggs

Like birds today, dinosaurs laid eggs with a tough shell that kept the growing babies safe until hatching. Eggs were laid in a nest made by scraping a hollow or digging a burrow. Some dinosaurs sat on their eggs to warm them, while others buried their eggs and then left.

Shape and Size

The eggs of plant-eaters were usually round, but meat-eaters' eggs were longer and thinner. The smallest eggs were 4.5 cm (1.8 in) long. The biggest, laid by a large meat-eater, were 60 cm (24 in) long.

Oviraptor used its feathery wings to warm its nest of eggs.

These fossilized eggs were laid by a plant-eater.

A female *Oviraptor* laid around 15 eggs in a nest.

DID YOU KNOW? Many of the biggest dinosaurs were tiny when they hatched: The 5-m (16-ft) sauropodomorph *Massospondylus* started life just 15 cm (6 in) long.

Caring or Not?

The dinosaurs that sat on their nests also took care of their babies after they were born. However, big plant-eaters would have run out of food near their nests if they stayed around, so their newborn babies had strong legs and were left to find their own food.

Maiasaura (which means "good mother lizard") looked after her babies for at least a year.

Oviraptor's name means "egg-stealer," as its fossil was found with eggs once believed to belong to another dinosaur—but now known to be the dinosaur's own eggs.

MILLIONS OF YEARS AGO	PALEOZOIC	TRIASSIC	JURASSIC	CRETACEOUS	AGE OF MAMMALS
	541	251	206	145	66	present

75

Name: *Oviraptor*
(OH–vee–RAP–tor)
Family: Oviraptoridae
Height: 0.7 m (2.3 ft)
Length: 1.5 m (4.9 ft)
Weight: 38 kg (84 lb)

DINOSAUR PROFILE

Fast and Slow

We can make guesses about how fast dinosaurs walked and ran by looking at their leg bones and measuring their footprints. The fastest dinosaurs could run quicker than any human adult, while the slowest could have been outrun by a child.

Slowest

A series of dinosaur footprints, called a trackway, can give clues about how fast the animal was walking or running. To make guesses about speed, paleontologists use measurements of the size and depth of the footprints, as well as the distance between them. They work out which dinosaur may have made the prints by comparing features, such as the number of toes, with local dinosaur bones. Large plant-eaters weighed up to 100 tonnes (110 tons), as much as 50 family cars. Like today's elephants, they usually walked slowly on their four thick legs. Adults had no need to run, as their size kept them safe from meat-eaters.

Brachiosaurus's legs were suited to holding its great weight rather than to sprinting.

Fastest

Paleontologists also base their speed guesses on foot shape, leg length, and body shape and weight. Slim meat-eaters, such as *Gallimimus*, were the fastest runners. They ran on their back legs. Like today's ostrich, their legs were long and muscly. Possibly some could run as fast as ostriches: up to 72 km/h (45 mph) an hour.

Gallimimus used its long tail for balance as it ran.

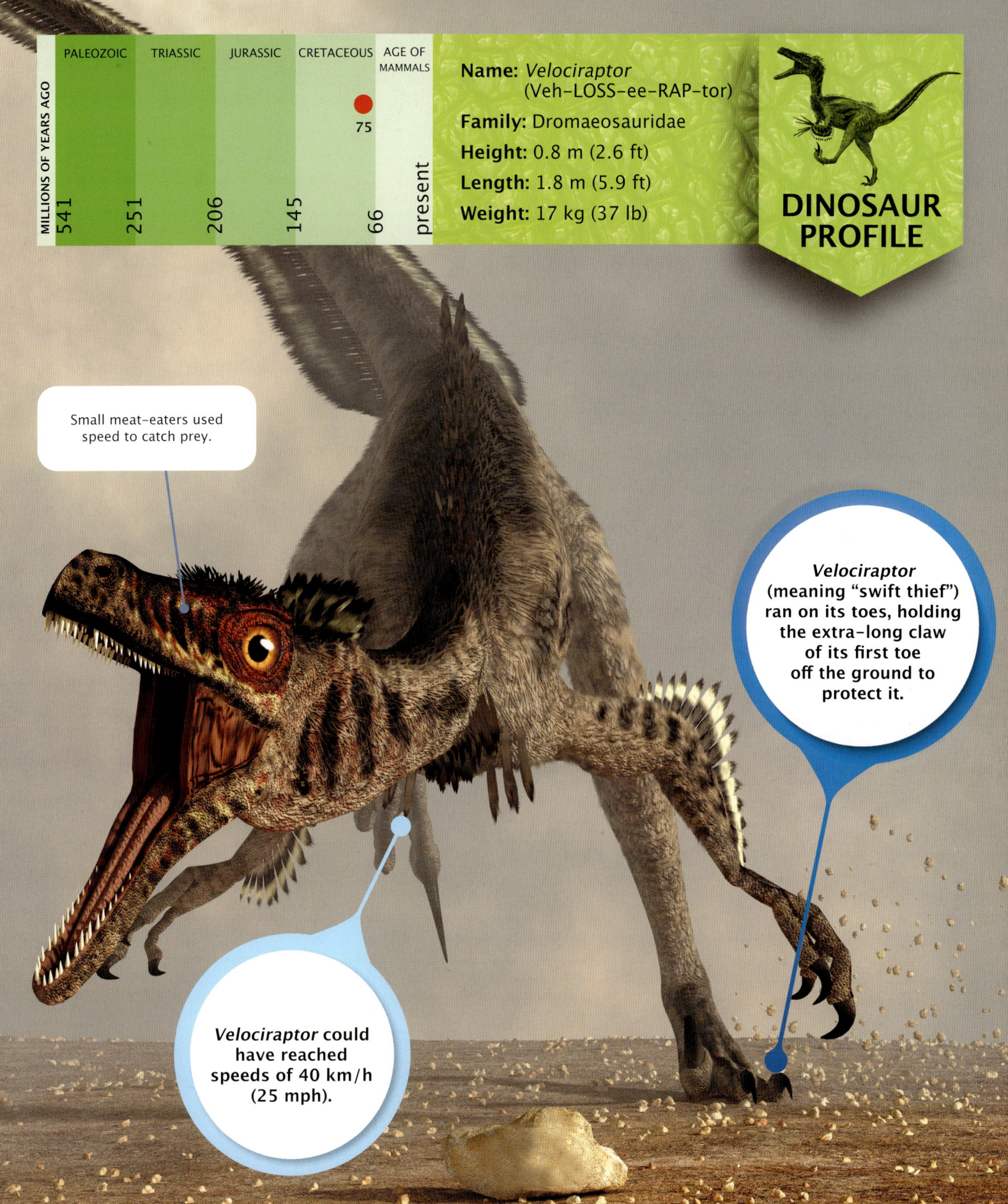

	PALEOZOIC	TRIASSIC	JURASSIC	CRETACEOUS	AGE OF MAMMALS
MILLIONS OF YEARS AGO	541	251	206	145	66	present

75

Name: *Velociraptor*
(Veh–LOSS–ee–RAP–tor)
Family: Dromaeosauridae
Height: 0.8 m (2.6 ft)
Length: 1.8 m (5.9 ft)
Weight: 17 kg (37 lb)

DINOSAUR PROFILE

Small meat–eaters used speed to catch prey.

Velociraptor (meaning "swift thief") ran on its toes, holding the extra–long claw of its first toe off the ground to protect it.

Velociraptor could have reached speeds of 40 km/h (25 mph).

DID YOU KNOW? The fastest running speed calculated from any trackway is about 43 km/h (26.7 mph)—a little faster than the best human sprinters.

Communication

By making sounds or using body language, dinosaurs could warn each other about threats, frighten off attackers, and attract a mate. Paleontologists base their ideas about dinosaur communication on the way that modern birds and reptiles behave.

Calls

Rather than roaring like a lion, dinosaurs may have made low grunting, rumbling, and booming sounds with their mouths closed. Such sounds, made by pushing air up through the throat, are used by birds and reptiles today. Like these modern animals, dinosaurs may have been capable of a range of different sounds, from alarms to mating calls. Studies on the bones around dinosaur ears have shown that they were probably good at hearing low sounds. Low sounds travel long distances, so they could be heard by a scattered herd, or by distant females at mating time.

The hadrosaur *Olorotitan* might have blown air through its hollow nose crest, making its honking calls louder.

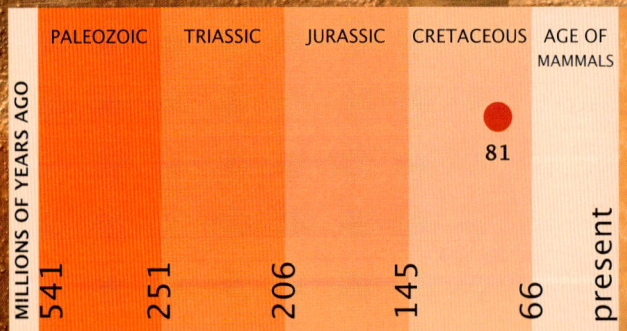

	PALEOZOIC	TRIASSIC	JURASSIC	CRETACEOUS	AGE OF MAMMALS
MILLIONS OF YEARS AGO	541	251	206	145	66 · present

81

Name: *Diabloceratops* (Dee-OB-low-SEH-ruh-tops)

Family: Ceratopsidae

Height: 2.8 m (9.2 ft)

Length: 4 m (13 ft)

Weight: 1.3 tonnes (1.4 tons)

DINOSAUR PROFILE

DID YOU KNOW? Scientists base their ideas about dinosaur calls on the rumbles of crocodiles, which share an ancestor with dinosaurs that lived 250 million years ago.

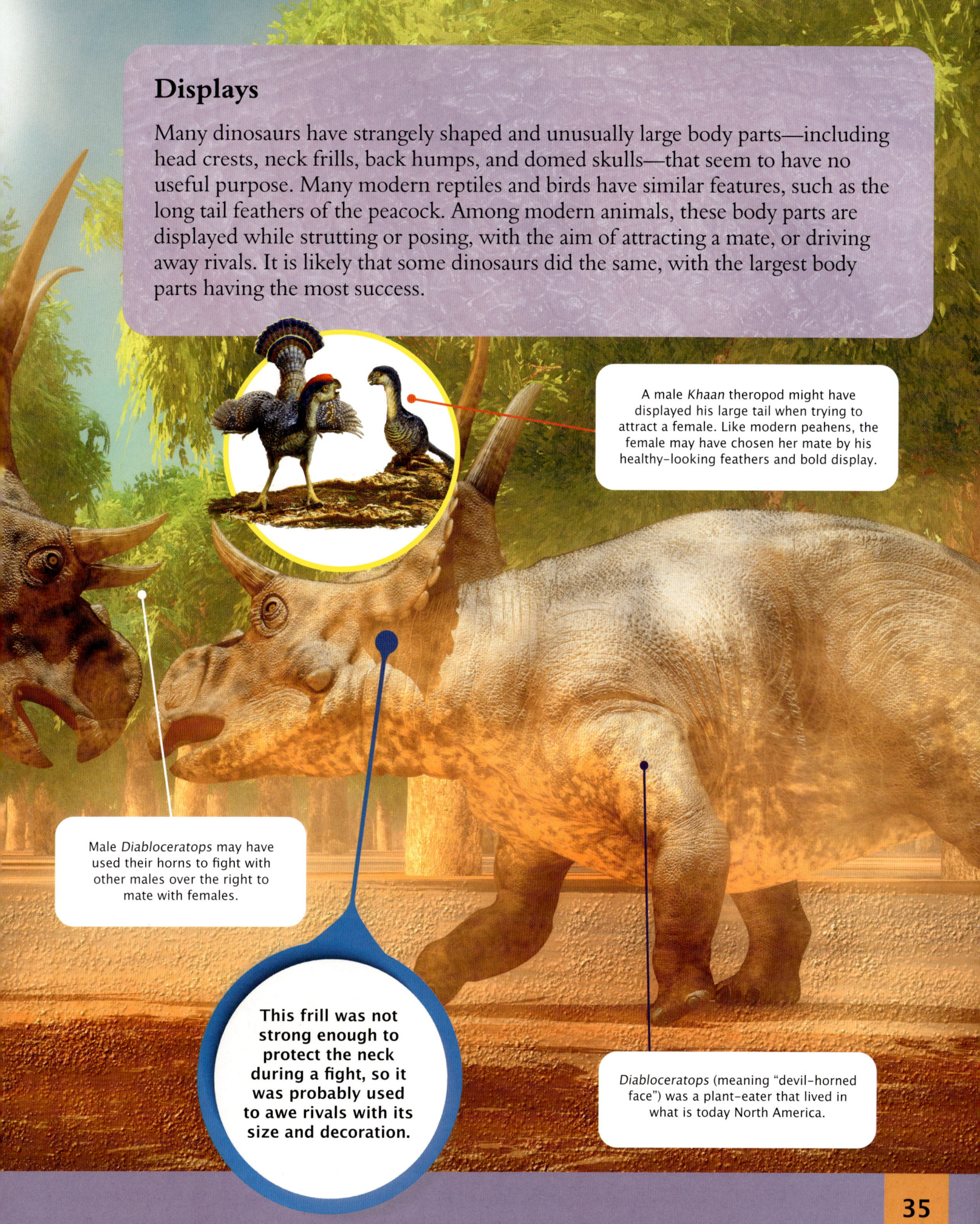

Displays

Many dinosaurs have strangely shaped and unusually large body parts—including head crests, neck frills, back humps, and domed skulls—that seem to have no useful purpose. Many modern reptiles and birds have similar features, such as the long tail feathers of the peacock. Among modern animals, these body parts are displayed while strutting or posing, with the aim of attracting a mate, or driving away rivals. It is likely that some dinosaurs did the same, with the largest body parts having the most success.

A male *Khaan* theropod might have displayed his large tail when trying to attract a female. Like modern peahens, the female may have chosen her mate by his healthy-looking feathers and bold display.

Male *Diabloceratops* may have used their horns to fight with other males over the right to mate with females.

This frill was not strong enough to protect the neck during a fight, so it was probably used to awe rivals with its size and decoration.

Diabloceratops (meaning "devil-horned face") was a plant-eater that lived in what is today North America.

Evolution of Birds

Today, there are around 10,000 species of birds, from plant-eating pigeons to meat-eating eagles. All these birds are the descendants of theropod dinosaurs. Over millions of years, some dinosaurs evolved to have more birdlike features: smaller bodies, feathers, toothless beaks, and long arms that could be flapped as wings.

Becoming Birds

Around 160 million years ago, some small, long-armed, feathered coelurosaur theropods started to climb into trees to hide from predators, or to look for leaves and insects that were not reachable from the ground. After a while, some of these birdlike dinosaurs were able to glide down from trees, by opening wide their long, feathered arms. Eventually, birdlike dinosaurs could flap their wings to fly longer distances. By 130 million years ago, the first true birds were soaring through the sky.

This is a fossil of *Archaeopteryx*, a birdlike dinosaur that lived 150 million years ago. The imprints of long, stiff feathers can be seen, their stalks growing from the skin and softer vanes spreading from the stalks.

Dinosaurs Are Alive!

When a giant asteroid wiped out the dinosaurs 66 million years ago, some birds survived. The birds that lived were probably small seed-eaters. As forests burned and ash filled the sky, killing plants from lack of sunlight, the leaf-eating birds died, followed by the meat-eaters, who could now find only skeletons. The seed-eaters, however, found enough food to survive until the skies cleared and plants regrew.

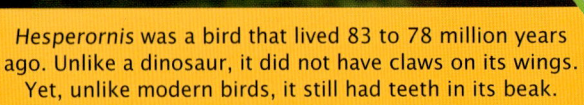

Hesperornis was a bird that lived 83 to 78 million years ago. Unlike a dinosaur, it did not have claws on its wings. Yet, unlike modern birds, it still had teeth in its beak.

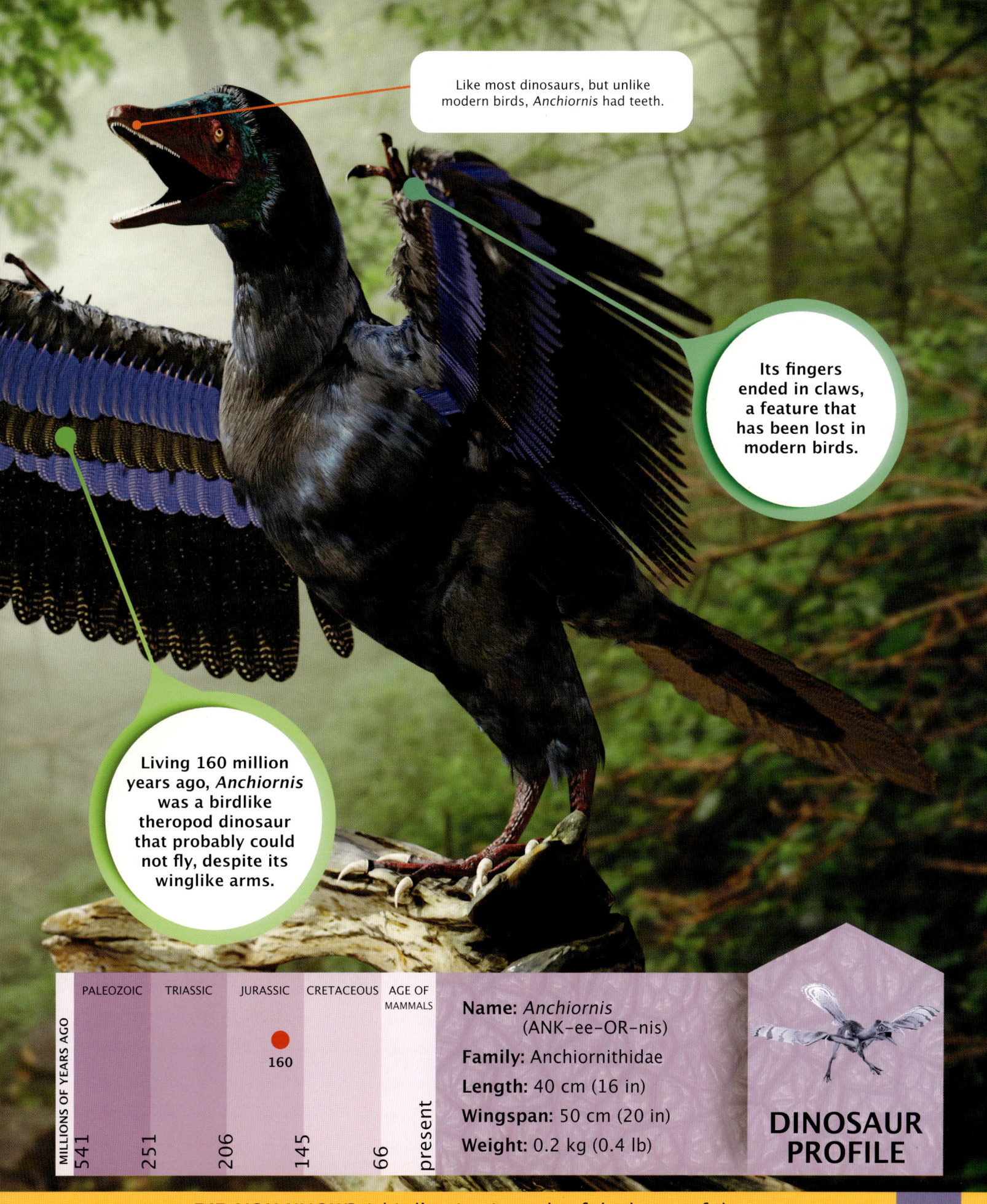

Like most dinosaurs, but unlike modern birds, *Anchiornis* had teeth.

Its fingers ended in claws, a feature that has been lost in modern birds.

Living 160 million years ago, *Anchiornis* was a birdlike theropod dinosaur that probably could not fly, despite its winglike arms.

MILLIONS OF YEARS AGO	PALEOZOIC	TRIASSIC	JURASSIC	CRETACEOUS	AGE OF MAMMALS	
			● 160			
	541	251	206	145	66	present

Name: *Anchiornis* (ANK–ee–OR–nis)

Family: Anchiornithidae

Length: 40 cm (16 in)

Wingspan: 50 cm (20 in)

Weight: 0.2 kg (0.4 lb)

DINOSAUR PROFILE

DID YOU KNOW? A bird's wing is made of the bones of the upper arm, forearm, and hand, along with muscles, skin, and feathers.

End of the Dinosaurs

Around 66 million years ago, a giant space rock, called an asteroid, hit Earth. The disaster killed all the dinosaurs, along with most other large animals. The only dinosaurs that survived were the small feathered ones that had already evolved into birds.

A few months after the asteroid, the plant-eating *Torosaurus* looks for food.

Asteroid Crash!

The asteroid, which was up to 15 km (9 miles) wide, fell into the sea near the coast of North America. The crash sent a cloud of dust into the sky, blocking out all sunlight for up to a year. Most plants died from lack of sunlight. Soon, plant-eating dinosaurs ran out of food. Without the plant-eaters, the meat-eating dinosaurs could not survive either.

The asteroid left a crater 180 km (112 miles) wide.

MILLIONS OF YEARS AGO	PALEOZOIC	TRIASSIC	JURASSIC	CRETACEOUS	AGE OF MAMMALS	
	541	251	206	145	68 • 66	present

Name: *Torosaurus* (TORE-oh-SAWR-us)

Family: Ceratopsidae

Height: 3 m (9.8 ft)

Length: 8.5 m (28 ft)

Weight: 5 tonnes (5.5 tons)

DINOSAUR PROFILE

38

Like all other dinosaurs, *Edmontosaurus* became extinct 66 million years ago.

Plants have died, but their fallen seeds may have survived.

Many species of frogs, such as *Xenopus*, survived. Frogs grew much more widespread in the following years, moving into new habitats such as trees.

Death and Survival

Very few land-living animals weighing over 25 kg (55 lb) survived. Large animals, which need more food, were soon unable to find enough to eat. Animals that ate only meat or only plants also mostly died. Some smaller animals survived if they ate seeds, insects, or dead animals until the skies cleared. Alongside the dinosaurs, the pterosaurs and many sea-living reptiles also died out. However, some reptiles did survive, including crocodiles, turtles, snakes, and lizards. Many fish, amphibians, mammals, and insects and other invertebrates also survived.

DID YOU KNOW? *Torosaurus* had one of the largest skulls of any known land animal: more than 2.5 m (8.2 ft) long.

39

Rise of the Mammals

The mammoth's tusks, which were actually teeth, grew up to 4.2 m (14 ft) long.

Only a quarter of Earth's animals survived the asteroid strike. Among the survivors were little mammals, which ate fallen seeds or worms until the clouds cleared. With the huge, fierce dinosaurs gone, mammals slowly evolved to be many different shapes and sizes.

Mammal Time

The first mammals evolved from reptiles around 225 million years ago. Their scales became hair. They also evolved to be warm blooded, which means they can produce their own body heat, rather than relying on their surroundings to keep them warm. These changes allowed mammals to move into a range of new habitats, from the cold poles to dark burrows. Instead of laying eggs, mammals began to give birth to live babies they fed on milk. In addition, mammals started to develop bigger brains, leading to a range of new and more complex activities.

Like its relatives the elephants, a woolly mammoth used its trunk for grasping plants to eat.

Mammals evolved from hairy reptiles like *Lycaenops*, which lived 270 to 251 million years ago.

Thick fur kept a woolly mammoth warm during the last ice age, when Earth's temperature was much lower than it is today.

New and Old

Over the years, new mammals have evolved and then died out. Today's mammals include dogs, cats, and humans. The first dogs evolved 37 million years ago, while cats appeared 25 million years ago. Humans have been around for only 350,000 years.

Smilodon was a big cat that lived from 2.5 million to 10,000 years ago.

MILLIONS OF YEARS AGO	PALEOZOIC	TRIASSIC	JURASSIC	CRETACEOUS	AGE OF MAMMALS	
	541	251	206	145	66	present
						0.4

Name: Woolly mammoth (WOOL-ee MAM-uth)

Family: Elephantidae

Height: 3 m (9.8 ft)

Length: 6 m (19.7 ft)

Weight: 5 tonnes (5.5 tons)

MAMMAL PROFILE

DID YOU KNOW? Woolly mammoths died out around 4,000 years ago, probably due to warming temperatures and hunting by humans.

Timeline of Life

Dinosaurs ruled the Earth for millions of years, but their time on our planet was only a small fraction of Earth's long history. If the planet's 4.5 billion years are likened to a 24-hour day, the dinosaurs walked the Earth for less than an hour. Humans have been in existence for the last seven seconds of this "day."

Amazing Advances

Scientists do not know why the first simple living cells came into being in Earth's oceans. After this unexplained event, evolution moved very slowly for at least 1.5 billion years, before something almost as amazing happened: the first complex cells, called eukaryotes, developed. All animals and plants are made entirely of eukaryote cells.

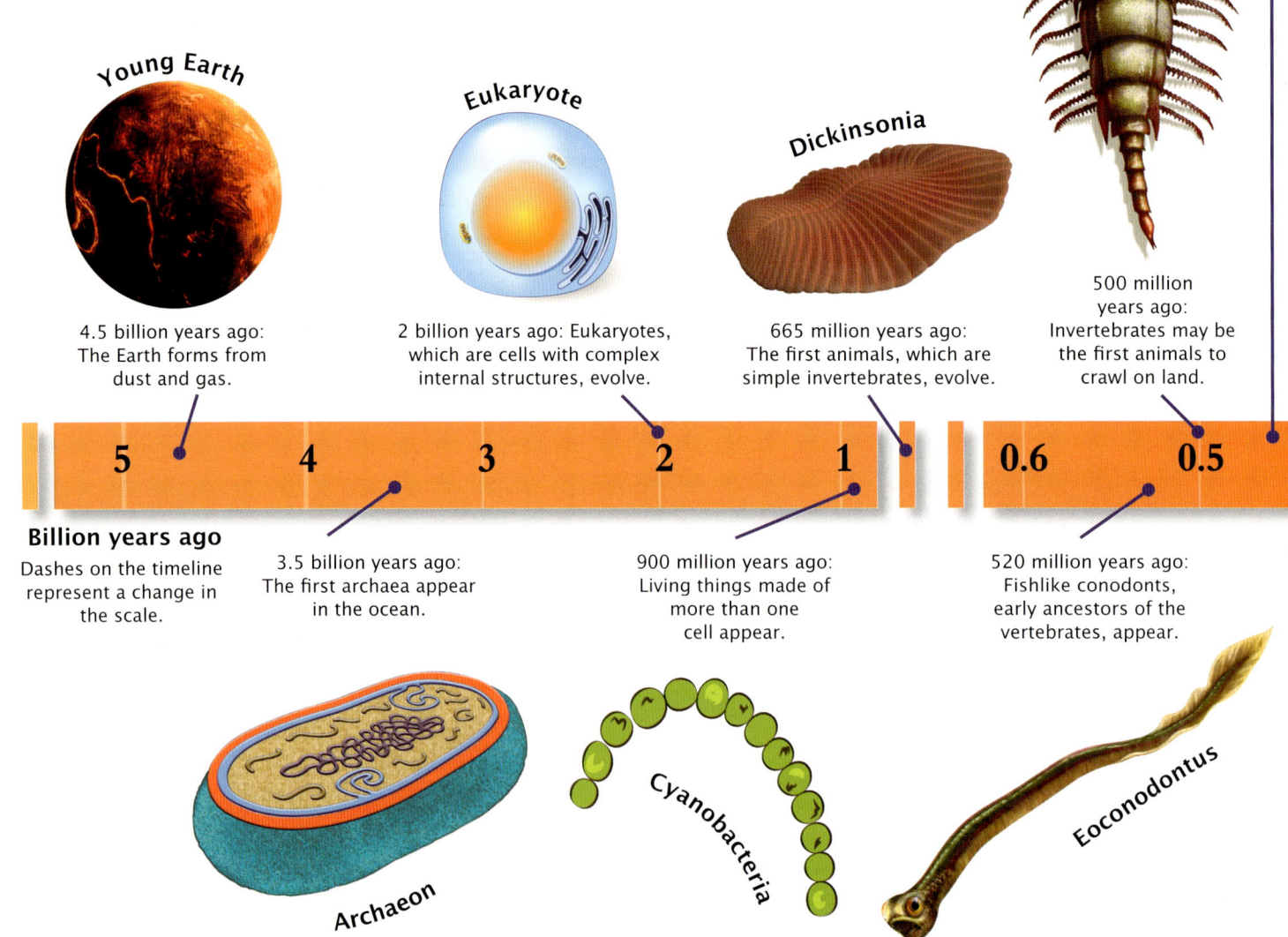

Euthycarcinus

Young Earth

Eukaryote

Dickinsonia

500 million years ago: Invertebrates may be the first animals to crawl on land.

4.5 billion years ago: The Earth forms from dust and gas.

2 billion years ago: Eukaryotes, which are cells with complex internal structures, evolve.

665 million years ago: The first animals, which are simple invertebrates, evolve.

5 4 3 2 1 0.6 0.5

Billion years ago
Dashes on the timeline represent a change in the scale.

3.5 billion years ago: The first archaea appear in the ocean.

900 million years ago: Living things made of more than one cell appear.

520 million years ago: Fishlike conodonts, early ancestors of the vertebrates, appear.

Archaeon

Cyanobacteria

Eoconodontus

DID YOU KNOW? Until around 40,000 years ago, there were at least two other species of humans sharing our planet, the Neanderthals and the Denisovans.

Humans

Humans evolved very late in Earth's history, only around 350,000 years ago. Our species started to evolve from great apes, part of the primate order of mammals, between 4 and 7 million years ago. Today, we dominate the Earth, just as the dinosaurs once did. In the short time that humans have been on Earth, we have changed the landscape by planting fields of crops and building factories and great cities.

470 million years ago:
Plants are growing on land.

Ceratosaurus

Homo sapiens

Ichthyostega

367 million years ago:
Four-legged animals, called tetrapods, evolve. Among the earliest are amphibians.

233 million years ago:
A group of reptiles evolves into dinosaurs. By approximately 100 million years later, some dinosaurs have evolved into birds.

350,000 years ago:
Humans are walking the Earth.

0.3   **0.2**   **0.1**   **0.05**   **0.001**

312 million years ago:
Reptiles evolve from amphibians.

225 million years ago:
Mammals evolve from reptiles.

55 million years ago: Large-brained mammals called primates evolve.

Scutosaurus

Megacerops

Darwinius

Chapter 2

Theropods

The largest meat-eaters that ever walked the Earth were theropods. The theropods were a group of dinosaurs that evolved in the Late Triassic Period, around 231 million years ago. Most theropods walked on their strong back legs, using their shorter front limbs for grabbing or slashing.

Found in river valleys in Africa, *Suchomimus* was a large carnosaur theropod that both walked on land and waded or swam in water.

Long, strong claws may have been used for swiping at fish from the riverbank, as grizzly bears do today.

DID YOU KNOW? Nearly all meat-eating dinosaurs were theropods, but not every theropod was a meat-eater: Some later theropods evolved to eat plants.

MILLIONS OF YEARS AGO	PALEOZOIC	TRIASSIC	JURASSIC	CRETACEOUS	AGE OF MAMMALS
	541	251	206	145	66	present

125

Name: *Suchomimus* (SOOK-oh-MIM-us)
Family: Spinosauridae
Height: 3.2 m (10.5 ft)
Length: 10.3 m (33.8 ft)
Weight: 3.2 tonnes (3.5 tons)

DINOSAUR PROFILE

Its crocodile–like snout, with 122 pointed teeth, was suited to snapping up wriggling fish, as well as reptiles such as pterosaurs.

Theropod Groups

Many of the largest theropods, including *Giganotosaurus* and *Carcharodontosaurus*, were in the carnosaur subgroup. Another subgroup was the coelurosaurs, which included the ostrich-like *Ornithomimus* and the fierce *Tyrannosaurus*. Smaller coelurosaurs were covered in feathers. Other theropods probably had feathers only on some parts of their body, with most of their skin covered by scales. Birds are descendants of small coelurosaurs that evolved to have wings.

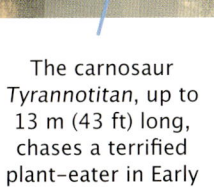

The carnosaur *Tyrannotitan*, up to 13 m (43 ft) long, chases a terrified plant–eater in Early Cretaceous Argentina.

Theropod Skeletons

Theropods were saurischian (lizard-hipped) dinosaurs. They had hollow bones, like today's birds. The theropods take their name from the ancient Greek for "beast-footed," but their feet were more like those of birds than a lion's or a bear's. Most theropods had three main toes, as well as three main fingers.

Like most theropods, *Ornithomimus* had three toes and fingers. However, this late theropod had no teeth. Its sharp beak was used for snapping up plants and small animals.

Herrerasaurus

One of the earliest carnivorous dinosaurs, *Herrerasaurus* lived in South America at the end of the Triassic Period. There were many plant-eaters in its jungle habitat, but few dinosaurs. The main predators were archosaurs and early mammals called synapsids.

Close Relatives

Paleontologists have argued about *Herrerasaurus*'s place in the dinosaur family tree. Some count it as a primitive theropod (two-legged, carnivorous dinosaur). Others say it cannot be a theropod because it does not have opposable thumbs. They place *Herrerasaurus* in a group of its own.

Herrerasaurus was a speedy runner, thanks to its strong back legs.

From the Same Rocks

The first *Herrerasaurus* fossils were found in rocky mountains outside the city of San Juan in northwestern Argentina in 1959. The species is named after the farmer who discovered it, Victorino Herrera. The dinosaur *Eoraptor* was later found in the same rocks. Its name means "dawn lizard," and both of these hunters were around at the very beginning of the dinosaur age.

Eoraptors pause for a drink in their swampy forest home.

DID YOU KNOW? By studying *Herrerasaurus* coprolites (fossilized dung), scientists know that this carnivore crunched up and digested bone.

MILLIONS OF YEARS AGO

PALEOZOIC	TRIASSIC	JURASSIC	CRETACEOUS	AGE OF MAMMALS
541	251	206	145	66 present

231

Name: *Herrerasaurus*
(Her–RARE–uh–SAWR–us)
Family: Herrerasauridae
Height: 1.5 m (5 ft)
Length: 3 m (10 ft)
Weight: 210 kg (460 lb)

DINOSAUR PROFILE

Herrerasaurus used sight and sound to find prey.

This small, stocky reptile is a rhynchosaur. Its beaky mouth clips off plant stems to eat.

Its front legs had grasping, curved claws.

The first complete *Herrerasaurus* skull was discovered in 1988. Before then, paleontologists had to work from fragments.

Coelophysis

Coelophysis was a fast runner, with light bones and a small, slender body. Its front limbs were used for grasping prey. *Coelophysis* was an early theropod, evolving in the Late Triassic Period.

Large Eyes

Coelophysis had large eyes that faced forward like the eyes of modern birds of prey, such as eagles and hawks. Forward-facing eyes allow binocular vision, when the two eyes work together to judge the distance and speed of prey. Like birds of prey, *Coelophysis* could probably spot fast-moving prey at a distance.

Studies of the rings of bone found in *Coelophysis*'s eyes suggest it was a daytime, or diurnal, hunter.

Coelophysis (meaning "hollow form" due to its hollow bones) lived in what is now the southwestern United States.

Like its ancestors but unlike later theropods, *Coelophysis* had four fingers, but the fourth finger was embedded in the flesh of its hand.

48

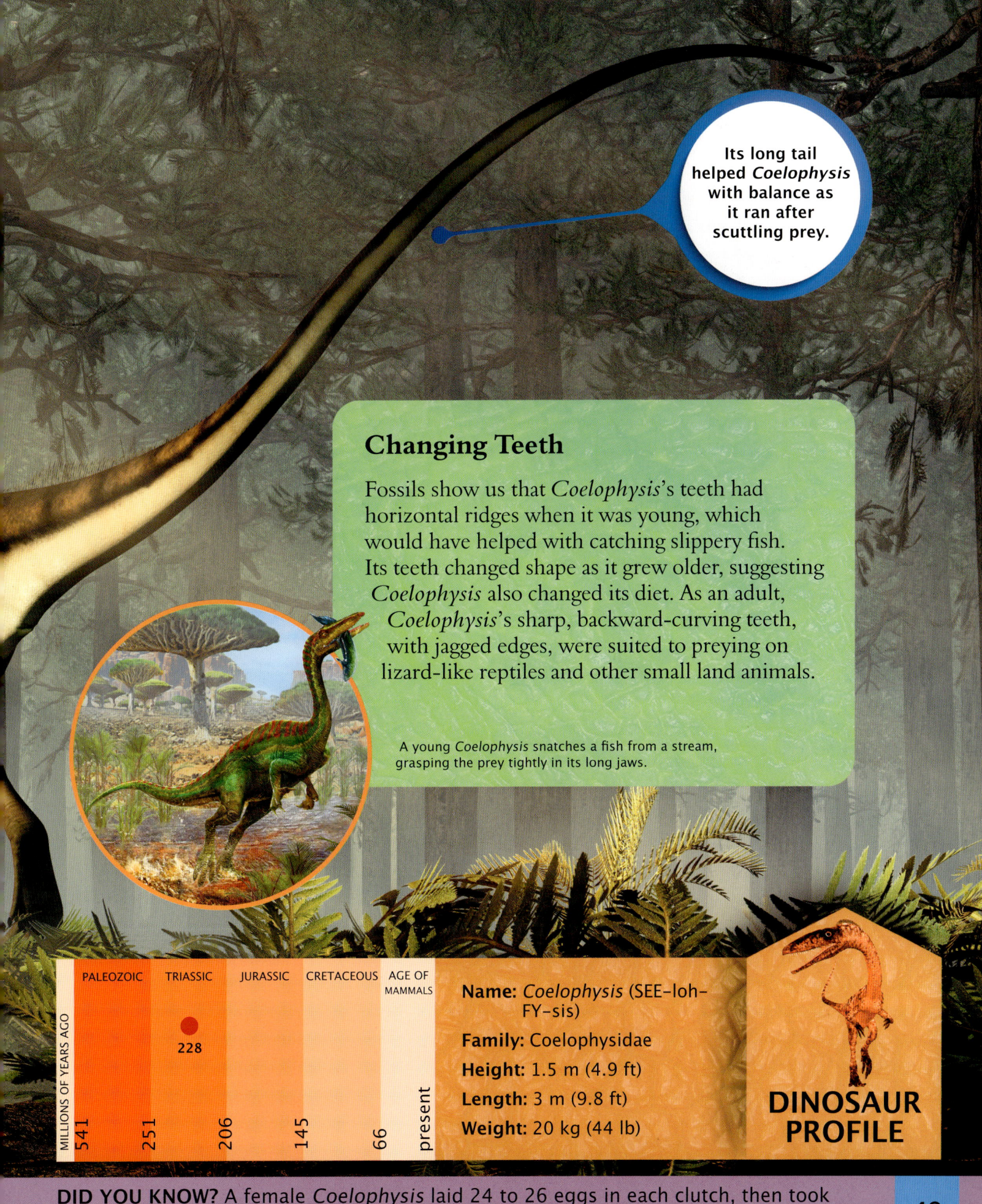

Its long tail helped *Coelophysis* with balance as it ran after scuttling prey.

Changing Teeth

Fossils show us that *Coelophysis*'s teeth had horizontal ridges when it was young, which would have helped with catching slippery fish. Its teeth changed shape as it grew older, suggesting *Coelophysis* also changed its diet. As an adult, *Coelophysis*'s sharp, backward-curving teeth, with jagged edges, were suited to preying on lizard-like reptiles and other small land animals.

A young *Coelophysis* snatches a fish from a stream, grasping the prey tightly in its long jaws.

	PALEOZOIC	TRIASSIC	JURASSIC	CRETACEOUS	AGE OF MAMMALS	
MILLIONS OF YEARS AGO	541	251	206	145	66	present

228

Name: *Coelophysis* (SEE–loh–FY–sis)

Family: Coelophysidae

Height: 1.5 m (4.9 ft)

Length: 3 m (9.8 ft)

Weight: 20 kg (44 lb)

DINOSAUR PROFILE

DID YOU KNOW? A female *Coelophysis* laid 24 to 26 eggs in each clutch, then took some care of her hatchlings until they grew to around 1.5 m (4.9 ft) long.

Dilophosaurus

Around 193 million years ago, *Dilophosaurus* was the largest meat-eater in North America. Later North American meat-eaters, such as *Tyrannosaurus*, grew much larger. *Dilophosaurus* means "two-crested lizard." It had 33 slim, curving teeth for seizing prey.

Dilophosaurus did not have a powerful bite, so it used its front teeth for tearing at prey rather than biting.

Its arms were strong enough to grasp plant-eating dinosaurs, such as the early sauropodomorph *Sarahsaurus*, which grew up to 4 m (13 ft) long.

Dilophosaurus weighed the same as a modern horse.

50 **DID YOU KNOW?** In 1940, the first three *Dilophosaurus* fossilized skeletons were found in Arizona, in the United States, by Jesse Williams, a member of the Navajo Nation.

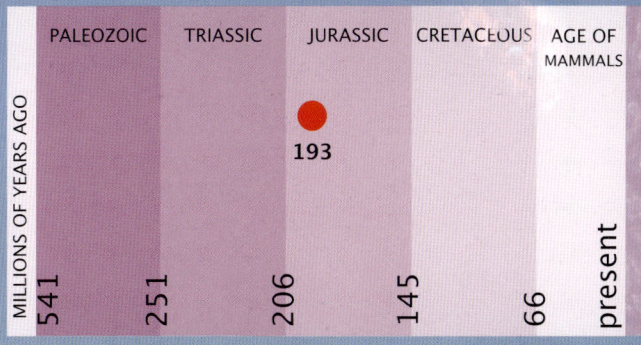

MILLIONS OF YEARS AGO	PALEOZOIC	TRIASSIC	JURASSIC	CRETACEOUS	AGE OF MAMMALS	present
	541	251	206	145	66	

193

Name: *Dilophosaurus* (Dye-LOF-oh-SAWR-us)
Family: Dilophosauridae
Height: 2 m (6.6 ft)
Length: 6.5 m (21.3 ft)
Weight: 350 kg (770 lb)

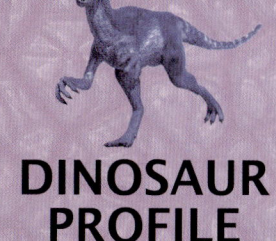

DINOSAUR PROFILE

Having a Rest

One *Dilophosaurus* left dents in the sand when it was resting. The sand was baked hard by the Sun, then covered by more sand. The dents stayed in the sandstone rock as it formed. The dents showed us how *Dilophosaurus* held its hands, with the palms facing each other.

Showing Off

Dilophosaurus's skull bones formed two crests. The crest bones were too thin to be strong enough for fighting, so the crests were probably for display. Males may have shown them off to attract females.

The crest bones were covered by tough horn and skin, making the crest taller.

The *Dilophosaurus* trace fossil gave a rare insight into the posture of a crouching, resting dinosaur.

51

Allosaurus

This large meat-eater had up to 44 sharp teeth with jagged edges. These teeth sometimes fell out as *Allosaurus* ripped through flesh, so they are common fossils. *Allosaurus* bite marks have been found in dinosaurs as large as *Stegosaurus*.

Hunting Techniques

Each hand had three fingers, armed with long curved claws. *Allosaurus* could not reach forward easily with its short arms. However, once prey was in its mouth, the hook-like claws stopped escape. Despite its big skull, *Allosaurus* may have had weaker jaw muscles and a weaker bite than today's crocodiles and lions. *Allosaurus* probably fed by jabbing its narrow jaws into prey, then ripping out flesh by pulling with clamped teeth. As well as hunting live prey, *Allosaurus* probably fed on dead animals it came across.

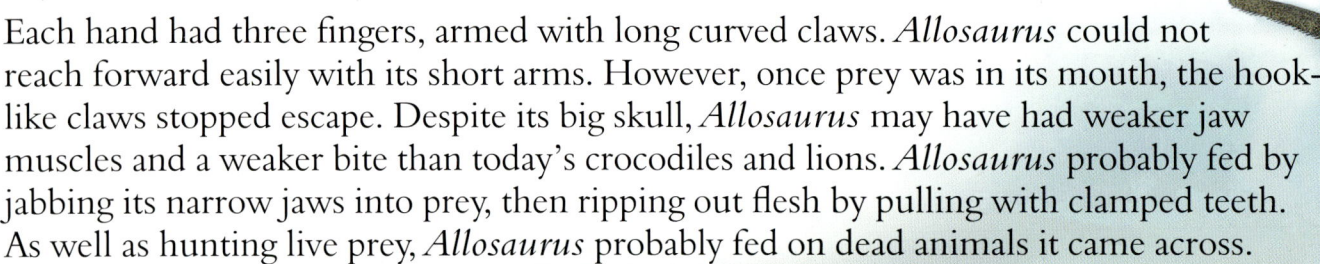

An *Allosaurus* claw could grow over 18 cm (7 in) long.

	MILLIONS OF YEARS AGO	PALEOZOIC	TRIASSIC	JURASSIC	CRETACEOUS	AGE OF MAMMALS
		541	251	206	145	66	present

● 155

Name: *Allosaurus* (AL-oh-SAWR-us)
Family: Allosauridae
Height: 5 m (16.4 ft)
Length: 8.5 m (28 ft)
Weight: 1.7 tonnes (1.9 tons)

DINOSAUR PROFILE

Allosaurus had a horn above each eye. Like today's animals with horns or antlers, such as deer, these features may have been used to attract a mate.

Growing Up

Allosaurus reached its full size by around 15 years old. Every year as it grew, it gained around 150 kg (330 lb)—the weight of 40 human babies. Most *Allosauruses* lived to be around 25 years old.

Allosaurus was big enough to attack young or sick *Diplodocuses*.

Allosaurus lived in forests and plains in North America and Europe.

The bodies of several *Allosauruses* have been found side by side, which suggests these dinosaurs hunted together.

DID YOU KNOW? Until the evolution of the tyrannosaurs around 75 million years later, the allosaur family were the largest and deadliest predators in North America.

53

Ceratosaurus

Unusually for a theropod, *Ceratosaurus* had a line of small bony plates running along its back.

This medium-sized meat-eater had a horn on its snout and a pair of horns over its eyes. These small horns were possibly not useful weapons, but may have helped a *Ceratosaurus* recognize other *Ceratosauruses*.

Ceratosaurus waded into swamps and lakes to catch fish.

Competing Dinosaurs

Ceratosaurus lived in the same area at the same time as *Allosaurus*. To avoid competing with the bigger dinosaur for food, *Ceratosaurus* may often have fed on water-living animals, such as lungfish, crocodiles, and turtles. *Ceratosaurus* teeth, which were shed while attacking prey, are most common in and around water such as lake edges, swamps, and floodplains.

MILLIONS OF YEARS AGO	PALEOZOIC	TRIASSIC	JURASSIC	CRETACEOUS	AGE OF MAMMALS
	541	251	206 ● 161	145	66 present

Name: *Ceratosaurus* (Seh-RAT-oh-SAWR-us)

Family: Ceratosauridae

Height: 2.2 m (7.2 ft)

Length: 6.3 m (20.7 ft)

Weight: 600 kg (1,320 lb)

DINOSAUR PROFILE

54

The name of this North American dinosaur comes from the ancient Greek words for "horn lizard."

Ceratosaurus's teeth were blade-like and grew up to 9.3 cm (3.7 in) long.

Unlike most meat-eaters, *Ceratosaurus* had four fingers on each hand.

Helpful Bones

Like other theropods, *Ceratosaurus* had bones that were hollow. This made them lighter and more likely to bend than break in a fall. Together with this dinosaur's long, muscly back legs, lightweight bones also allowed it to run swiftly, possibly at up to 32 km/h (20 mph). Its jaw had a particularly flexible joint, allowing it to open wide enough to swallow whole prey or large chunks of flesh.

DID YOU KNOW? The parts of the brain dedicated to sense of smell, known as olfactory bulbs, were much smaller in *Ceratosaurus* than in *Tyrannosaurus*.

Compsognathus

This delicate little dinosaur lived on islands of the Tethys Sea, in what is now France and Germany. It had a very long tail, which helped it balance as it raced and swerved after fast-running prey. *Compsognathus* means "dainty jaw" in ancient Greek.

Lizard Lover

We know what *Compsognathus* ate, because one of its fossils had the remains of its last meal inside its stomach. This *Compsognathus* had gulped down a small, long-tailed lizard. Lizards evolved around 199 million years ago. The last common ancestor of lizards and dinosaurs lived around 250 to 260 million years ago, after which time the two groups evolved differently.

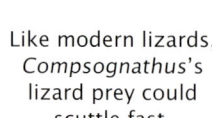

Like modern lizards, *Compsognathus*'s lizard prey could scuttle fast.

DID YOU KNOW? The first *Compsognathus* fossil was discovered in 1859, but it was initially mistaken for a species of lizard.

	PALEOZOIC	TRIASSIC	JURASSIC	CRETACEOUS	AGE OF MAMMALS	
MILLIONS OF YEARS AGO			● 150			present
	541	251	206	145	66	

Name: *Compsognathus* (Comp-sog-NAY-thus)
Family: Compsognathidae
Height: 30 cm (12 in)
Length: 1 m (3.3 ft)
Weight: 1.5 kg (3.3 lb)

DINOSAUR PROFILE

Large eyes helped *Compsognathus* to spot small, fast-moving prey.

In this fossil, *Compsognathus*'s head and neck are bent round, over its back.

For decades, *Compsognathus* was the smallest known dinosaur, but smaller species—such as *Microraptor* (found in 2000)—were discovered much later.

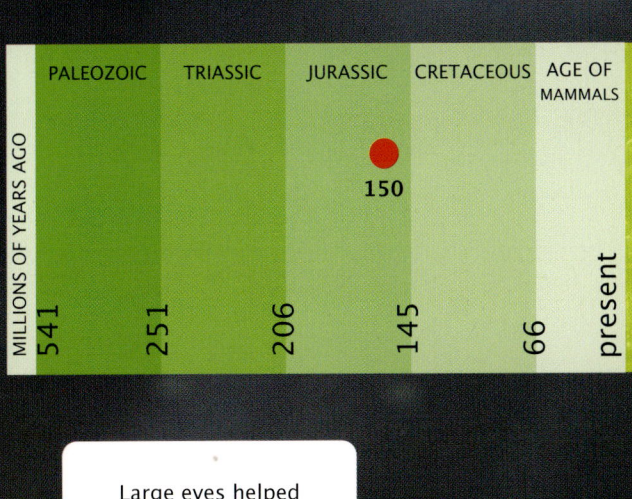

Slim and Speedy

Compsognathus was built for speed, with long back legs and a slim, light skeleton. Its neck and jaws were also long, so it could snatch prey that was hiding under rocks or plants. This dinosaur had more than 50 teeth, which were small and pointed, ideally shaped for a diet of little vertebrates and possibly insects, too.

The long tail had around 40 small bones, known as caudal vertebrae.

Archaeopteryx

Over millions of years, some dinosaurs grew to look more and more like birds. By 150 million years ago, dinosaurs like *Archaeopteryx* could use their feathered arms to make short flights. By 130 million years ago, the first true birds had evolved from their dinosaur grandparents.

Dinosaur or Bird?

The first *Archaeopteryx* skeleton was discovered in Germany in 1861. Until the early 21st century, *Archaeopteryx* was believed to be the oldest bird. Yet older birdlike dinosaurs, such as *Anchiornis*, have been discovered since. Today, *Archaeopteryx* is understood to be a "transition fossil": a midpoint in the evolution of dinosaurs into birds. *Archaeopteryx* had features of both dinosaurs and birds. Like most dinosaurs but unlike modern birds, it had teeth. However, its arm muscles and bones had evolved into wide wings, allowing it to make short flights to catch prey or escape danger.

Archaeopteryx used its sharp little teeth for snapping insects.

Twelve body fossils of *Archaeopteryx* have been found—all of them in the limestone of Germany's Solnhofen.

Its bony tail was much longer than a modern bird's.

A Black Feather

In 2011, scientists studied a fossilized *Archaeopteryx* wing feather under a powerful microscope in order to find melanosomes, which make the tint-creating pigment melanin. The melanosomes were compared with those of modern birds, and the scientists revealed—with 95 percent certainty—that the feather was black. Black feathers are common on wings, as black melanosomes also strengthen feathers for flight.

The results of the study do not mean that *Archaeopteryx* was entirely black, only that it had some black feathers on its wings.

Unlike today's birds, *Archaeopteryx* had clawed fingers.

PALEOZOIC	TRIASSIC	JURASSIC	CRETACEOUS	AGE OF MAMMALS

MILLIONS OF YEARS AGO

150

541 251 206 145 66 present

Name: *Archaeopteryx* (ARK-ee-OPT-er-ix)

Family: Archaeopterygidae

Length: 50 cm (20 in)

Wingspan: 70 cm (28 in)

Weight: 0.7 kg (1.5 lb)

DINOSAUR PROFILE

DID YOU KNOW? *Archaeopteryx*, which means "ancient wing" in ancient Greek, is sometimes called by its German name Urvogel, meaning "original bird."

Utahraptor

Utahraptor was an intelligent, agile, and swift hunter. It had a stiff tail to help it stay balanced as it pounced on its prey. As heavy as a large bear, it was one of the biggest of the dromaeosaurids, or "running lizards."

Killer Claws

Utahraptor had a longer, sickle-shaped claw on its second toe (the first toe was not functional). This claw was raised off the ground as it ran, but when the muscles of the toe were contracted, the claw swept down quickly. The 24-cm- (9-in-) long blade could tear at *Utahraptor*'s prey, or cling on like a climbing crampon. With a powerful kick, the claw could have brought down another dinosaur, often killing it instantly.

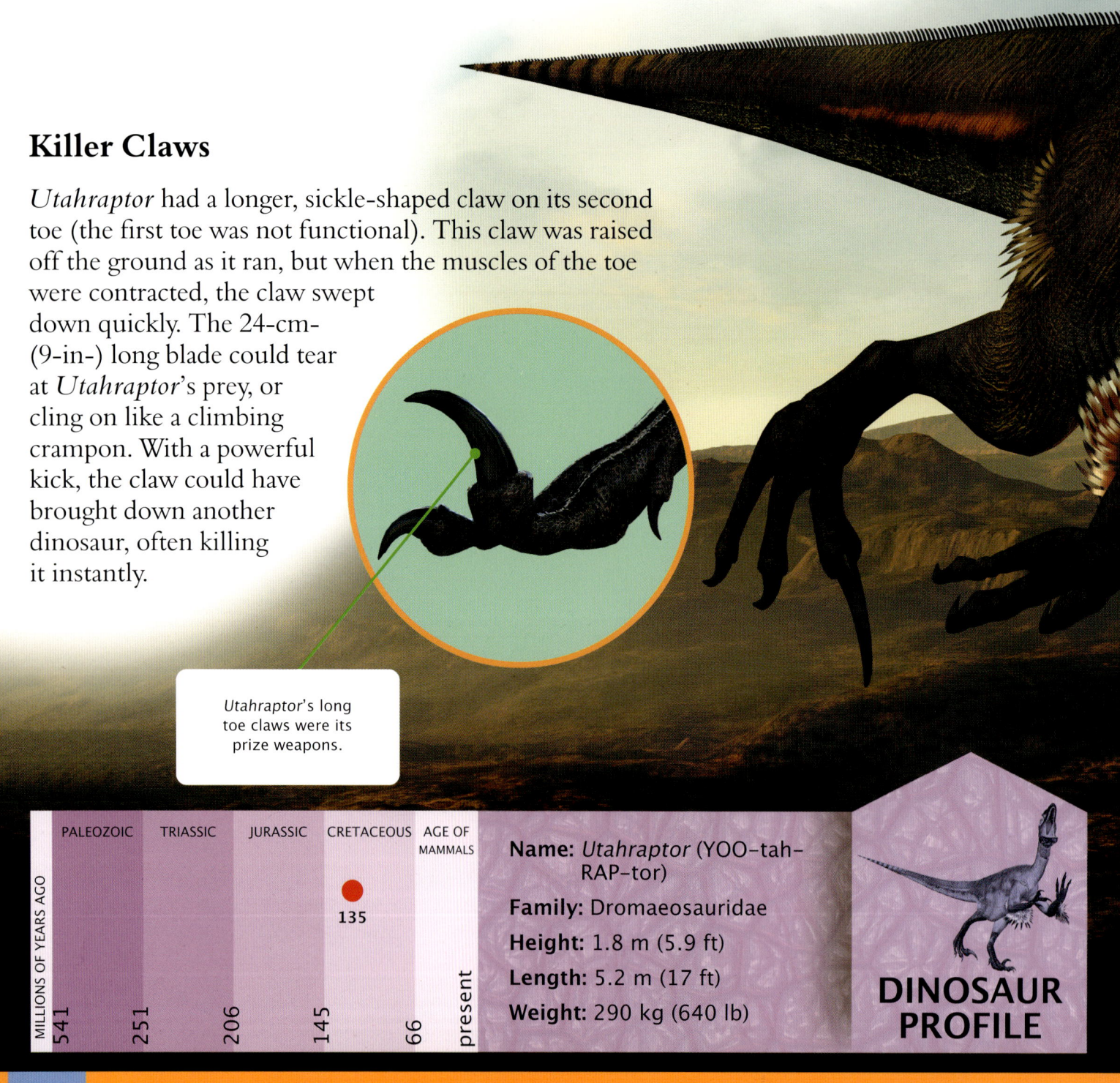

Utahraptor's long toe claws were its prize weapons.

	PALEOZOIC	TRIASSIC	JURASSIC	CRETACEOUS	AGE OF MAMMALS	
MILLIONS OF YEARS AGO	541	251	206	135 ● 145	66	present

Name: *Utahraptor* (YOO–tah–RAP–tor)

Family: Dromaeosauridae

Height: 1.8 m (5.9 ft)

Length: 5.2 m (17 ft)

Weight: 290 kg (640 lb)

DINOSAUR PROFILE

DID YOU KNOW? In 2018, *Utahraptor* was made the state dinosaur of Utah, replacing *Allosaurus*, which became the state fossil.

The first fossils of *Utahraptor* were found in the US state of Utah in 1975.

Utahraptor had powerful jaws, with which it bit and tore at prey until its victims were exhausted.

Due to its bulkier build, *Utahraptor* was probably not as fast a runner as its relatives *Velociraptor* and *Deinonychus*.

Utahraptor's fluffy feathery covering would have been for warmth or for show to attract a mate, since this dinosaur could not fly.

Bird Relatives

Studies of dromaeosaurid bones reveal they were among the theropods most closely related to birds—and possibly that birds were their direct descendants. Scientists believe *Utahraptor* may have been covered in feathers. Fossils of close relatives have been discovered with downy feathers, but no evidence of feathers has yet been found for *Utahraptor*.

Microraptor

The trees of Early Cretaceous China were home to *Microraptor*, a small, four-winged dromaeosaur. Like *Archaeopteryx*, it is one of the missing links between dinosaurs and birds. It probably used its wings to glide and parachute, rather than to truly fly.

Microraptor stretched out its limbs and tail to be as aerodynamic as possible.

Speedy Killer

Microraptor was an opportunist—in other words, it ate whatever prey came its way. It must have been an agile, speedy hunter. *Microraptor* fossils show the remains of small mammals, birds, and even fish inside its gut. One bird meal had been swallowed whole.

Skeleton Specimens

Microraptor was discovered in 2000, in the Jiufotang Formation, a layer of rock in Liaoning, northeastern China. During the Early Cretaceous, Liaoning was warm and swampy. Rocks from that time contain the fossilized remains of many creatures, including other feathered dinosaurs. So far, hundreds of *Microraptor* specimens have been found.

Microraptor had fine, delicate bones.

	PALEOZOIC	TRIASSIC	JURASSIC	CRETACEOUS	AGE OF MAMMALS
MILLIONS OF YEARS AGO	541	251	206	145	66 · present

120

Name: *Microraptor* (MY–kro–rap–tor)

Family: Dromaeosauridae

Length: 65 cm (2.1 ft)

Wingspan: 92 cm (36 in)

Weight: 650 g (1.4 lb)

DINOSAUR PROFILE

DID YOU KNOW? *Microraptor* was not the only four-winged dinosaur. *Changyuraptor*, also from Cretaceous China, was the largest, measuring 1.3 m (4.3 ft) from nose to tail.

Experts think *Microraptor* had gleaming, blackish feathers. Like starlings, it was iridescent, appearing in different shades in different lighting.

Microraptor hunted small, fast prey, including birds.

Microraptor's teeth were serrated on only one side.

Microraptor means "small one who seizes." It used its hand-claws to grip meat or branches.

Deinonychus

The dromaeosaur *Deinonychus* lived in North America during the Early Cretaceous. It probably hunted in packs to bring down prey much larger than itself. Its name means "terrible claw" and its killer weapon was the sickle-shaped claw on its second toe.

Pack Hunter

Paleontologists believe *Deinonychus* hunted in a pack. *Deinonychus* teeth have been found with fossils of the 7-m (23-ft) long ornithopod *Tenontosaurus*, which a *Deinonychus* could not have attacked alone. In addition, groups of *Deinonychus* skeletons have been found in several locations.

Working together, a team of *Deinonychus* could kill a juvenile *Tenontosaurus*. An adult was probably too large for them to attack.

In a Flap

Like all dromaeosaurs, *Deinonychus* had feathers. Experts believe that feathers evolved from reptilian scales that had frayed and grown fluffy. They helped dinosaurs to stay warm. In time, feathers were used for display, too. It is possible that *Deinonychus* juveniles could even fly from danger by flapping their arms.

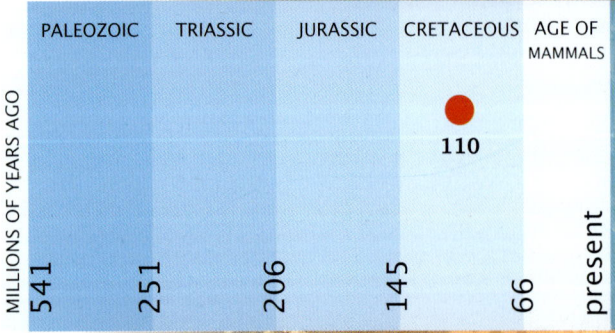

MILLIONS OF YEARS AGO	PALEOZOIC	TRIASSIC	JURASSIC	CRETACEOUS	AGE OF MAMMALS
	541	251	206	145	66 present

110

Name: *Deinonychus* (Dye-NON-ik-us)

Family: Dromaeosauridae

Height: 1.2 m (4 ft)

Length: 3.4 m (11.2 ft)

Weight: 85 kg (187 lb)

DINOSAUR PROFILE

Tenontosaurus, the most common plant-eater in its habitat, was often hunted by Deinonychus.

Deinonychus's hooked, second toe was about 13 cm (5 in) long.

Deinonychus's killing method was to stab prey with its claws and then wait for it to bleed to death.

Deinonychus gripped its prey firmly with its claws. A kick could not shake it off.

DID YOU KNOW? *Deinonychus* was first discovered in 1931—but it was not actually given a name until 1969.

Hesperonychus

This Late Cretaceous dromaeosaur is the smallest known predatory dinosaur from North America. A member of the microraptor group of small dromaeosaurs, it looked much like its larger cousin *Velociraptor*—but unlike *Velociraptor*, it probably spent some of its time in trees.

Gliding for Safety

Hesperonychus was covered with feathers, but it could not fly like a bird. Instead, it may have glided on its wings between the branches of trees as it looked for food. *Hesperonychus* was small enough to go unnoticed by many large dinosaurs, but it would have made a good meal for others, so it kept off the forest floor.

Hesperonychus had long fingers and toes that were suited to gripping tree branches.

The first *Hesperonychus* fossil was discovered by American-Canadian student paleontologist Elizabeth Nicholls in 1982.

DID YOU KNOW? The name *Hesperonychus* comes from the Latin and Greek for "western claw," since it was one of the first small dromaeosaurs found in the western hemisphere.

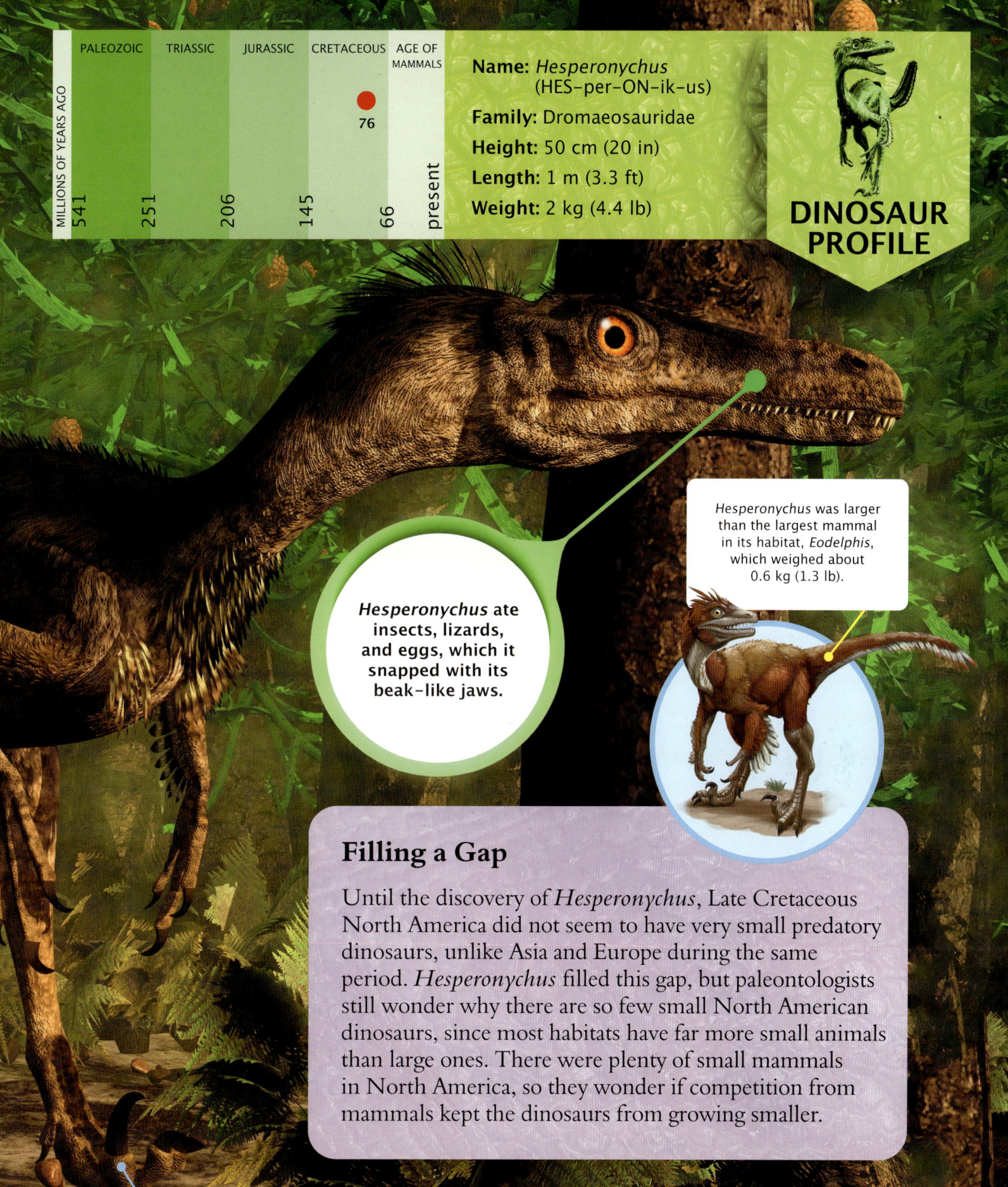

	PALEOZOIC	TRIASSIC	JURASSIC	CRETACEOUS	AGE OF MAMMALS	
MILLIONS OF YEARS AGO	541	251	206	145	66	present

76

Name: *Hesperonychus*
(HES–per–ON–ik–us)
Family: Dromaeosauridae
Height: 50 cm (20 in)
Length: 1 m (3.3 ft)
Weight: 2 kg (4.4 lb)

DINOSAUR PROFILE

Hesperonychus was larger than the largest mammal in its habitat, *Eodelphis*, which weighed about 0.6 kg (1.3 lb).

Hesperonychus ate insects, lizards, and eggs, which it snapped with its beak–like jaws.

Filling a Gap

Until the discovery of *Hesperonychus*, Late Cretaceous North America did not seem to have very small predatory dinosaurs, unlike Asia and Europe during the same period. *Hesperonychus* filled this gap, but paleontologists still wonder why there are so few small North American dinosaurs, since most habitats have far more small animals than large ones. There were plenty of small mammals in North America, so they wonder if competition from mammals kept the dinosaurs from growing smaller.

At around 2.5 cm (1 in) long, the sickle–shaped second claw was smaller than those of most dromaeosaurs.

Baryonyx

In 1983, an amateur fossil hunter made a startling discovery in Surrey, England. He unearthed the fossil of a 25-cm (10-in) thumb claw. Beneath the claw was the skeleton of an unknown dinosaur that was named *Baryonyx*, meaning "heavy claw" in ancient Greek.

Baryonyx had 96 long, pointed, ridged teeth, suited to piercing slippery fish.

Stomach Contents

Fossils have revealed both fish scales and the remains of an *Iguanodon* in *Baryonyx*'s stomach. As one of the largest meat-eating dinosaurs discovered in its habitat, it seems that *Baryonyx* could choose what it ate, mixing its diet between land- and water-dwelling prey.

Baryonyx had a jaw similar to the gharial, a modern crocodilian, suggesting it had a similar, fish–based diet.

When *Baryonyx* lived in Surrey, it was warmer than it is today and was covered by lagoons, mudflats, and marshes.

DID YOU KNOW? *Baryonyx* had denser, heavier bones than most theropods, which may have helped it sink to the bottom when it dived underwater in search of prey.

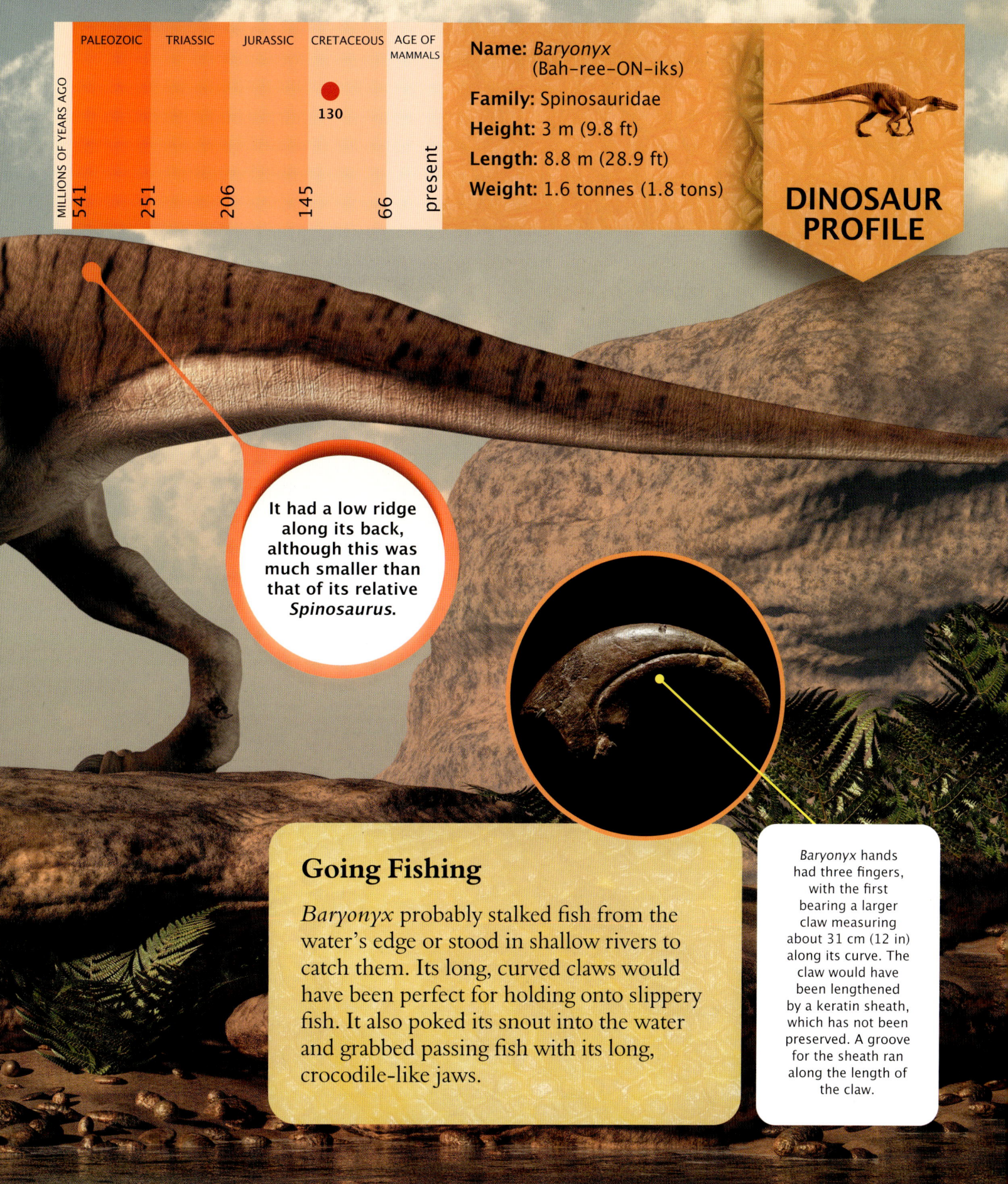

Name: *Baryonyx*
(Bah–ree–ON–iks)
Family: Spinosauridae
Height: 3 m (9.8 ft)
Length: 8.8 m (28.9 ft)
Weight: 1.6 tonnes (1.8 tons)

DINOSAUR PROFILE

It had a low ridge along its back, although this was much smaller than that of its relative *Spinosaurus.*

Going Fishing

Baryonyx probably stalked fish from the water's edge or stood in shallow rivers to catch them. Its long, curved claws would have been perfect for holding onto slippery fish. It also poked its snout into the water and grabbed passing fish with its long, crocodile-like jaws.

Baryonyx hands had three fingers, with the first bearing a larger claw measuring about 31 cm (12 in) along its curve. The claw would have been lengthened by a keratin sheath, which has not been preserved. A groove for the sheath ran along the length of the claw.

Spinosaurus

Spinosaurus was one of the biggest meat-eaters that ever lived. Its long, narrow skull looked rather like a modern crocodile's. This dinosaur used the long claws on its thumbs, as well as its sharp teeth, to grab slippery fish.

Spinosaurus had 68 teeth, which grew up to 15 cm (6 in) long.

The spines on *Spinosaurus*'s back were up to 1.6 m (5.4 ft) long.

Strange Sail

Spinosaurus is named for the Latin word for "spine" and the ancient Greek word for "lizard." Bony spines grew from *Spinosaurus*'s back. These were covered by skin, making a "sail." *Spinosaurus* may have shown off its sail to attract a mate. Today, peacocks use their long tails in the same way. The sail's large surface area may also have helped the dinosaur soak up sunlight in cold weather, and lose excess heat in hot weather.

This North African dinosaur lived around freshwater, as well as on the seashore among mudflats and mangrove forests.

Super Swimmer

Unlike most dinosaurs, *Spinosaurus* spent a lot of time in rivers and shallow seas. Its long, paddle-shaped tail could have powered it through the water. Like a modern crocodile, *Spinosaurus* was probably semiaquatic, hunting both in water and on land—and even leaping into the air to catch passing pterosaurs.

Its long back legs were suited to wading in shallow water.

Spinosaurus tries to snap up an *Onchopristis* fish.

PALEOZOIC	TRIASSIC	JURASSIC	CRETACEOUS	AGE OF MAMMALS
541	251	206	145	66 present

MILLIONS OF YEARS AGO

112

Name: *Spinosaurus* (SPINE-oh-SAWR-us)

Family: Spinosauridae

Height: 4.3 m (14 ft)

Length: 14 m (46 ft)

Weight: 7 tonnes (7.7 tons)

DINOSAUR PROFILE

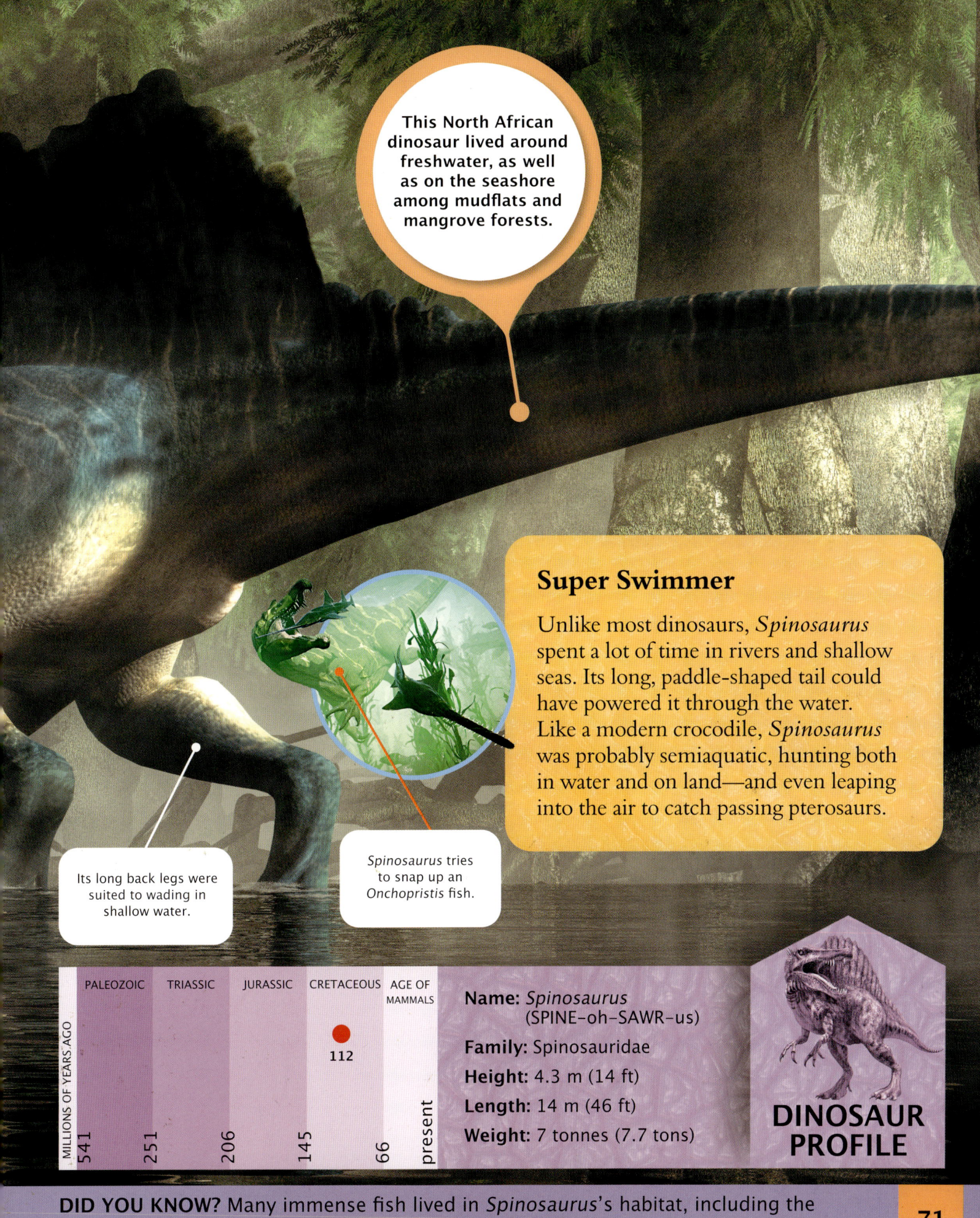

DID YOU KNOW? Many immense fish lived in *Spinosaurus*'s habitat, including the 3-m- (9.8-ft-) long *Bawitius* and the 5-m- (16-ft-) long *Mawsonia*.

Caudipteryx

With its small body, feathers, and beak, *Caudipteryx* looked very much like a bird. However, its arms were not long and strong enough to allow it to fly. Most paleontologists think *Caudipteryx* was an oviraptorosaur dinosaur, others suggest it was a flightless bird, and some think it was both!

Tail Feather

Caudipteryx means "tail feather" in ancient Greek. This dinosaur's tail had a fan of feathers. While its body was covered in short, fluffy feathers, the longest feathers on *Caudipteryx*'s arms were 20 cm (8 in) long. Feathers on the tail and arms helped to keep eggs warm when sitting on a nest.

Like a modern peacock, a male *Caudipteryx* may have shown off its tail to attract females.

Two meat-eating *Dilongs*, around 2 m (6.6 ft) long, have spotted little *Caudipteryx*.

Stone Swallower

This dinosaur is thought to have been an omnivore, eating both plants and small animals. Like some modern birds, *Caudipteryx* swallowed stones. Known as gastroliths, these ground up tough plants in a special, extra stomach called a gizzard. The gizzard walls had strong muscles that squeezed the food and stones.

Stones can be seen in the stomach of this *Caudipteryx* fossil.

MILLIONS OF YEARS AGO	PALEOZOIC	TRIASSIC	JURASSIC	CRETACEOUS	AGE OF MAMMALS
	541	251	206	145	66 present

125

Name: *Caudipteryx*
(Caw–DIP–tuh–riks)
Family: Caudipteridae
Height: 50 cm (20 in)
Length: 80 cm (31 in)
Weight: 2.3 kg (5 lb)

DINOSAUR PROFILE

Little *Caudipteryx* lived in forested river valleys in eastern Asia.

Caudipteryx's hard-edged beak held a few small, weak teeth.

DID YOU KNOW? Some paleontologists think *Caudipteryx* was a flightless bird descended from birds that could fly—but, like the ostrich, it lost the ability as it evolved.

Giganotosaurus

When *Giganotosaurus* was discovered in Argentina in 1993, the 12-m- (39-ft-) long carnivore was thought to be the largest theropod in the southern hemisphere—and possibly even the world. Its name means "giant southern lizard."

On the Run

Giganotosaurus is known from preserved tracks as well as fossilized bones. Experts have been able to work out how fast it could run by considering its body size and looking at the spacing between its footprints. Its top speed was probably around 50 km/h (31 mph). By comparison, *Tyrannosaurus* (pages 96–97) could reach only 40 km/h (25 mph).

Giganotosaurus

The Carcharodonts

Giganotosaurus was one of the carcharodonts: a group of dinosaurs named after the theropod *Carcharodontosaurus* that lived in North Africa during the Late Cretaceous. Their sharp, serrated teeth resemble those of the great white shark, *Carcharodon*. Both *Giganotosaurus* and *Carcharodontosaurus* had a gigantic skull with bony ridges overhanging the eyes, massive jaws, and long teeth.

Carcharodontosaurus

	PALEOZOIC	TRIASSIC	JURASSIC	CRETACEOUS	AGE OF MAMMALS
MILLIONS OF YEARS AGO	541	251	206	145	66 — present

98

Name: *Giganotosaurus* (JIG-an-oh-tuh-SAWR-us)

Family: Carcharodontosauridae

Height: 7 m (23 ft)

Length: 12 m (39 ft)

Weight: 7.3 tonnes (8 tons)

DINOSAUR PROFILE

Giganotosaurus had a weaker biting force than *Tyrannosaurus*, but could snap its jaws shut more quickly.

Giganotosaurus had low, horn–like projections on the bones above and in front of its eyes—just like *Carcharodontosaurus*.

Giganotosaurus was the apex (top) predator in its habitat.

Giganotosaurus's skull was about 1.8 m (6 ft) long.

Giganotosaurus had powerful, muscular back legs.

DID YOU KNOW? *Giganotosaurus* had a close cousin, *Mapusaurus*, which lived in Argentina at the same time and was just as large.

Carcharodontosaurus

During the Late Cretaceous Period, *Carcharodontosaurus* was one of the largest hunters in North Africa. Its head was larger than the *Tyrannosaurus* and it contained a mouthful of long, blade-like teeth. *Carcharodontosaurus* needed to eat 60 kg (130 lb) of meat every day to survive.

Battling Giants

Different species of large, predatory dinosaurs usually avoided each other. However, battles between them did take place, probably when one strayed into another's territory. We know about a battle between a *Spinosaurus* and *Carcharodontosaurus* because of a *Spinosaurus* bone that has been bitten in half by a *Carcharodontosaurus*. Unlike *Carcharodontosaurus*, which hunted only on land, *Spinosaurus* probably only sought prey on land when water levels dropped. This may have been what happened when it strayed into a *Carcharodontosaurus*'s territory, resulting in a mighty battle.

We do not know whether *Carcharodontosaurus* (left) or *Spinosaurus* (right) won the battle.

Based on the activities of modern predators, paleontologists think *Carcharodontosaurus* defended a hunting territory of around 500 sq km (200 sq miles).

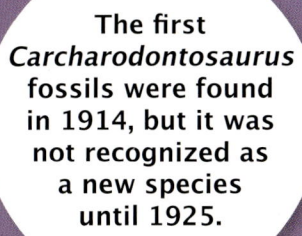

The first *Carcharodontosaurus* fossils were found in 1914, but it was not recognized as a new species until 1925.

Carcharodontosaurus was one of the biggest carnivorous dinosaurs, with a skull up to 1.63 m (5.3 ft) long.

Up to 20 cm (8 in) long, a *Carcharodontosaurus* tooth is relatively flat, with a jagged edge like a carving knife. A bite from this dinosaur left a gaping wound that leaked large quantities of blood, soon making prey drop to the ground.

Shark Teeth

The name *Carcharodontosaurus* means "shark-toothed lizard." It was named after a modern predator, the great white shark—which has the scientific name *Carcharodon*, composed of the ancient Greek words for "jagged" and "teeth"—because of the resemblance between their serrated teeth. Such teeth are well suited to slicing both flesh and bone.

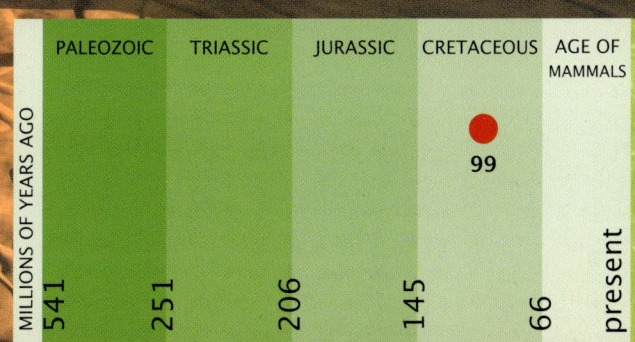

MILLIONS OF YEARS AGO	PALEOZOIC	TRIASSIC	JURASSIC	CRETACEOUS	AGE OF MAMMALS
	541	251	206	145	66 · present

99

Name: *Carcharodontosaurus* (CAR-car-oh-dont-oh-SAWR-us)

Family: Carcharodontosauridae

Height: 3.6 m (11.8 ft)

Length: 12 m (39 ft)

Weight: 5 tonnes (5.5 tons)

DINOSAUR PROFILE

DID YOU KNOW? A study showed that, based on the strength of its jaws and neck, *Carcharodontosaurus* could lift animals weighing up to 424 kg (935 lb) in its jaws.

Mapusaurus

Up to 35 m (115 ft) long, the plant-eater *Argentinosaurus* was perhaps the largest land animal that ever lived. It was thought unlikely that there was a predator big enough to hunt it, but in 2006, a discovery made experts think again. A new killer had been found—*Mapusaurus*—and it was capable of hunting a giant like *Argentinosaurus*.

Pack Hunter

Around 11 m (36 ft) long, *Mapusaurus* was too small to prey on *Argentinosaurus* alone. Instead, several *Mapusauruses* worked as a group to attack the great sauropod. One such group was discovered in a South American fossil bed in 2006. The skeletons of several *Mapusauruses* of different ages proved the theory that this killer was a pack hunter.

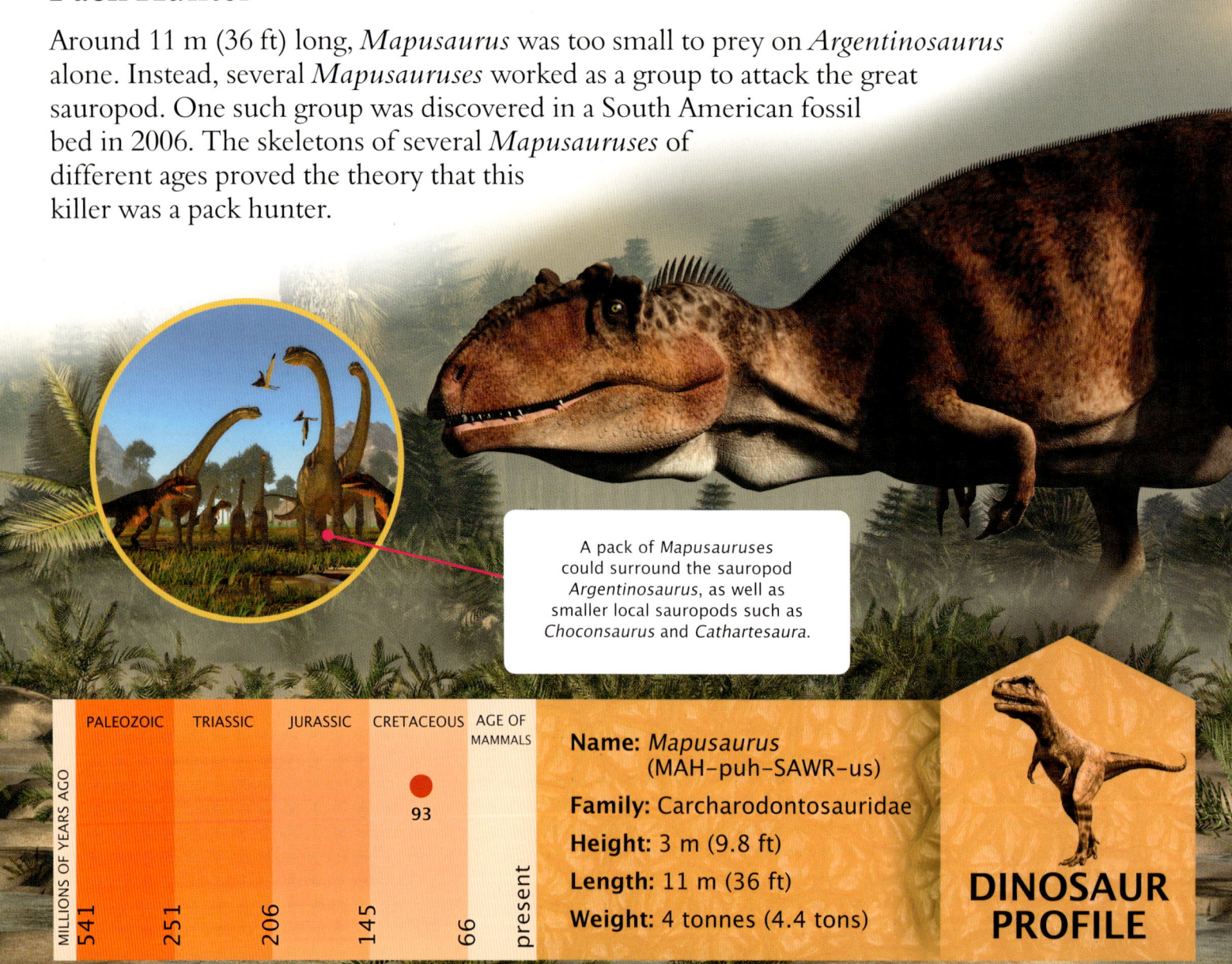

A pack of *Mapusauruses* could surround the sauropod *Argentinosaurus*, as well as smaller local sauropods such as *Choconsaurus* and *Cathartesaura*.

MILLIONS OF YEARS AGO	PALEOZOIC	TRIASSIC	JURASSIC	CRETACEOUS	AGE OF MAMMALS	
	541	251	206	145	66	present

93

Name: *Mapusaurus* (MAH–puh–SAWR–us)

Family: Carcharodontosauridae

Height: 3 m (9.8 ft)

Length: 11 m (36 ft)

Weight: 4 tonnes (4.4 tons)

DINOSAUR PROFILE

DID YOU KNOW? *Mapusaurus* was the largest meat-eater in its habitat, facing little competition from the smaller theropods *Skorpiovenator* and *Ilokelesia*.

Killing Style

Experts think that even a *Mapusaurus* pack would not have been able to bring down an adult *Argentinosaurus*. Instead, they think *Mapusaurus* took non-lethal bites out of *Argentinosaurus's* body but left the dinosaur standing. *Mapusaurus's* blade-like teeth were perfectly designed to slice off pieces of flesh in this way.

By treating *Argentinosaurus's* body like a table to take a snack from, *Mapusaurus* could come back and snack again in the future.

Fossilized pollen and other plant remains tell us that *Mapusaurus* lived among conifers, ferns, liverworts, and hornworts.

Found in Argentina, *Mapusaurus* was named for the word *mapu*, meaning "of the Earth" in the language of the Mapuche people of Argentina and Chile.

Mapusaurus was very similar in bone and tooth shape to its larger relative *Giganotosaurus*.

Gigantoraptor

Gigantoraptor was the largest known oviraptorosaur, a group of extremely bird-like dinosaurs with short, beaked, parrot-like skulls. Oviraptorosaurs were feathered and usually small, like *Caudipteryx*, but *Gigantoraptor* grew to 8 m (26 ft) long.

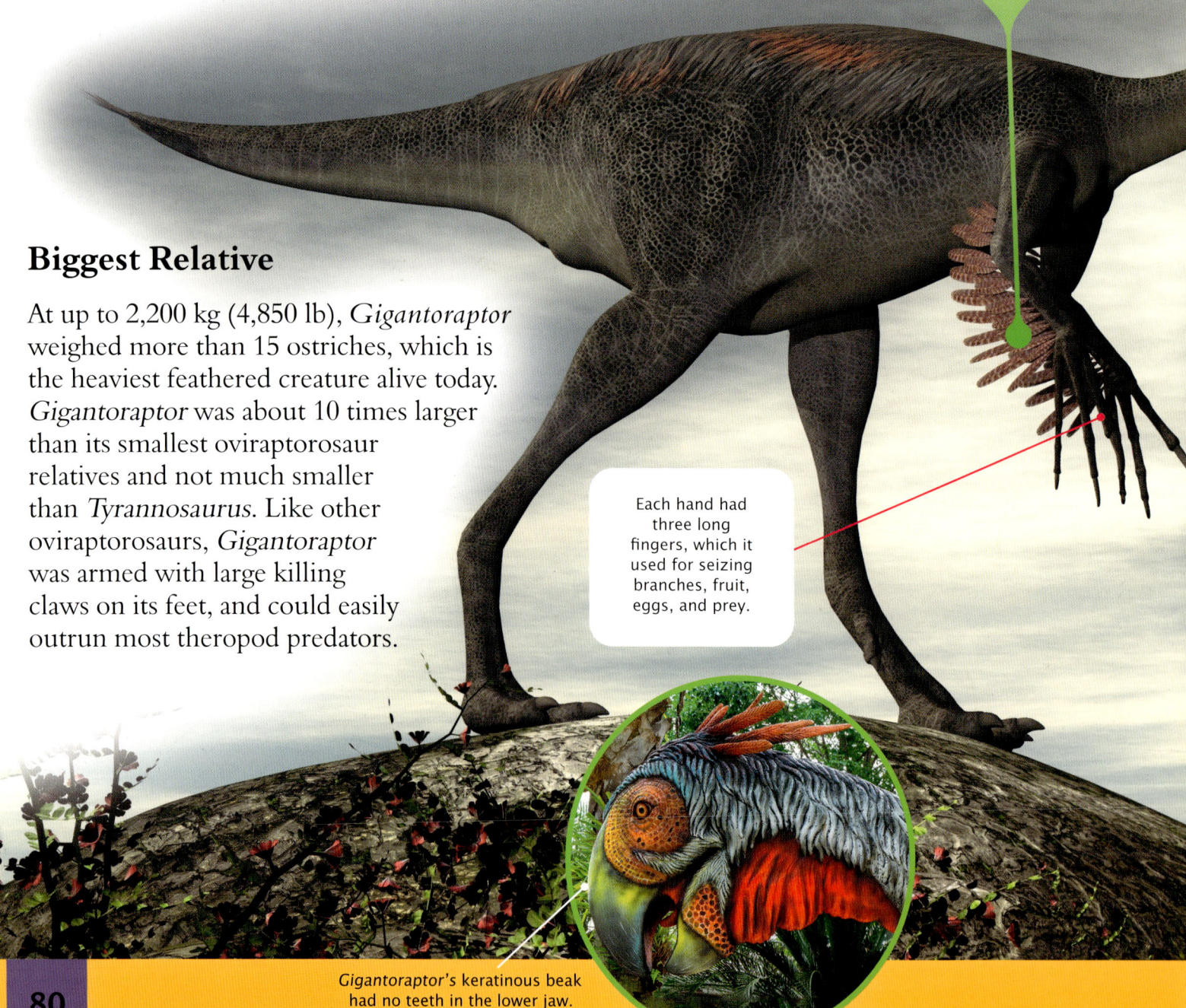

Gigantoraptor had wings, but probably flapped them only to attract a mate or to threaten predators and rivals.

Each hand had three long fingers, which it used for seizing branches, fruit, eggs, and prey.

Biggest Relative

At up to 2,200 kg (4,850 lb), *Gigantoraptor* weighed more than 15 ostriches, which is the heaviest feathered creature alive today. *Gigantoraptor* was about 10 times larger than its smallest oviraptorosaur relatives and not much smaller than *Tyrannosaurus*. Like other oviraptorosaurs, *Gigantoraptor* was armed with large killing claws on its feet, and could easily outrun most theropod predators.

Gigantoraptor's keratinous beak had no teeth in the lower jaw.

Not Cracking Eggs

A female *Gigantoraptor* laid her eggs in a ring up to 3 m (9.8 ft) across. The eggs were not covered by leaves or soil. Oviraptorosaur nests usually had eggs arranged in a circle, but smaller species left no gap at the middle of the nest, whereas large species such as *Gigantoraptor* did. This suggests that, while small oviraptorosaurs sat directly on their eggs to keep them warm, a *Gigantoraptor* sat on the area without eggs to avoid egg-crushing.

The eggs of large oviraptorosaurs were around 50 cm (20 in) long.

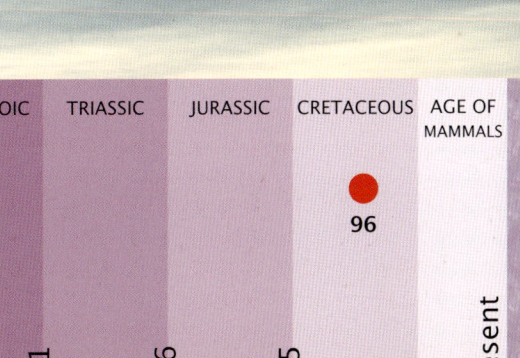

	PALEOZOIC	TRIASSIC	JURASSIC	CRETACEOUS	AGE OF MAMMALS

MILLIONS OF YEARS AGO

541 — 251 — 206 — 145 — 66 — present

96

Name: *Gigantoraptor* (JIG-ant-oh-RAP-tor)

Family: Caenagnathidae

Height: 3.5 m (11.5 ft)

Length: 8 m (26.2 ft)

Weight: 2.2 tonnes (2.4 tons)

DINOSAUR PROFILE

DID YOU KNOW? A *Gigantoraptor* probably reached full size at around 10 years old, gaining about 128-140 kg (282-309 lb) per year during its early life.

Troodon

Birdlike *Troodon* lived across North America in the Late Cretaceous. Its name means "wounding teeth." When it was first discovered in 1856, it was known from just one fossil, a small and extremely sharp tooth.

Clever Carnivore

Troodon is sometimes described as the most intelligent dinosaur. Compared to other dinosaurs its size, it probably was. Its brain was about six times heavier than its counterparts. However, it was only as large as an emu's brain today, so *Troodon* cannot have been *that* smart.

Neat Nests

Troodon laid its eggs in bowl-shaped nests over a period of about a week. Just like ostriches today, it is likely that the males and females took turns sitting on the nest to keep the eggs warm. A typical nest contained between 16 and 24 eggs.

Troodon preyed on other dinosaurs, such as young hadrosaurs. It also hunted small mammals and lizards.

Part of a nest of *Troodon* eggs, preserved in rock.

Troodon had binocular vision—forward-pointing eyes that allowed it to judge distances.

Troodon's covering of feathers kept its body warm.

Troodon used its jaws, hands, or feet to grip prey.

PALEOZOIC	TRIASSIC	JURASSIC	CRETACEOUS	AGE OF MAMMALS

MILLIONS OF YEARS AGO

77

541 251 206 145 66 present

Name: *Troodon* (TRO–uh–don)
Family: Troodontidae
Height: 0.9 m (3 ft)
Length: 2.4 m (7.9 ft)
Weight: 50 kg (110 lb)

DINOSAUR PROFILE

DID YOU KNOW? *Troodon's* relatively large eyes let in plenty of light. It could hunt at dawn, at dusk, or even in the middle of the night.

83

Ornithomimus

Ornithomimus means "bird mimic"—and its feathers and body shape made it look a lot like a modern ostrich. Yet *Ornithomimus* was not a bird: It was a theropod in the ornithomimosaur group. The ornithomimosaurs had feathers, slender arms and claws, long legs, and it could achieve fast running speeds.

Ornithomimus lived in North America, probably in a large flock.

Its legs were suited to fast running, with a tibia (lower leg bone) around 20 percent longer than the femur (upper leg bone).

Omnivore Beak

We know that *Ornithomimus* ate plants as well as meat, because it had a long, scissor-like beak. This would have been used to pick up insects and small reptiles, but also to strip and slice through leaves and other plant material. *Ornithomimus*'s long fingers would have been useful for grasping branches and fruit, as well as poking insect nests.

Unusually for theropods, *Ornithomimus* and its close relatives were toothless.

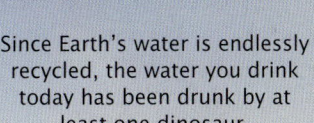

Examination of the bones around *Ornithomimus*'s eyes suggest it was active for short periods throughout the day and night, a habit known as cathemerality.

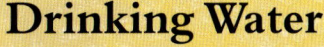

Since Earth's water is endlessly recycled, the water you drink today has been drunk by at least one dinosaur.

Drinking Water

Scientists have studied eggs laid by dinosaurs such as *Ornithomimus* for traces of the water they drank. By measuring the levels of minerals such as magnesium and iron inside an egg, it is possible to discover whether the mother drank rainwater, river water, or swamp water. The results show that female dinosaurs seemed to stick to one source of fresh, running water before egg-laying, suggesting they stayed in one well-watered spot.

	PALEOZOIC	TRIASSIC	JURASSIC	CRETACEOUS	AGE OF MAMMALS
MILLIONS OF YEARS AGO	541	251	206	145	66 present

76

Name: *Ornithomimus* (OR–nith–OM–im–us)
Family: Ornithomimidae
Height: 1.5 m (4.9 ft)
Length: 3.8 m (12.5 ft)
Weight: 170 kg (375 lb)

DINOSAUR PROFILE

DID YOU KNOW? The brain of *Ornithomimus* was large compared to its body size, with large portions dedicated to coordinating movements.

Deinocheirus

Like *Ornithomimus*, *Deinocheirus* was part of the ornithomimosaur group of theropods. It fed on plants and small animals. The dinosaur's large claws earned it the name *Deinocheirus*, which means "horrible hand." Yet the claws were blunt and probably used only for digging up plants.

The tail ended in fused bones known as a pygostyle, which probably supported a fan of feathers.

Scary Sail

On its back, *Deinocheirus* had bony spines that made a "sail." The sail made Deinocheirus look bigger to meat-eaters thinking of an attack. Ligaments (strong, rope-like tissues) extending from the back spines also helped to support the dinosaur's huge stomach. This spine-and-ligament structure was a little like human-built bridges that use towers and cables to support roads.

In hot weather, the sail helped *Deinocheirus* cool down, as it gave more skin surface to lose heat from.

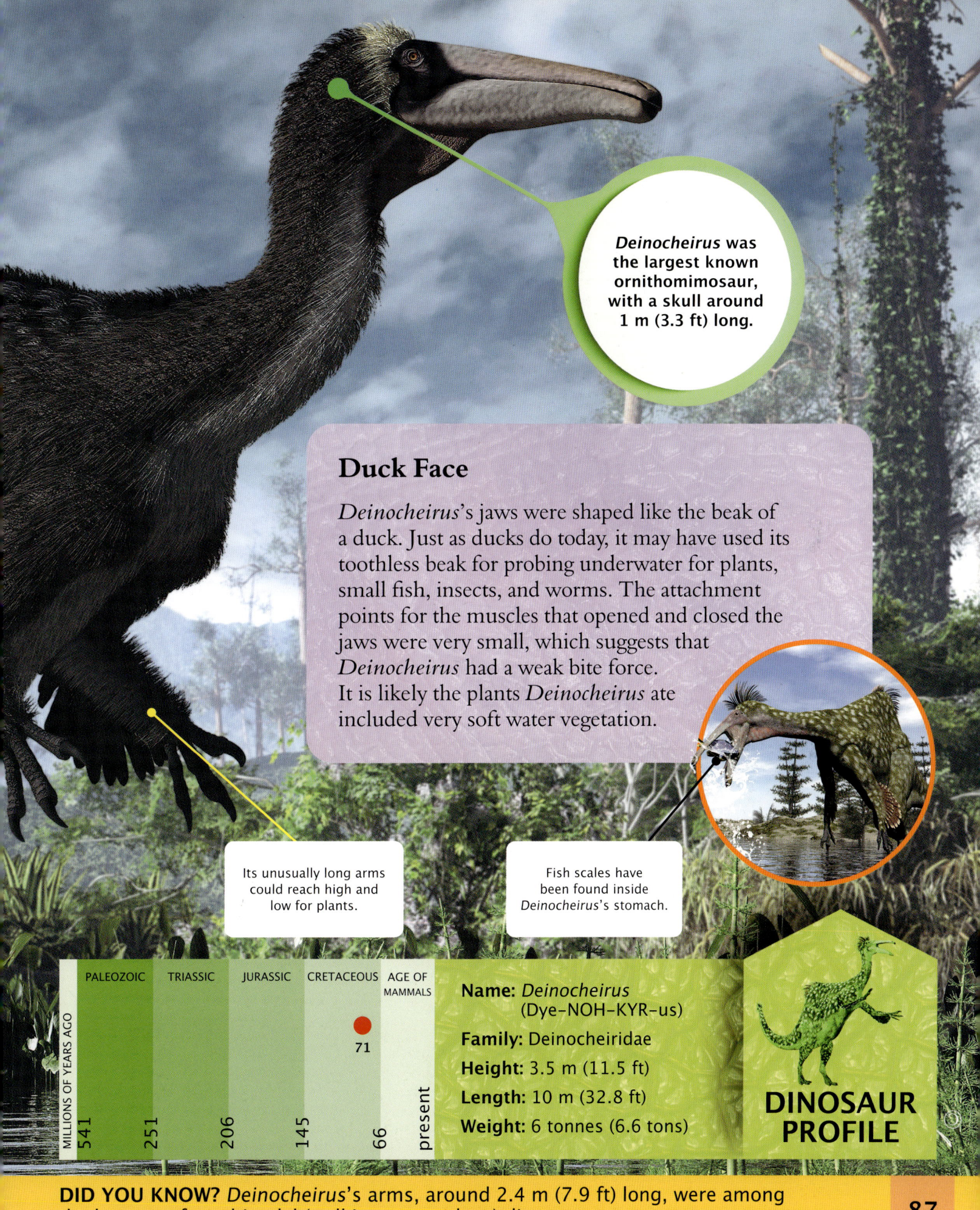

Deinocheirus was the largest known ornithomimosaur, with a skull around 1 m (3.3 ft) long.

Duck Face

Deinocheirus's jaws were shaped like the beak of a duck. Just as ducks do today, it may have used its toothless beak for probing underwater for plants, small fish, insects, and worms. The attachment points for the muscles that opened and closed the jaws were very small, which suggests that *Deinocheirus* had a weak bite force. It is likely the plants *Deinocheirus* ate included very soft water vegetation.

Its unusually long arms could reach high and low for plants.

Fish scales have been found inside *Deinocheirus*'s stomach.

	PALEOZOIC	TRIASSIC	JURASSIC	CRETACEOUS	AGE OF MAMMALS
MILLIONS OF YEARS AGO	541	251	206	145	66 present

71

Name: *Deinocheirus* (Dye–NOH–KYR–us)

Family: Deinocheiridae

Height: 3.5 m (11.5 ft)

Length: 10 m (32.8 ft)

Weight: 6 tonnes (6.6 tons)

DINOSAUR PROFILE

DID YOU KNOW? *Deinocheirus*'s arms, around 2.4 m (7.9 ft) long, were among the longest of any bipedal (walking on two legs) dinosaur.

Majungasaurus

During the Late Cretaceous Period, two types of killer dinosaurs dominated Earth. The northern hemisphere was ruled by tyrannosaurs, and the southern hemisphere by abelisaurs. Abelisaurs, including *Majungasaurus* and *Carnotaurus*, were just as dangerous as their northern counterparts—and some also had a disturbing habit: cannibalism.

Cretaceous Cannibals

Majungasaurus was a common abelisaur that left many fossils behind. The bones of these fossils have revealed a series of deep bite marks made by other *Majungasauruses*. These marks show that the dinosaurs not only fought each other, but that they also ate the flesh off each others' bones. It is the first direct evidence of cannibalism in dinosaurs.

A long tail stabilized the weight of the head and body, so the dinosaur was balanced over its hips.

Although cannibalism is quite rare among modern animals, the largest modern species of lizard, the Komodo dragon, sometimes kills members of its species when competing for access to carcasses.

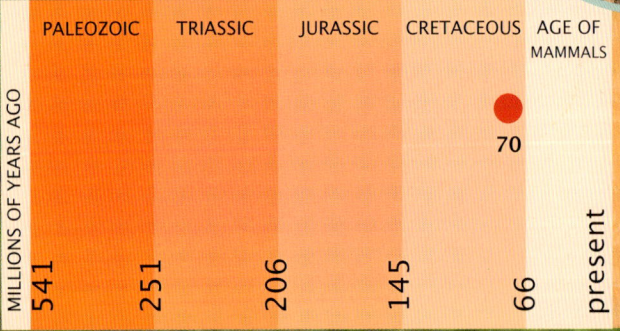

PALEOZOIC	TRIASSIC	JURASSIC	CRETACEOUS	AGE OF MAMMALS
541	251	206	145	66	present

MILLIONS OF YEARS AGO

70

Name: *Majungasaurus* (Mah-JOONG-ah-SAWR-us)

Family: Abelisauridae

Height: 2 m (6.6 ft)

Length: 6.3 m (20.7 ft)

Weight: 1.1 tonnes (1.2 tons)

DINOSAUR PROFILE

DID YOU KNOW? *Majungasaurus* was named after the old Mahajanga Province of northwestern Madagascar, a large island off the coast of Africa.

Killing Technique

Abelisaurs had a much shorter skull than the tyrannosaurs, and they had different ways of killing their prey. Instead of tearing chunks off a victim until it was dead, *Majungasaurus* may have clamped its jaws full of sharp teeth down tight on its prey's neck. This bite-and-hold technique was similar to that used by modern lions and was brutally effective.

The front teeth of the upper jaw of *Majungasaurus* were stronger than the rest to provide an anchor point for its long-lasting, slow-killing bites.

A small, dome-like horn protruded from the fused bones of *Majungasaurus*'s forehead.

Majungasaurus lived in Madagascar until 66 million years ago, when it was wiped out after an asteroid hit Earth.

Carnotaurus

Carnotaurus means "flesh-eating bull." With two horns and a powerful, bulky body, this theropod certainly had a bull-like appearance. It had a hunter's forward-facing vision and muscly legs that could chase prey at high speed.

Scent Stalker

Carnotaurus probably followed its nose to find prey. The shape of its deep skull suggests the brain's olfactory lobes (responsible for smell) were large, giving the dinosaur an above-average sense of smell for a theropod. In contrast, the optic lobes, which were responsible for sight, were relatively small.

Carnotaurus probably stalked its prey by following its scent.

Carnotaurus had a relatively weak bite (3,390 Newtons, compared with *Tyrannosaurus*'s 35,000 Newtons), but could make many small, quick bites that would have weakened large prey.

Its arms were extremely short, had no wristbone, and had almost immobile fingers, so *Carnotaurus* could not grasp prey with its hands.

				AGE OF MAMMALS	
PALEOZOIC	TRIASSIC	JURASSIC	CRETACEOUS		

MILLIONS OF YEARS AGO

541 · 251 · 206 · 145 · 66 · present

71

Name: *Carnotaurus*
(CAR–no–TAWR–us)
Family: Abelisauridae
Height: 2.8 m (9.2 ft)
Length: 8 m (26.2 ft)
Weight: 1.7 tonnes (1.9 tons)

DINOSAUR PROFILE

Carnotaurus lived in South America during the Late Cretaceous Period.

Horn Fighter

Carnotaurus's horns stuck out sideways just above the eyes, and may have been used in male-on-male fights. They may also have been used to help knock out its prey, or for display in the mating season. Its strong neck would have given *Carnotaurus* colossal power if it butted a rival. For extra protection in sparring or attacks, *Carnotaurus* had extra-hard, larger, pebbly scales over its head, neck, and back.

The flexible joints of *Carnotaurus's* jaw and skull could absorb more pressure during head butts or bites than those of other theropods.

DID YOU KNOW? *Carnotaurus's* arms were vestigial, which means they had evolved to be useless—like the coccyx (tailbone) in humans.

91

Therizinosaurus

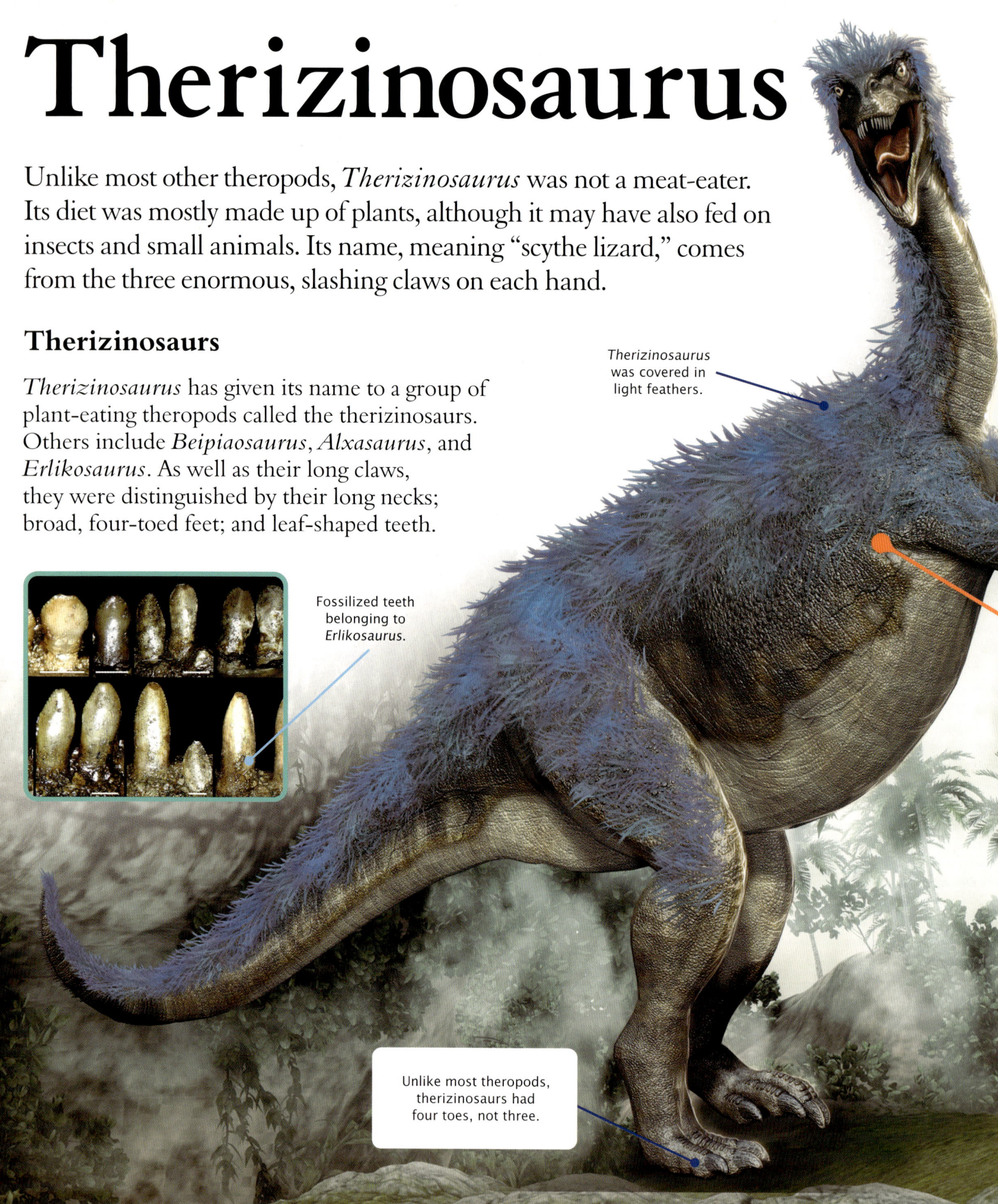

Unlike most other theropods, *Therizinosaurus* was not a meat-eater. Its diet was mostly made up of plants, although it may have also fed on insects and small animals. Its name, meaning "scythe lizard," comes from the three enormous, slashing claws on each hand.

Therizinosaurs

Therizinosaurus has given its name to a group of plant-eating theropods called the therizinosaurs. Others include *Beipiaosaurus*, *Alxasaurus*, and *Erlikosaurus*. As well as their long claws, they were distinguished by their long necks; broad, four-toed feet; and leaf-shaped teeth.

Therizinosaurus was covered in light feathers.

Fossilized teeth belonging to *Erlikosaurus.*

Unlike most theropods, therizinosaurs had four toes, not three.

DID YOU KNOW? Therizinosaurs probably nested in groups. Seventeen clutches of eggs were found close to each other in the Gobi Desert, in China, in 2013.

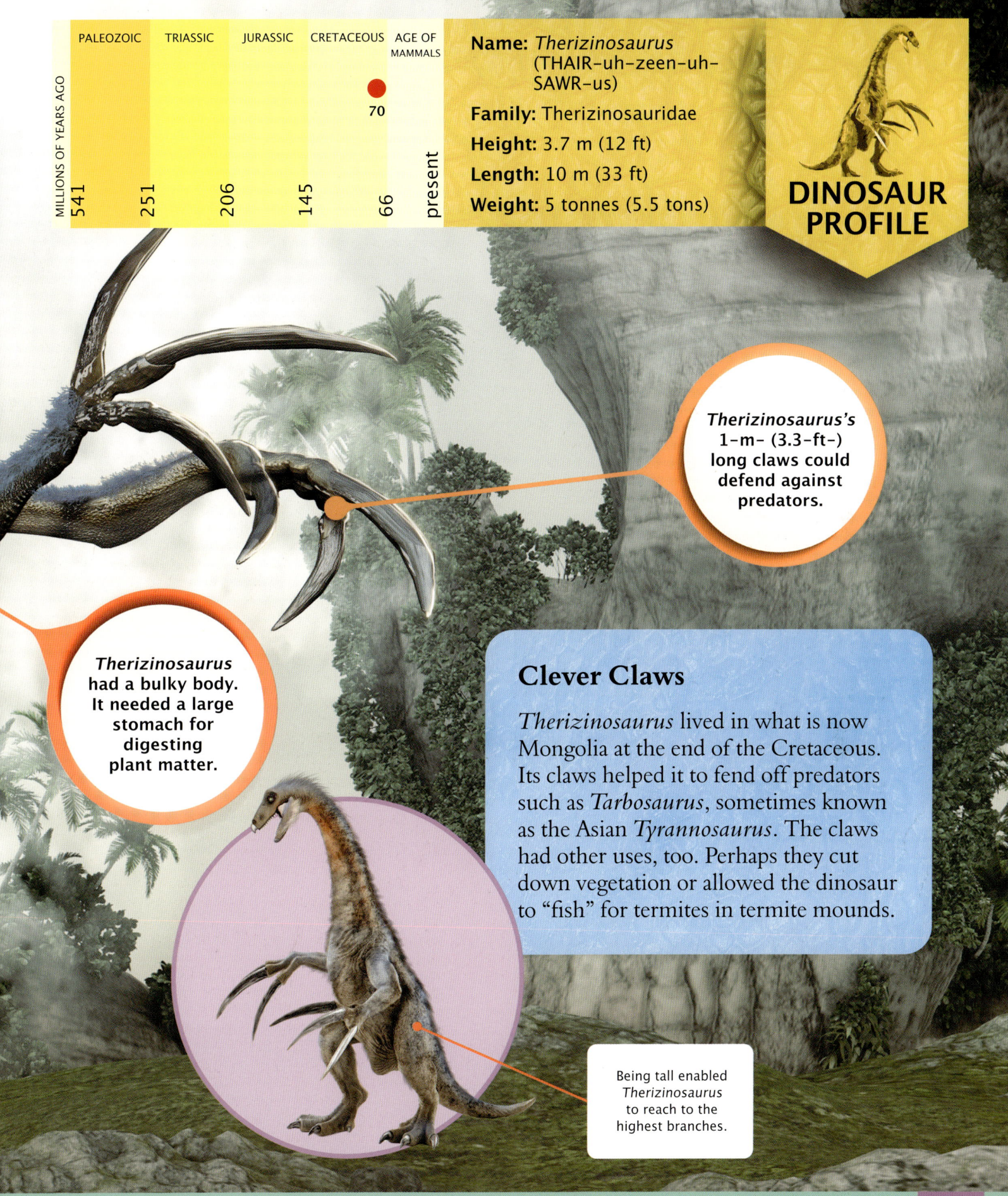

	PALEOZOIC	TRIASSIC	JURASSIC	CRETACEOUS	AGE OF MAMMALS
MILLIONS OF YEARS AGO	541	251	206	145	66	present

70

Name: *Therizinosaurus*
(THAIR-uh-zeen-uh-
SAWR-us)
Family: Therizinosauridae
Height: 3.7 m (12 ft)
Length: 10 m (33 ft)
Weight: 5 tonnes (5.5 tons)

DINOSAUR PROFILE

Therizinosaurus's 1-m- (3.3-ft-) long claws could defend against predators.

Therizinosaurus had a bulky body. It needed a large stomach for digesting plant matter.

Clever Claws

Therizinosaurus lived in what is now Mongolia at the end of the Cretaceous. Its claws helped it to fend off predators such as *Tarbosaurus*, sometimes known as the Asian *Tyrannosaurus*. The claws had other uses, too. Perhaps they cut down vegetation or allowed the dinosaur to "fish" for termites in termite mounds.

Being tall enabled *Therizinosaurus* to reach to the highest branches.

93

Daspletosaurus

When the remains of a *Daspletosaurus* were discovered in Canada, it was obvious that the dinosaur was an ancestor to *Tyrannosaurus*. *Daspletosaurus* resembled *Tyrannosaurus* in almost every way, except it was smaller and lighter.

Taking the Chance

Like a lion in a pride, *Daspletosaurus* was a pack hunter that would cooperate with other *Daspletosauruses* to bring down prey. However, *Daspletosaurus* was more of an opportunist than a thinker, so it is unlikely that these group kills were well organized. Instead, several *Daspletosauruses* would have grabbed their chance to join together and attack an isolated plant-eater.

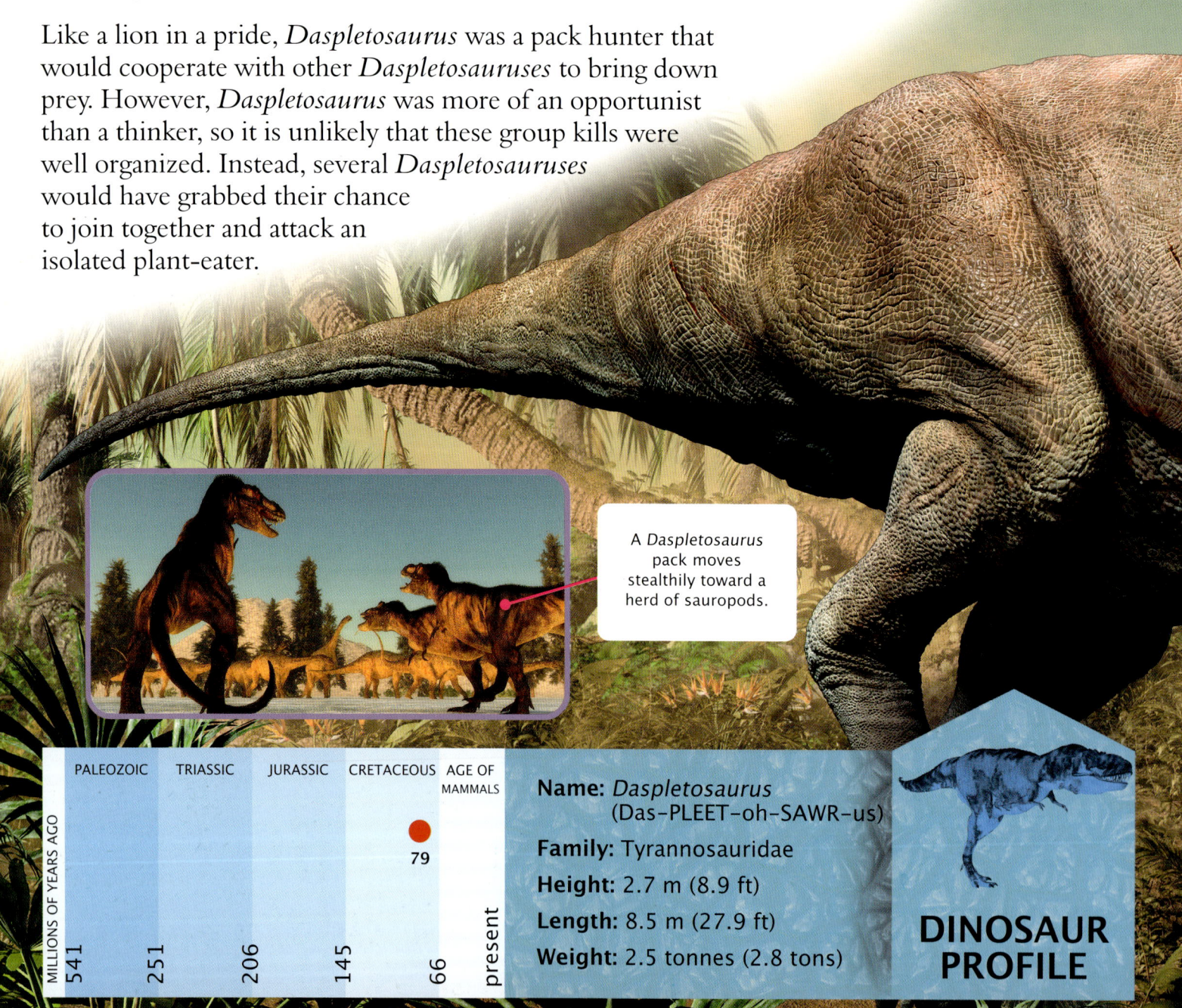

A *Daspletosaurus* pack moves stealthily toward a herd of sauropods.

	PALEOZOIC	TRIASSIC	JURASSIC	CRETACEOUS	AGE OF MAMMALS
MILLIONS OF YEARS AGO	541	251	206	145	79 / 66 / present

Name: *Daspletosaurus* (Das-PLEET-oh-SAWR-us)
Family: Tyrannosauridae
Height: 2.7 m (8.9 ft)
Length: 8.5 m (27.9 ft)
Weight: 2.5 tonnes (2.8 tons)

DINOSAUR PROFILE

Although some smaller, earlier tyrannosaurs had downy feathers to keep them warm, many paleontologists think *Daspletosaurus* had scales.

Daspletosaurus (meaning "frightful lizard") was an apex predator, at the top of its food chain.

Larger scales on the snout protected *Daspletosaurus* during prey capture and fights with rivals.

Daspletosauruses may have fought over territory or resources, or for dominance within a social group.

Taking Bites

After a *Daspletosaurus* kill had been made, it would have been every dinosaur for itself, with the strongest taking all. This explains some of the *Daspletosaurus* teeth marks found on the bones of other *Daspletosauruses*: The killers might have been scrapping over pieces of meat. Some of the bite marks had healed over, indicating that the dinosaur survived the bite.

DID YOU KNOW? *Daspletosaurus* lived alongside another tyrannosaur, but the smaller *Gorgosaurus* mainly hunted duckbill dinosaurs, while *Daspletosaurus* took ceratopsians.

Tyrannosaurus

Tyrannosaurus was the biggest meat-eater that ever lived in North America. An adult *Tyrannosaurus* had no need to fear any other animal. However, this deadly beast was wiped out when a giant space rock hit Earth, around 66 million years ago.

Powerful Bite

Tyrannosaurus had one of the strongest bites of any animal that has lived. Its bite force was equal to the weight of three small cars. Its thick, strong jaw bones could open very wide, before powerful muscles snapped them closed. After getting a firm grip on flesh and muscle, *Tyrannosaurus* probably clamped its teeth, then shook its head to free a bite-sized chunk, in the manner of crocodiles feeding today.

Tyrannosaurus's jaws crushed bone.

Although young *Tyrannosauruses* may have had some downy feathers, it is likely that fully grown adults had tough scales.

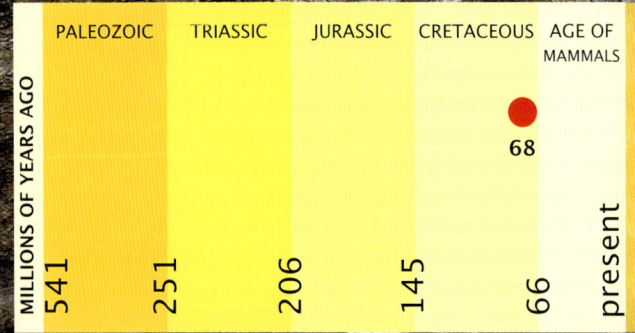

	PALEOZOIC	TRIASSIC	JURASSIC	CRETACEOUS	AGE OF MAMMALS
MILLIONS OF YEARS AGO	541	251	206	145	66 · present

68

Name: *Tyrannosaurus* (Ty–RAN–oh–SAWR–us)

Family: Tyrannosauridae

Height: 4 m (13 ft)

Length: 12.6 m (41.3 ft)

Weight: 7 tonnes (7.7 tons)

DINOSAUR PROFILE

Tyrannosaurus's 60 jagged-edged, knife-like teeth grew up to 30 cm (12 in) long.

Hunting and Scavenging

Tyrannosaurus may have run at 15 to 30 km/h (9 to 18 mph). This was much slower than smaller, lighter theropods such as dromaeosaurs, but fast enough to catch slow-moving plant-eaters such as sauropods and ceratopsians. Many paleontologists think *Tyrannosaurus* was both a hunter and a scavenger. Scavengers eat animals they find dead or dying. Some of today's big meat-eaters, such as lions, are also both hunters and scavengers. *Tyrannosaurus* needed to feed often, so it probably ate whatever animals it came across, alive or dead.

Like modern meat-eaters, from great white sharks to wolves, *Tyrannosaurus* had a very good sense of smell, which enabled it to track plant-eating dinosaurs for many miles.

It had short arms, around 1 m (3.3 ft) long, with only two clawed fingers, which pinned and pierced prey.

DID YOU KNOW? In 1905, this dinosaur was given the full name *Tyrannosaurus rex*, meaning "tyrant lizard king" due to its dominance over all other animals in its habitat.

Chapter 3
Sauropodomorphs

The sauropodomorphs were plant-eaters with long necks and tails. Early sauropodomorphs were small and slender. Over millions of years, these dinosaurs became larger and heavier. Eventually, sauropodomorphs were larger than any other land animal that has ever lived.

Getting Bigger

When sauropodomorphs first evolved, around 231 million years ago, they were light enough and short-necked enough to walk just on their two back legs. They may have been omnivores, eating both plants and small animals. As sauropodomorphs adapted to eating only plants, they grew bigger, and their huge size protected them from all but the largest meat-eaters. Like modern elephants, sauropodomorphs were far too heavy to balance only on their back legs. They walked slowly on their four sturdy legs, their long tails balancing their long necks.

Living 200 to 195 million years ago, the early sauropodomorph *Anchisaurus* was around 2 m (6.6 ft) long. It could walk on four legs or two legs, which left its hands free to grasp food.

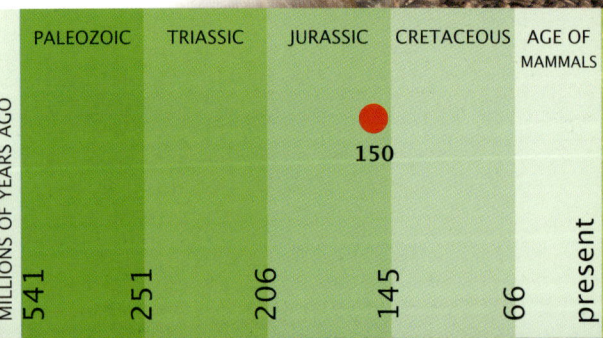

MILLIONS OF YEARS AGO	PALEOZOIC	TRIASSIC	JURASSIC	CRETACEOUS	AGE OF MAMMALS	present
	541	251	206	145	66	

● 150

Name: *Giraffatitan* (Ji–RAF–uh–TIE–tan)
Family: Brachiosauridae
Height: 12 m (39.4 ft)
Length: 22 m (72.2 ft)
Weight: 40 tonnes (44 tons)

DINOSAUR PROFILE

A bony bulge on its forehead may have helped its calls to reverberate—like the hollow chamber of a guitar—making them louder.

Apatosaurus had 15 air-filled vertebrae in its neck. Modern giraffes, as well as humans, have just seven vertebrae.

This large sauropodomorph, *Giraffatitan*, lived in Africa from 150 to 145 million years ago.

Long Necks

Sauropodomorph necks enabled them to reach high or distant plants, so they did not need to compete with smaller plant-eaters. The longest necks were over 15 m (49 ft) long. For these dinosaurs to lift such long necks, the neck and skull bones needed to be extremely light. Sauropodomorph skulls were very small compared to their bodies. The bones of the neck, called vertebrae, had many large air-filled spaces.

Giraffatitan had much longer front legs than back legs, which helped it hold its neck up straighter than many sauropodomorphs.

DID YOU KNOW? *Giraffatitan*'s brain measured around 300 cu cm (18.3 cu in), which, like those of other sauropods, was small compared with its massive body size.

99

Melanorosaurus

One of the earliest sauropodomorphs, or long-necked plant-eating dinosaurs, *Melanorosaurus* lived between 227 and 208 million years ago. Its name means "Black Mountain lizard" after the place where it was first discovered: Black Mountain in Transkei, South Africa.

First of the Line

In time, sauropodomorphs would become the largest land animals ever. Early species were much smaller—*Melanorosaurus* was just a quarter the length of *Argentinosaurus* (pages 114–115) and far lighter. However, it was still too bulky to walk on two legs and had to lumber along on all fours.

Volcanoes continually reshaped the land during the Late Triassic.

All in the Hips

Sauropodomorphs belong to the dinosaur group called the saurischians, or "lizard-hipped" dinosaurs. Their hips were arranged like those of modern lizards. Sauropodomorphs were plant-eaters, but the meat-eating theropods were lizard-hipped, too. The other group of dinosaurs are the ornithischians, or "bird-hipped" dinosaurs. They were all plant-eaters.

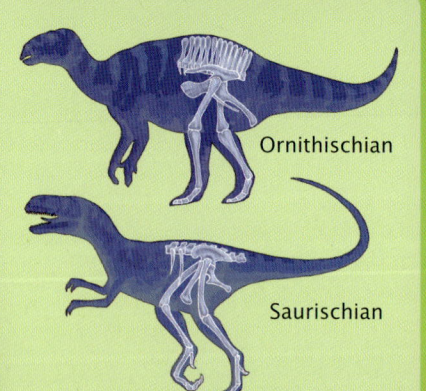

Ornithischian

Saurischian

Melanorosaurus's long neck allowed it to save energy. It could gather vegetation from a large area without the need to move its whole body.

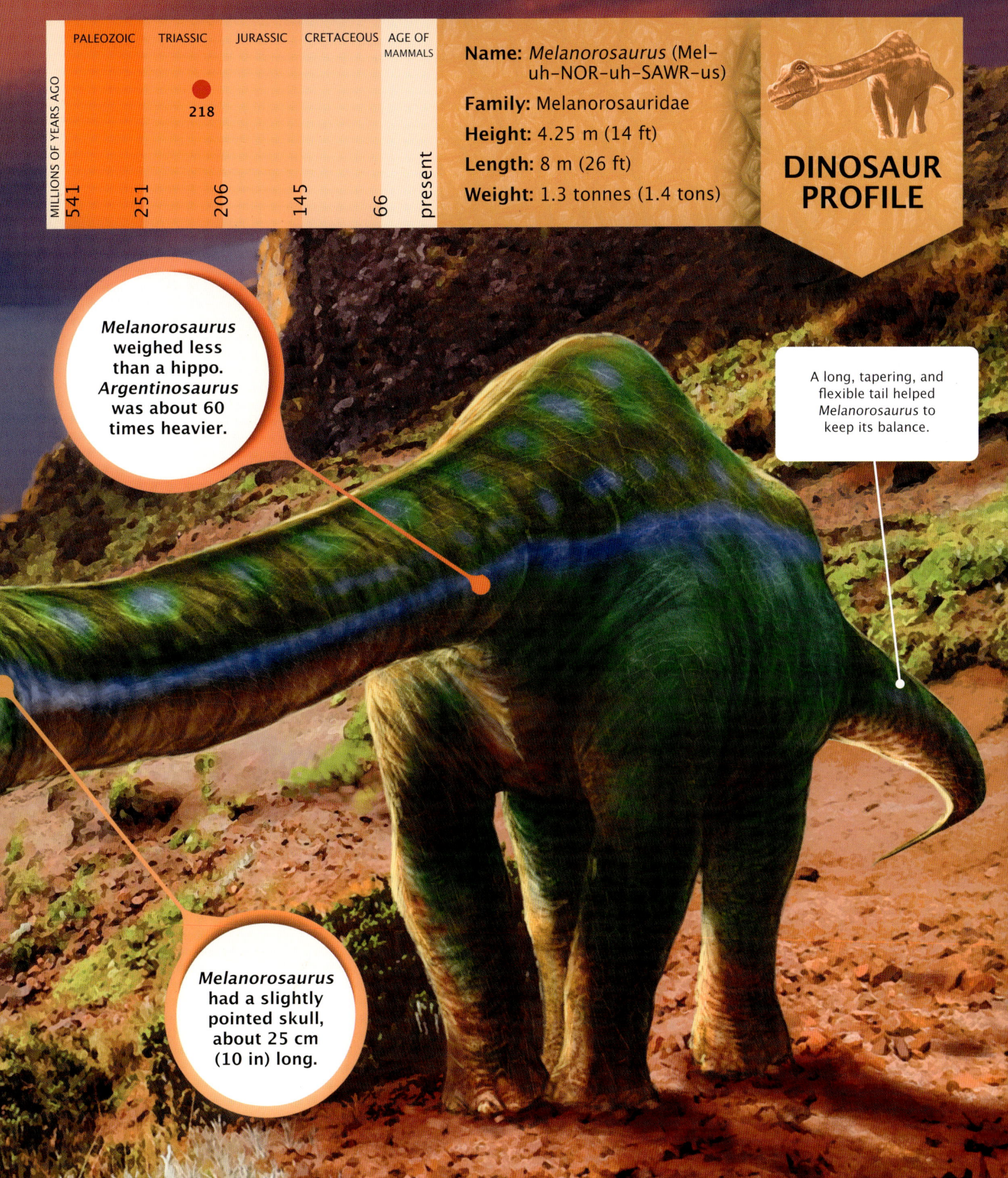

	PALEOZOIC	TRIASSIC	JURASSIC	CRETACEOUS	AGE OF MAMMALS

218

MILLIONS OF YEARS AGO

541 251 206 145 66 present

Name: *Melanorosaurus* (Mel–uh–NOR–uh–SAWR–us)

Family: Melanorosauridae

Height: 4.25 m (14 ft)

Length: 8 m (26 ft)

Weight: 1.3 tonnes (1.4 tons)

DINOSAUR PROFILE

Melanorosaurus weighed less than a hippo. *Argentinosaurus* was about 60 times heavier.

A long, tapering, and flexible tail helped *Melanorosaurus* to keep its balance.

Melanorosaurus had a slightly pointed skull, about 25 cm (10 in) long.

DID YOU KNOW? Two close relatives of *Melanorosaurus* lived in the Late Triassic, too: *Eucnemesaurus*, also from South Africa, and *Riojasaurus* from South America.

Plateosaurus

Since the first fossils were discovered in 1834, *Plateosaurus* has been reconstructed in many ways. It has been shown with its limbs sticking out from its sides like an iguana's and—correctly —with them starting from directly under its body.

Walking the Walk

Experts have also puzzled over whether *Plateosaurus* was quadrupedal (walking on four legs) or bipedal (walking on two). Today, most agree that this European dinosaur was bipedal. Standing on two legs gave it an advantage, because it could reach high in the trees for vegetation.

Plateosaurus's long, narrow jaw had wide, serrated teeth that could shear through tough plant stems.

Compared to other prosauropods, *Plateosaurus* had short arms.

Prosauropods

Plateosaurus belonged to a group called the prosauropods—the sauropodomorphs' early relatives. They walked on two legs, whereas the later, larger sauropodomorphs had to walk on four. Some paleontologists think prosauropods had a more varied diet, eating some meat as well as plants. *Melanorosaurus* (pages 100–101) used to be classed as a prosauropod, too.

DID YOU KNOW? *Plateosaurus* is one of the best-known dinosaurs. More than 100 of its skeletons have been found and studied.

	PALEOZOIC	TRIASSIC	JURASSIC	CRETACEOUS	AGE OF MAMMALS	

MILLIONS OF YEARS AGO

209

541   251   206   145   66   present

Name: *Plateosaurus* (PLAY–tee–uh–SAWR–us)

Family: Plateosauridae

Height: 3 m (9.8 ft)

Length: 7 m (23 ft)

Weight: 1.8 tonnes (2 tons)

DINOSAUR PROFILE

Ten bones, called vertebrae, supported its long, bendy neck.

There were two *Plateosaurus* species. This skull belongs to *Plateosaurus engelhardti*, named after Johann Engelhardt, the German doctor who discovered it.

Plateosaurus grips a branch with its clawed hands.

Mamenchisaurus

Mamenchisaurus lived in what is now China between 160 and 145 million years ago. So far, seven species have been discovered. They vary greatly in size but all share one characteristic—an extra-long neck that makes up around half of their total body length.

Great and Small

The first *Mamenchisaurus* fossils, found in the 1950s, belonged to a species called *Mamenchisaurus constructus* (the *constructus* part of the name came from it being discovered on a building site). The record-breaker of the family was named in the 1990s. Known as *Mamenchisaurus sinocanadorum*, it was three times as long, with a body length of 35 m (115 ft) and an 18-m (59-ft) neck.

Hunters such as *Yangchuanosaurus* had to team up to bring down a *Mamenchisaurus.*

Mamenchisaurus's main predator was an allosaur called Yangchuanosaurus.

PALEOZOIC	TRIASSIC	JURASSIC	CRETACEOUS	AGE OF MAMMALS	
		● 153			
541	251	206	145	66	present

MILLIONS OF YEARS AGO

DINOSAUR PROFILE

Name: *Mamenchisaurus* (Mah-MEN-chih-SAWR-us)
Family: Mamenchisauridae
Height: 12 m (40 ft)
Length: 35 m (115 ft)
Weight: 12 tonnes (13 tons)

DID YOU KNOW? One species of *Mamenchisaurus* is thought to have had a defensive tail club.

Reaching Out

Mamenchisaurus's long neck could have reached up high, but most experts believe that this dinosaur fed mostly on low-lying vegetation. Having a long neck was still an advantage. *Mamenchisaurus* could reach out for food across a large area without having to use up energy moving its body from place to place.

No one can be sure what noises sauropods made.

Mamenchisaurus **could rear up to frighten off predators.**

A small group of *Mamenchisauruses* go to the river to drink. Like all sauropodomorphs, this dinosaur lived in herds.

Brachiosaurus

When it was discovered in 1903, *Brachiosaurus* was the largest known dinosaur. Paleontologists did not believe that such an enormous animal could have supported its own weight on land. They thought that it must have lived in water.

Nose Knowhow

In early reconstructions, *Brachiosaurus*'s nostrils were located on a bump between its eyes, where they could be used to breathe even when the rest of the head was submerged. Today, paleontologists know *Brachiosaurus* lived on land, not water, and position the nostrils further down the snout in reconstructions. The nostrils were relatively large, so the dinosaur probably had a good sense of smell.

Brachiosaurus had 58 leaf-shaped teeth for stripping plants of shoots, leaves, and cones.

Eating Machines

Just like today's large herbivores, sauropodomorphs moved in herds, constantly eating and seeking out new feeding grounds. Experts estimate that *Brachiosaurus* consumed 120 kg (264 lb) of vegetation a day. Despite this, it shared its environment with other plant-eating giants, including *Apatosaurus* and *Diplodocus*.

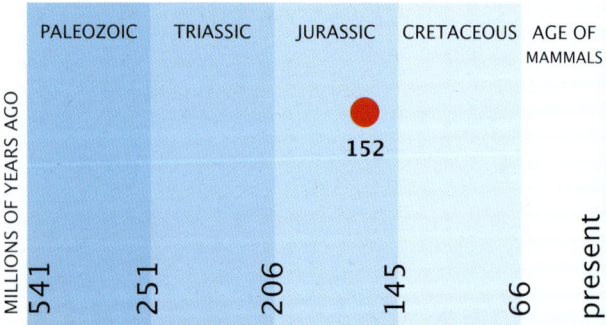

MILLIONS OF YEARS AGO	PALEOZOIC	TRIASSIC	JURASSIC	CRETACEOUS	AGE OF MAMMALS
	541	251	206	145	66	present

152

Name: *Brachiosaurus* (BRACK-ee-uh-SAWR-us)

Family: Brachiosauridae

Height: 9 m (30 ft)

Length: 30 m (98 ft)

Weight: 70 tonnes (77 tons)

DINOSAUR PROFILE

Unlike other sauropods, *Brachiosaurus* had longer front legs than back ones. Its back sloped down toward the tail.

Brachiosaurus held its neck upright, like a giraffe. One early species has since been renamed *Giraffatitan.*

Brachiosaurus lived in Late Jurassic North America.

***Brachiosaurus*'s huge bulk helped it to conserve its body heat.**

DID YOU KNOW? *Brachiosaurus* means "arm lizard." The name comes from it having longer front legs, or arms.

Diplodocus

The huge size of this peaceful dinosaur protected it from attack. Even the largest local meat-eaters, *Allosaurus* and *Ceratosaurus*, could not kill an adult *Diplodocus*. This giant lived in North America toward the end of the Jurassic Period.

Feeding High and Low

Its long neck enabled *Diplodocus* to feed on low plants a distance away, saving the energy needed to walk toward them. It could also rear up on its back legs to reach branches up to 11 m (36 ft) high. Signs of wear on the tips of *Diplodocus*'s blunt, peglike teeth suggest that it fed by stripping all the leaves from branches, by pulling its almost-closed teeth along them.

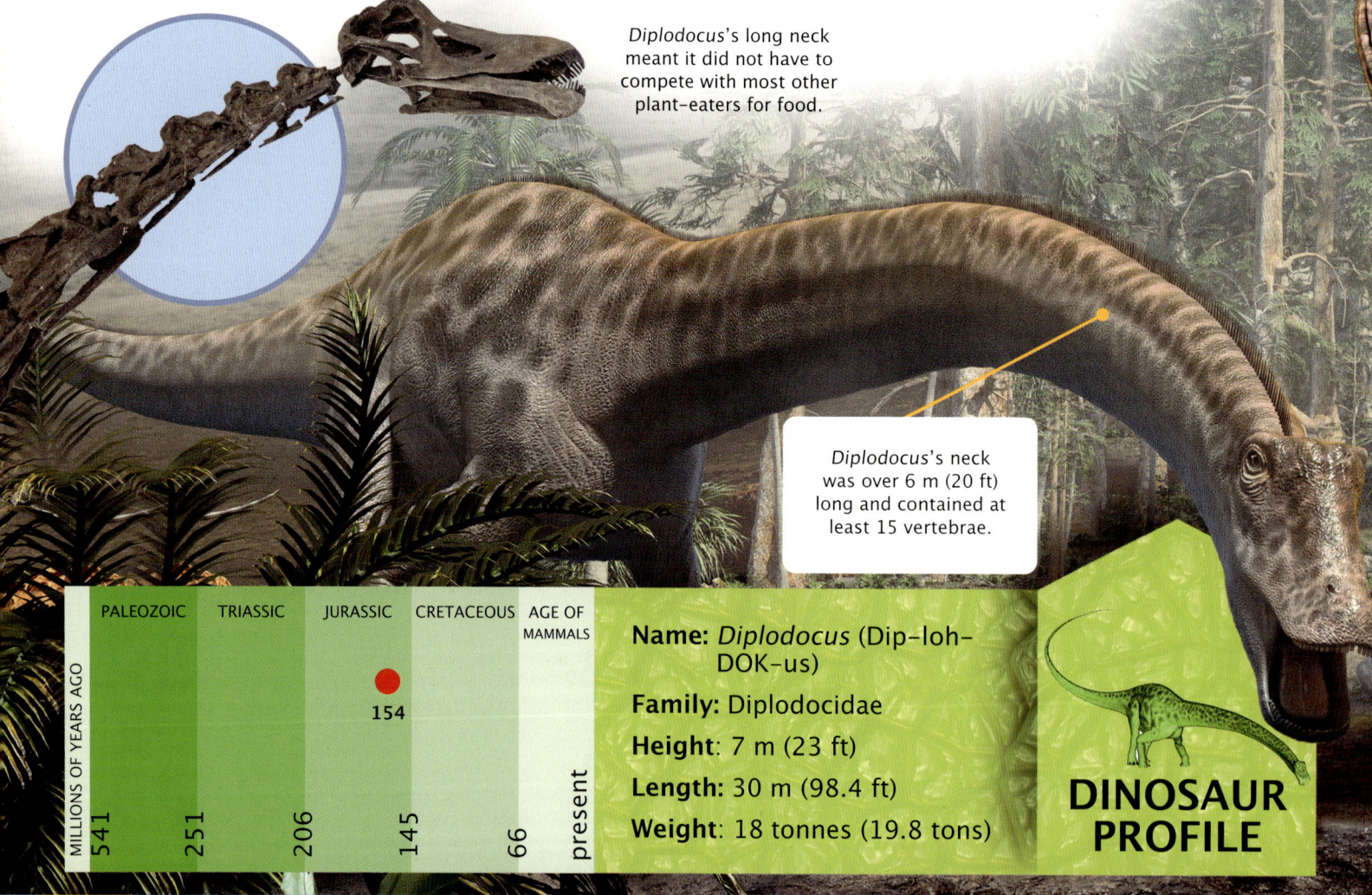

Diplodocus's long neck meant it did not have to compete with most other plant-eaters for food.

Diplodocus's neck was over 6 m (20 ft) long and contained at least 15 vertebrae.

	PALEOZOIC	TRIASSIC	JURASSIC	CRETACEOUS	AGE OF MAMMALS	present
MILLIONS OF YEARS AGO	541	251	206 ● 154	145	66	

Name: *Diplodocus* (Dip-loh-DOK-us)
Family: Diplodocidae
Height: 7 m (23 ft)
Length: 30 m (98.4 ft)
Weight: 18 tonnes (19.8 tons)

DINOSAUR PROFILE

DID YOU KNOW? *Diplodocus* means "double beam" in ancient Greek, in reference to the strangely shaped bones on the underside of its tail.

Cracking a Whip

Diplodocus's tail grew to 14 m (46 ft) long. Made of 80 small bones, it was very bendy. The dinosaur could crack it like a whip, making a sudden loud noise that frightened away predators. As it walked along in its herd, *Diplodocus* may also have used its tail to feel the dinosaurs behind and to the sides, helping the group to stay together.

Diplodocus's tail was longer than the longest buses.

When its front feet were on the ground, *Diplodocus* probably could not lift its neck very high, instead using it to reach for leaves over a wide area.

Each front foot had only one large claw, which may have been used against attackers.

109

Amargasaurus

One of the smallest sauropodomorphs, 10-m- (33-ft-) long *Amargasaurus* lived 125 million years ago in what is now Argentina. The spines along its neck and back might have been to defend against predators, or to show off to rivals or mates.

Double Find

Amargasaurus was found on an expedition led by the Argentinian paleontologist José Bonaparte. The team discovered an almost complete skeleton. They found another dinosaur on that trip: the Late Cretaceous predator *Carnotaurus*. Like *Amargasaurus*, it is known from only one skeleton.

One theory is that *Amargasaurus*'s spines supported sails of skin that helped to keep its temperature steady.

The one *Amargasaurus* skeleton that has been found was discovered in 1984.

Feeding Strategy

Amargasaurus is one of the dicraeosaurids. The family is named after *Dicraeosaurus*, a small sauropodomorph of Late Jurassic Tanzania, eastern Africa. Being smaller than other sauropodomorphs meant that dicraeosaurids did not have to compete for plants. They were browsing for vegetation at a different level.

Amargasaurus's broad snout was lined with long, cylinder–shaped teeth.

DID YOU KNOW? *Amargasaurus* was found at a place in Argentina called La Amarga Arroyo. Its name means "lizard from La Amarga."

Amargasaurus's neck was short for a sauropod. It made up just a quarter of its total body length.

Two rows of tall spines ran down *Amargasaurus*'s neck and back.

PALEOZOIC	TRIASSIC	JURASSIC	CRETACEOUS	AGE OF MAMMALS	

125

| 541 | 251 | 206 | 145 | 66 | present |

MILLIONS OF YEARS AGO

Name: *Amargasaurus*
(Ah–MAR–guh–SAWR–us)
Family: Dicraeosauridae
Height: 2.4 m (7.9 ft)
Length: 10 m (33 ft)
Weight: 8 tonnes (8.8 tons)

DINOSAUR PROFILE

Nigersaurus

Named after the West African country where it was discovered in the 1970s, *Nigersaurus* was an unusual, elephant-sized sauropodomorph. Its fossilized remains were found in the Sahara Desert, but in the Early Cretaceous, this landscape was a great floodplain with rivers and lush vegetation.

Nigersaurus was a very primitive member of *Diplodocus*'s superfamily, the diplodocoids.

Tooth Talk

Nigersaurus's straight-edged snout was packed with more than 500 teeth for munching on low-growing plants. At least 50 tiny teeth lined the front of its mouth—with about eight rows of replacement teeth behind them, ready and waiting. Cutting through fibrous vegetation was a tough job. Each tooth lasted only a couple of weeks.

Having teeth at the front of the muzzle allowed *Nigersaurus* to "mow" plants close to the ground.

	PALEOZOIC	TRIASSIC	JURASSIC	CRETACEOUS	AGE OF MAMMALS
MILLIONS OF YEARS AGO	541	251	206	145	66 ← present

110

Name: *Nigersaurus* (NI–juh–SAWR–us)
Family: Rebbachisauridae
Height: 1.9 m (6.2 ft)
Length: 9 m (30 ft)
Weight: 4 tonnes (4.4 tons)

DINOSAUR PROFILE

DID YOU KNOW? The smallest *Nigersaurus* fossil is a jawbone that belonged to a tiny hatchling. It is less than 2.5 cm (1 in) across.

Fellow Fossils

Nigersaurus was found in the Elrhaz Formation, a band of Early Cretaceous rock in Niger, West Africa. Other dinosaurs discovered there include the fish-eating spinosaur *Suchomimus* and the hadrosaur *Ouranosaurus*. The super-crocodile *Sarcosuchus* is also known from the Elrhaz Formation.

Nigersaurus kept its head close to the ground, raising it only to look for predators.

Nigersaurus's snout broadened out at the end.

Nigersaurus had huge eyes for a sauropodomorph, but its nostrils were small. It probably had a poor sense of smell.

Nigersaurus fed on mosses, ferns, and horsetails.

Argentinosaurus

The area that is now South America was warm and wet at the end of the Cretaceous, and home to some enormous, plant-eating dinosaurs. *Argentinosaurus* ("Argentina lizard") was one of the largest animals to have ever lived on land. Each of its vertebrae (spine bones) was almost as tall as a person of average height.

Its long neck allowed the dinosaur to reach for food without moving much.

Record-Breakers

A farmer found the first *Argentinosaurus* fossil by accident in 1987. At first, he mistook the massive leg bone for a petrified tree trunk. *Argentinosaurus* was the outright record-breaker for more than two decades, until a new species of titanosaur was discovered. Known as *Patagotitan*, it was around the same size, perhaps 37 m (121 ft) long and weighing 69 tonnes (76 tons).

This unnamed titanosaur was even bigger than *Argentinosaurus*—as tall as a seven-floor building!

PALEOZOIC	TRIASSIC	JURASSIC	CRETACEOUS	AGE OF MAMMALS
541	251	206	145	66 present

MILLIONS OF YEARS AGO

95

DINOSAUR PROFILE

DID YOU KNOW? *Argentinosaurus* eggs were about the size of rugby balls—around 42 cm (16.5 in) long.

Titanosaur Teeth

Argentinosaurus was in a group of sauropodomorphs called titanosaurs that flourished after the large Jurassic sauropodomorphs had died out. Their nostrils were high on the snout, and they had a jaw packed with peglike teeth.

Argentinosaurus probably could not raise its neck much above shoulder height.

The long tail stuck out behind for balance.

Argentinosaurus may have taken 40 years to reach its adult size.

Thick, sturdy legs supported its heavy bulk.

Saltasaurus

Herds of the titanosaur *Saltasaurus* lived in Argentina at the end of the Cretaceous. When this dinosaur was discovered, it was the first sauropodomorph known to have bony bumps, called osteoderms, on its skin. These may have helped to protect *Saltasaurus*, which was relatively small for a sauropod.

Saltasaurus had small feet and short, stubby legs.

Titanosaur Nursery

A *Saltasaurus* nesting site was discovered in Argentina in 1997. The dinosaurs had used it for hundreds of years. Most of the time, the female *Saltasaurus* laid their eggs, the eggs hatched, and the youngsters left the site; however, the site was on a floodplain. Every so often the river flooded and eggs were buried in the mud and fossilized.

Saltasaurus did not guard its nest, but may have covered it with earth or plants to keep the eggs warm and hidden from predators.

	PALEOZOIC	TRIASSIC	JURASSIC	CRETACEOUS	AGE OF MAMMALS
MILLIONS OF YEARS AGO	541	251	206	145	66 present

70

Name: *Saltasaurus* (Salt–uh–SAWR–us)
Family: Saltasauridae
Height: 5 m (16.4 ft)
Length: 12 m (40 ft)
Weight: 7 tonnes (7.7 tons)

DINOSAUR PROFILE

Saltasaurus's head was supported on a small neck. The tail was short, too.

Skin Story

Saltasaurus's species name, *loricatus*, means "protected by plates." Its skin had osteoderms in two sizes. The larger ones were 12 cm (4.7 in) long and oval. Between these were small, round ones, just 0.7 cm (0.3 in) across. Paleontologists now know of other sauropodomorphs with osteoderms, such as the 18-m- (60-ft-) long *Laplatasaurus*, also from Late Cretaceous Argentina.

There is only one known species of *Saltasaurus*: *Saltasaurus loricatus*.

Saltasaurus ate around 205 kg (452 lb) of plant matter a day.

DID YOU KNOW? A *Saltasaurus* egg was just 12 cm (4.7 in) across—not even as large as an ostrich egg.

Rapetosaurus

Many titanosaurs are known from only a few bones, but *Rapetosaurus*'s fossils included a nearly complete skeleton. This dinosaur lived 70 million years ago on the island of Madagascar, off the east coast of Africa.

Stomach Stones

Like all sauropods, *Rapetosaurus* did not chew its food properly. Instead, it swallowed stones called gastroliths to grind up the plant food in its stomach.

These gastroliths were smoothed and polished inside a dinosaur's stomach.

Rapetosaurus had bony bumps, called osteoderms, on its skin.

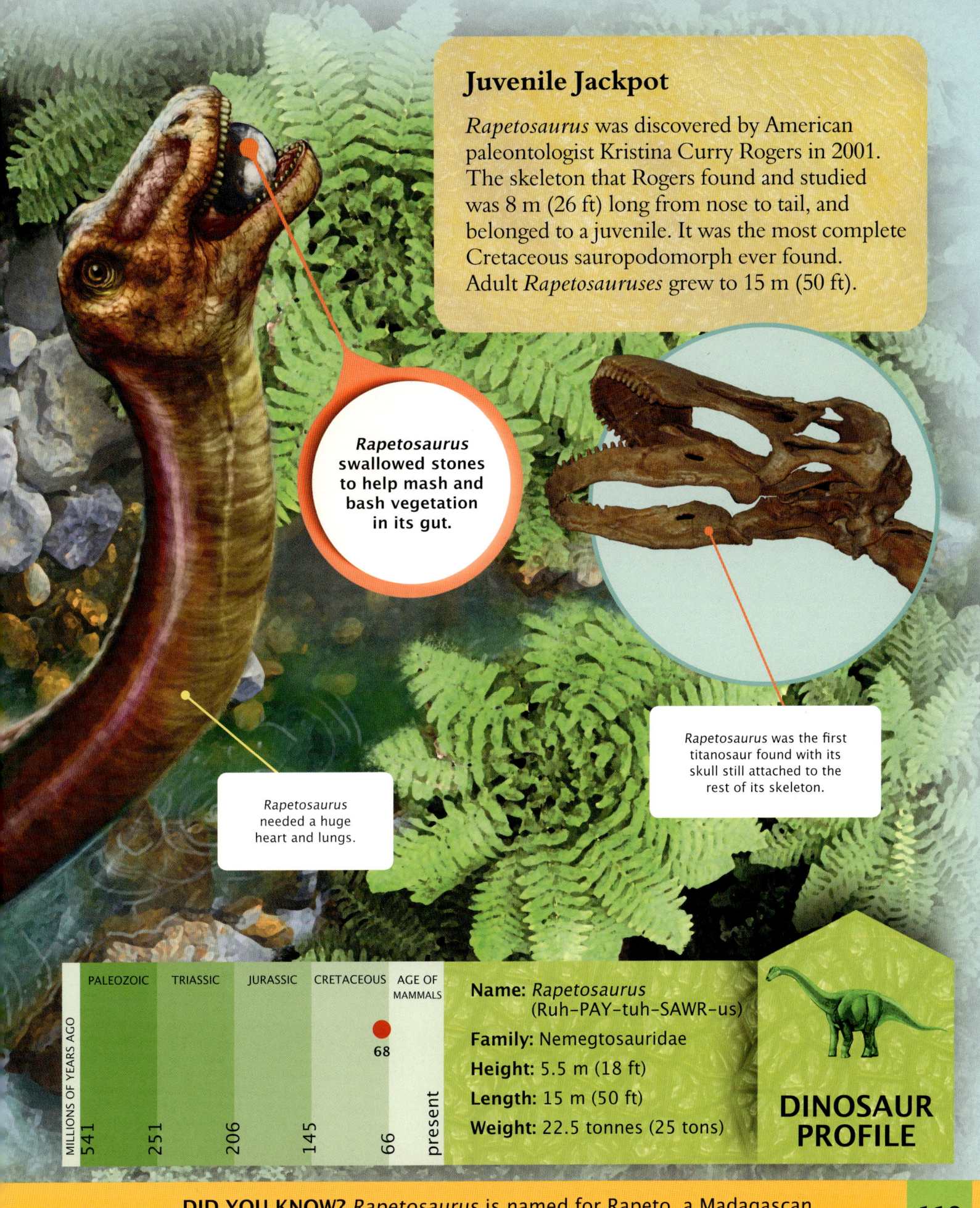

Juvenile Jackpot

Rapetosaurus was discovered by American paleontologist Kristina Curry Rogers in 2001. The skeleton that Rogers found and studied was 8 m (26 ft) long from nose to tail, and belonged to a juvenile. It was the most complete Cretaceous sauropodomorph ever found. Adult *Rapetosauruses* grew to 15 m (50 ft).

Rapetosaurus swallowed stones to help mash and bash vegetation in its gut.

Rapetosaurus was the first titanosaur found with its skull still attached to the rest of its skeleton.

Rapetosaurus needed a huge heart and lungs.

MILLIONS OF YEARS AGO	PALEOZOIC	TRIASSIC	JURASSIC	CRETACEOUS	AGE OF MAMMALS
	541	251	206	145	66	present

68

Name: *Rapetosaurus* (Ruh-PAY-tuh-SAWR-us)
Family: Nemegtosauridae
Height: 5.5 m (18 ft)
Length: 15 m (50 ft)
Weight: 22.5 tonnes (25 tons)

DINOSAUR PROFILE

DID YOU KNOW? *Rapetosaurus* is named for Rapeto, a Madagascan god who was responsible for shaping mountains and valleys.

Chapter 4

Cerapods

These plant-eaters had beak-like jaws for snapping stems and twigs. Cerapods also had a thicker coating, called enamel, on the insides of their lower front teeth. As a result, their teeth wore away unevenly during chewing, making sharp ridges that were perfect for mushing plants.

Maiasaura was a hadrosaur—or duckbilled dinosaur—in the ornithopod group of cerapods.

It cropped branches, bark, and leaves with its flat beak, which was typical of hadrosaurs.

Maiasaura could walk both on four legs and on two, when it used its hands to grasp food.

MILLIONS OF YEARS AGO	PALEOZOIC	TRIASSIC	JURASSIC	CRETACEOUS	AGE OF MAMMALS	present
	541	251	206	145	66	

76

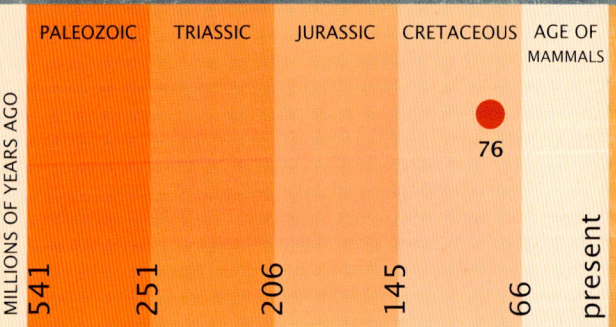

Name: *Maiasaura* (MAI-ah-SAWR-uh)

Family: Hadrosauridae

Height: 3 m (9.8 ft)

Length: 9 m (29.5 ft)

Weight: 4 tonnes (4.4 tons)

DINOSAUR PROFILE

DID YOU KNOW? The first cerapods evolved in the Jurassic Period, around 164 million years ago, and died out 66 million years ago, at the end of the Cretaceous Period.

Cerapod Groups

The cerapods can be divided into ornithopods (from the ancient Greek word for "bird feet") and marginocephalians ("fringed heads"). Ornithopods were named for their usually three-toed feet, which were a little like those of modern birds. They had rows of grinding teeth, and cheek pouches for holding food. Ornithopods included hypsilophodonts, iguanodonts, and hadrosaurs. Marginocephalians had a bony shelf at the back of their skull and can be divided into two groups: ceratopsians ("horned faces") and pachycephalosaurs ("thick-headed lizards").

Kosmoceratops was a ceratopsian in the marginocephalian group.

Cerapod Beaks

The cerapods were ornithischian ("bird-hipped") dinosaurs, with hip bones that looked like those of birds. Ornithischians had an extra bone at the front of their lower jaw, helping to form a beak. Both upper and lower jaws were covered in hard, horny keratin, which is also found in claws.

Like other ornithischians, the ceratopsian *Styracosaurus* had an extra bone in its jaw, called the predentary.

Heterodontosaurus

One of the earliest ornithischians, or "bird-hipped" dinosaurs, *Heterodontosaurus* lived in South Africa about 195 million years ago. Its name means "different toothed lizard." Unlike most reptiles, it had teeth of several different shapes.

Tooth Types

Heterodontosaurus's square cheek teeth were used for grinding and chewing. At the front of its beak-like, horny snout, it had smaller front teeth for snipping off plant stems. Finally, it had a pair of curved tusks.

Heterodontosaurus probably used its tusks to show off to rivals.

Discoveries

The first *Heterodontosaurus* fossil was a skull, discovered in 1961. Five years later another skull was found—this time attached to an almost perfect skeleton. Since then, more finds have surfaced. The most complete skeleton was found in 2005, but it could not be excavated because it had fossilized in such hard rock.

This cast is of a *Heterodontosaurus* skeleton that was discovered in 1966.

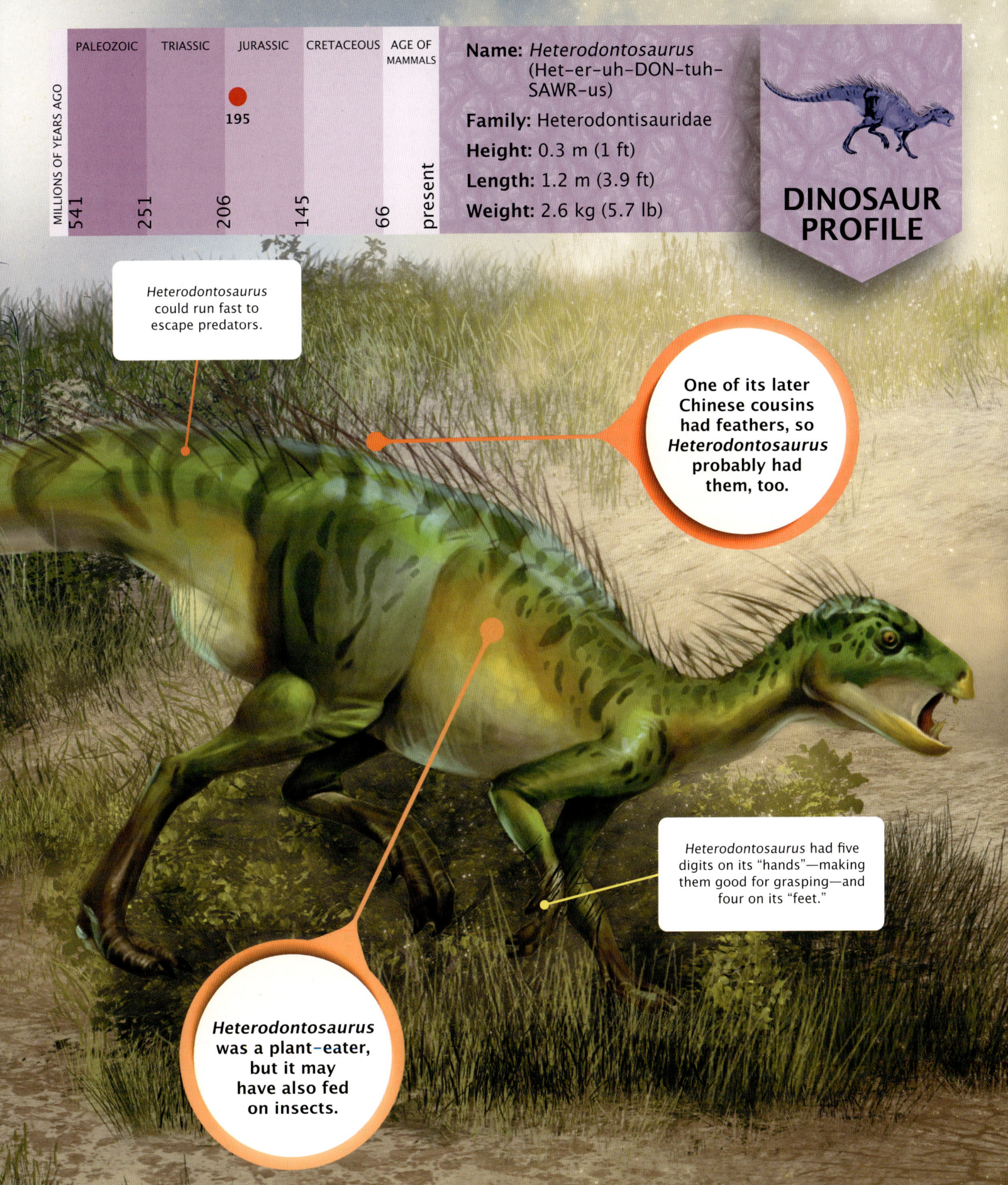

MILLIONS OF YEARS AGO	PALEOZOIC	TRIASSIC	JURASSIC	CRETACEOUS	AGE OF MAMMALS
	541	251	206 ● 195	145	66 — present

Name: *Heterodontosaurus* (Het-er-uh-DON-tuh-SAWR-us)
Family: Heterodontisauridae
Height: 0.3 m (1 ft)
Length: 1.2 m (3.9 ft)
Weight: 2.6 kg (5.7 lb)

DINOSAUR PROFILE

Heterodontosaurus could run fast to escape predators.

One of its later Chinese cousins had feathers, so *Heterodontosaurus* probably had them, too.

Heterodontosaurus had five digits on its "hands"—making them good for grasping—and four on its "feet."

Heterodontosaurus was a plant-eater, but it may have also fed on insects.

DID YOU KNOW? *Fruitadens* was the smallest heterodontosaurid. It was just 70 cm (27.5 in) long and lived in Late Jurassic North America.

Hypsilophodon

During the Early Cretaceous, the Isle of Wight, a small island off the south coast of England, was home to a small, fast-moving dinosaur called *Hypsilophodon*. It browsed on tough plants like ferns and cycads, and it probably lived in herds for safety.

Threatening Theropods

The main hunters in *Hypsilophodon's* habitat were *Baryonyx*, *Eotyrannus*, and *Neovenator*. *Baryonyx* had a narrow jaw and was probably a specialist fish-eater. *Eotyrannus* was a pony-sized tyrannosaur. The top predator was a 7.6-m- (25-ft-) long allosaur called *Neovenator* ("new hunter").

Hypsilophodon's short, beak-like snout was ideal for snapping off low-growing plants.

The landscape was hot and usually dry. Any rain caused flash floods.

	PALEOZOIC	TRIASSIC	JURASSIC	CRETACEOUS	AGE OF MAMMALS	
MILLIONS OF YEARS AGO	541	251	206	145	66	present

128

Name: *Hypsilophodon* (Hip-sih-LO-fuh-don)

Family: Hypsilophodontidae

Height: 0.6 m (2 ft)

Length: 1.8 m (5.9 ft)

Weight: 20 kg (44 lb)

DINOSAUR PROFILE

DID YOU KNOW? More than 100 *Hypsilophodon* skeletons have been found on one Isle of Wight beach, Brighstone Bay.

Hypsilophodon, like Heterodontosaurus (pages 122–123), was bipedal. It was one of the earliest ornithischians.

Hypsilophodon had a stiff tail that stuck out behind it for balance.

Hypsilophodon had a lightweight skeleton that helped it to be fast-moving.

A quadrupedal Hypsilophodon (left) and a kangaroo–like one (right).

Different Postures

Many 19th-century reconstructions of Hypsilophodon wrongly showed it on four legs, like a lizard. There was also a theory that this dinosaur used its grasping hands to move about in trees. Today, paleontologists agree that Hypsilophodon was a ground dweller.

125

Iguanodon

The large plant-eater *Iguanodon* roamed across Europe and North America during the Early and Middle Cretaceous. More than 25 species are known. *Iguanodon* moved in herds for protection against predators such as *Deinonychus* (pages 64–65).

Iguanodon walked on all fours, with its body and tail parallel to the ground.

Some experts think that *Iguanodon* may have had cheek pouches for storing food.

Iguanodon sometimes reared up to reach for food or look for danger.

DID YOU KNOW? English geologist Gideon Mantell named *Iguanodon* in 1825— 17 years before paleontologist Richard Owen coined the word "dinosaur."

Eating Technique

Iguanodon had a toothless beak for cropping off tough horsetails and ferns, and wide cheek teeth for mashing and pulping plant matter. The teeth were similar to a modern-day iguana's (*Iguanodon* means "iguana tooth").

Iguanodon's tail stuck out stiffly behind it.

Iguanodon had a vicious thumb spike to stab at would-be attackers.

Early Finds

Iguanodon was only the second dinosaur to be named (the first was *Megalosaurus*). The first fossils were a few teeth from southern England. The most spectacular finds came from a coal mine at Bernissart in Belgium. Nearly 40 *Iguanodon* skeletons were uncovered there in 1878.

An *Iguanodon* skeleton from Bernissart, Belgium, is shown being mounted for display.

MILLIONS OF YEARS AGO	PALEOZOIC	TRIASSIC	JURASSIC	CRETACEOUS	AGE OF MAMMALS	present
	541	251	206	145	66	

121

Name: *Iguanodon* (Ig-WAN-oh-don)

Family: Iguanodontidae

Height: 3.25 m (10.7 ft)

Length: 10 m (33 ft)

Weight: 3.1 tonnes (3.4 tons)

DINOSAUR PROFILE

Parasaurolophus

This plant-eater lived in herds in North America. Together, the herd could watch for danger in all directions. When searching for leaves, *Parasaurolophus* strolled on all fours. When it needed to escape danger, it ran fast on its back legs.

A Duck's Bill

Like its relatives, *Parasaurolophus* was a hadrosaur, or duckbilled dinosaur. *Parasaurolophus* had long, flat jaw bones, making its mouth a little like a duck's bill. It clipped off twigs with its hard jaws, and then mashed food with the teeth at the back of its mouth.

Although the front of *Parasaurolophus*'s beak was toothless, the back of its jaws held hundreds of tiny teeth suited to grinding plants. Only a handful of these teeth were used at one time, with the other teeth stacked beneath them, ready to move upward when the one above fell out.

The fingers were joined by flesh and skin, making a tough pad.

MILLIONS OF YEARS AGO	PALEOZOIC	TRIASSIC	JURASSIC	CRETACEOUS	AGE OF MAMMALS	present
	541	251	206	145	66	

75

Name: *Parasaurolophus* (Par-ah-SAWR-OL-uh-fus)
Family: Hadrosauridae
Height: 3.6 m (12 ft)
Length: 11 m (36 ft)
Weight: 2.5 tonnes (2.8 tons)

DINOSAUR PROFILE

Noisy Crest

Parasaurolophus had a long, hollow crest on its head. This made the dinosaur's calls louder—similar to how the tubes of a trumpet enable its player to make really loud sounds. Some paleontologists think the crest had another use: It is possible that *Parasaurolophus* could lose excess body heat through its crest, to stop it becoming too hot. Elephant ears perform the same function, as their large surface area allows them to radiate heat.

Parasaurolophus could call to other members of its herd from far away.

A stiff tail helped *Parasaurolophus* to balance on its back legs.

Bones surrounding the eyes have been compared with those of modern birds and lizards. The results suggest that hadrosaurs were active for short periods throughout the day and night.

DID YOU KNOW? *Parasaurolophus* means "like *Saurolophus*," as it was thought to be a close relative of another hadrosaur, *Saurolophus* (meaning "crested lizard").

Leaellynasaura

Large-eyed *Leaellynasaura* lived about 110 million years ago. During the winter months this plant-eater had to cope with total darkness and cooler temperatures, because its forest habitat lay inside the Antarctic Circle.

The Antarctic Circle was warmer in the Cretaceous than it is today.

Like all hypsilophodonts, *Leaellynasaura* was small and speedy. It moved around on two legs.

Leaellynasaura relied on its excellent eyesight to look out for predators.

Leaellynasaura's long tail contained more than 70 vertebrae.

110

Name: *Leaellynasaura* (Lee–ELL–in-ah–SAWR–ah)
Family: Hypsilophontidae
Height: 0.6 m (2 ft)
Length: 1.8 m (5.9 ft)
Weight: 20 kg (44 lb)

DINOSAUR PROFILE

Dinosaur Cove

Leaellynasaura was discovered in 1989 at Dinosaur Cove in Victoria, on the coast of southeast Australia. The sand- and mudstone cliffs there formed in the Early Cretaceous. Other dinosaurs found at the site include another two-legged plant-eater, *Atlascopcosaurus*, and a small theropod called *Timimus*.

This image of *Leaellynasaura* was created for an Australian postage stamp.

Keeping Warm

During the Early Cretaceous, the southern tip of Australia was within the Antarctic Circle. Temperatures were milder than they are today. However, there still would have been less food during the long winter months, when that part of Earth was facing away from the Sun. There is no evidence that *Leaellynasaura* hibernated, but it may have sheltered in burrows.

In the Early Cretaceous, Dinosaur Cove was a floodplain. There were conifers, gingkos, and monkey puzzle trees.

DID YOU KNOW? The paleontologists who discovered *Leaellynasaura*, Thomas Rich and Patricia Vickers–Rich, named it after their daughter, Leaellyn.

131

Gasparinisaura

Speedy little plant-eater *Gasparinisaura* lived in Argentina around 85 million years ago. It belonged to the same family as the much larger *Iguanodon* (pages 126–127) and fed on tough vegetation, including conifers and cycads.

Daily Grind

Stones called gastroliths (page 72) have been found with *Gasparinisaura*. Its stomach could contain as many as 140 stones, each measuring less than 1 cm (0.4 in) across. Plant matter was ground up as it passed between the stones, making it easier to digest.

Tiny *Gasparinisaura* skeletons are on display in Copenhagen, Denmark.

Large eyes high on its head, gave *Gasparinisaura* good all-round vision, so that it could spot danger.

	PALEOZOIC	TRIASSIC	JURASSIC	CRETACEOUS	AGE OF MAMMALS
MILLIONS OF YEARS AGO	541	251	206	145 ● 85	66 present

Name: *Gasparinisaura* (Gas-pah-reen-ee-SAWR-uh)

Family: Iguanodontidae

Height: 0.8 m (2.6 ft)

Length: 1.7 m (5.6 ft)

Weight: 13 kg (6.6 lb)

DINOSAUR PROFILE

DID YOU KNOW? *Gasparinisaura* was named after the Argentinian paleontologist Zulma Brandoni de Gasparini. Two members of her team discovered the dinosaur.

Living with Giants

Gasparinisaura fossils come from rock that formed in what is now Patagonia, Argentina, during the Late Cretaceous. Other species found nearby include the titanosaurs *Argentinosaurus* (pages 114–115), *Saltasaurus* (pages 116–117), and *Antarctosaurus*, and the theropods *Aucasaurus* and *Abelisaurus*.

Gasparinisaura shared its habitat with one of the largest ever sauropods, *Argentinosaurus*.

Gasparinisaura probably had a thumb spike like its cousin, *Iguanodon*.

Lambeosaurus

All the hollow-crested hadrosaurs are known as the lambeosaurines, after *Lambeosaurus*. Like *Parasaurolophus* (pages 128–129), *Lambeosaurus* lived in North America around 75 million years ago. It was named after Lawrence Lambe, the Canadian paleontologist who first studied it.

Dinosaur Park Formation

The layer of rock in Alberta, Canada, where *Lambeosaurus* was discovered is called the Dinosaur Park Formation. It contains other hadrosaurs, including *Parasaurolophus* and *Corythosaurus*, pachycephalosaurs such as *Stegoceras* (pages 148–149), ceratopsians including *Styracosaurus* (pages 150–151), and ankylosaurs such as *Edmontonia* (pages 182–183) and *Euoplocephalus* (pages 184–185).

The crest looked like an axehead.

Lambeosaurus had more than 100 teeth in its cheeks for chewing.

The American paleontologist Barnum Brown excavated the first *Corythosaurus* specimen in 1912.

Complicated Cousin

Corythosaurus, whose name means "helmeted lizard," was the same size as *Lambeosaurus* and lived in the same habitat. The main difference between the two dinosaurs was the complex passages inside *Corythosaurus*'s crest. These would have turned any calls that *Corythosaurus* made into very deep, low-pitched sounds that could travel great distances.

	PALEOZOIC	TRIASSIC	JURASSIC	CRETACEOUS	AGE OF MAMMALS

MILLIONS OF YEARS AGO

541 251 206 145 66 present

75

Name: *Lambeosaurus* (LAM–be–uh–SAWR–us)

Family: Hadrosauridae

Height: 4 m (13 ft)

Length: 10 m (32 ft)

Weight: 4.5 tonnes (5 tons)

DINOSAUR PROFILE

The crest may have been for display, to amplify sounds, and to improve *Lambeosaurus*'s sense of smell.

The plant–eater lived in swampy forests.

Lambeosaurus moved around on four legs or two, so it could reach plants growing at different heights.

DID YOU KNOW? In the past, some paleontologists argued that *Lambeosaurus* was aquatic and that its crest acted as a snorkel!

Shantungosaurus

Not all duckbilled dinosaurs had a crest. *Shantungosaurus*, one of the largest known hadrosaurs, did not have one. Instead, it may have had its own method of making its calls distinctive—an inflatable flap of skin near its nostrils that made sounds.

From Shandong

Shantungosaurus means "Shandong lizard," after the province of eastern China where the dinosaur was discovered. It was named in 1973, and five incomplete skeletons have been dug up to date. When *Shantungosaurus* was alive, the environment was a humid floodplain.

Shantungosaurus has knocked over a predatory *Tarbosaurus* with a powerful swipe of its tail.

DID YOU KNOW? *Shantungosaurus*'s femur (thighbone) was 1.7 m (5.6 ft) long—taller than an average woman.

MILLIONS OF YEARS AGO	PALEOZOIC	TRIASSIC	JURASSIC	CRETACEOUS	AGE OF MAMMALS	present
	541	251	206	145	66	

74

Name: *Shantungosaurus* (Shan-TUNG-o-SAWR-us)
Family: Hadrosauridae
Height: 5 m (16.4 ft)
Length: 15.5 m (51 ft)
Weight: 16 tonnes (18 tons)

DINOSAUR PROFILE

The 1.6-m (5.3-ft) skull ended with a toothless beak. The jaws contained 1,500 tiny teeth.

Good Mothers

One of the best-known duckbills is *Maiasaura*, whose name means "good mother lizard." *Maiasaura* nurseries have been uncovered, and experts believe that this dinosaur incubated its eggs and may even have cared for its young. Perhaps other hadrosaurs also did this.

Shantungosaurus hatchlings may have been too helpless to find food for themselves.

Hadrosaurs laid round eggs.

Edmontosaurus

One of the largest hadrosaurs, *Edmontosaurus* lived at the end of the dinosaur age. It was the North American cousin of Asian *Shantungosaurus* (pages 136–137). It was named after Edmonton, capital city of Alberta, the Canadian province where *Edmontosaurus* was found.

Walking and Running

Usually, herbivorous *Edmontosaurus* walked on all fours. It could run at speeds faster than 50 km/h (31 mph), typically on two legs but sometimes on four. Running was its best way to escape predators. One *Edmontosaurus* was found with a theropod bite on its tail bone.

Edmontosaurus had a small crest, or comb. It was made of skin and scales, not bone.

Edmontosaurus's backbone was held horizontally above the hip bone.

	PALEOZOIC	TRIASSIC	JURASSIC	CRETACEOUS	AGE OF MAMMALS
MILLIONS OF YEARS AGO	541	251	206	145	66 / present

70

Name: *Edmontosaurus* (Ed–MON–tuh–SAWR–us)

Family: Hadrosauridae

Height: 3.5 m (11.5 ft)

Length: 12 m (39 ft)

Weight: 4 tonnes (4.4 tons)

DINOSAUR PROFILE

The long, narrow skull ended in a beaky mouth.

Paleontologists have been able to study fossilized *Edmontosaurus* skin.

No Limits

Some experts think that *Edmontosaurus* could have grown as large as *Shantungosaurus*—if an individual managed to live long enough. Their evidence is a 7.6-m (25-ft) *Edmontosaurus* tail. Unfortunately, most *Edmontosaurus* seem to have died before reaching that size because of predators, disease, or some other disaster.

As *Edmontosaurus* grew older, its skull became longer and flatter.

DID YOU KNOW? Many species of *Edmontosaurus* have been identified over the years. At the moment, just two are officially recognized.

139

Thescelosaurus

The first *Thescelosaurus* fossil was found in 1891, but was then stored in a crate and ignored for more than 20 years. When it was finally studied, it was named *Thescelosaurus neglectus* (*Thescelosaurus* means "wonderful lizard" and *neglectus* means "ignored").

Willo's Heart of Stone

In 2000, experts in North Carolina, USA, introduced the most complete *Thescelosaurus* skeleton. They called it Willo and claimed it had a heart. Fossilized hearts are extremely rare, because hearts are made of soft tissue. Unfortunately, experts now think the "heart" is just a lump of rock that formed during fossilization.

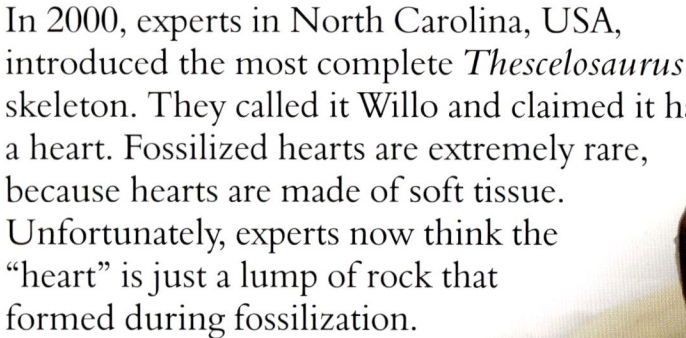

Paleontologists thought this dark ring inside Willo's chest might have been its heart.

Thescelosaurus's thighs were longer than its calves. (Fast-running ornithopods had the opposite—longer calves and shorter thighs.)

MILLIONS OF YEARS AGO	PALEOZOIC	TRIASSIC	JURASSIC	CRETACEOUS	AGE OF MAMMALS
	541	251	206	145	66 present

66

Name: *Thescelosaurus* (Theh–SEL–uh–SAWR–us)

Family: Thescelosauridae

Height: 1.75 m (5.7 ft)

Length: 3.75 m (12.3 ft)

Weight: 250 kg (550 lb)

DINOSAUR PROFILE

Just Plants?

Thescelosaurus has been found across North America, from Canada to New Mexico. It lived on floodplains, along riverbanks, and next to lakes. It had the leaf-shaped teeth at the back of its mouth that most herbivores have. However, it also had short, pointy front teeth, which might mean that it also ate some meat.

This *Thescelosaurus* skeleton came from the Hell Creek Formation in Montana, USA.

Thescelosaurus's small front teeth suggest that it might have been an omnivore.

Thescelosaurus ran upright on two legs.

DID YOU KNOW? The *Thescelosaurus* Willo contains organic, cell–like material. It could be from plants that it ate—or it could be from Willo itself.

Yinlong

The best-known of the ceratopsians (dinosaurs with horned faces) is *Triceratops* (pages 156–157), who lived during the Late Cretaceous. However, the first dinosaurs in this group appeared much earlier. *Yinlong* is the oldest, most primitive ceratopsian that is known.

Ceratopsian Characteristics

Plant-eating *Yinlong* did not have the dramatic horns of later ceratopsians, or much of a frill. It is counted as part of the family because of its parrot-like beak, formed by a bony lump on its upper jaw. Later ceratopsians were much larger and moved on all fours, but *Yinlong* was small, bipedal, and speedy.

Yinlong had three-fingered hands at the end of short, slim arms. It had chunky, muscular back legs.

Yinlong had a deep, wide skull. The tip of the snout was like a parrot's beak.

Made in China

Chinese paleontologist Xu Xing has named more dinosaurs than any other living paleontologist. *Yinlong* and *Guanlong* owe their names to him, as well as the therizinosaur *Beipiaosaurus*, dromaeosaur *Sinornithosaurus*, and birdlike *Mei*.

Beipiaosaurus was found near Beipiao, a city in northeastern China.

MILLIONS OF YEARS AGO	PALEOZOIC	TRIASSIC	JURASSIC	CRETACEOUS	AGE OF MAMMALS
	541	251	206	145	66 present

158

Name: *Yinlong* (YIN-long)
Family: Ceratopsidae
Height: 45 cm (18 in)
Length: 1.2 m (3.9 ft)
Weight: 15 kg (33 lb)

DINOSAUR PROFILE

The tyrannosaur *Guanlong* preyed on *Yinlong*. It was around earlier than its American cousin *Tyrannosaurus* (pages 96–97) and it was smaller, too—just 1 m (3.3 ft) tall.

Sinornithosaurus was only the fifth feathered dinosaur to be discovered.

DID YOU KNOW? *Yinlong* was discovered in the Chinese province where a movie called *Crouching Tiger, Hidden Dragon* (2000) was filmed. Its name means "hidden dragon."

Psittacosaurus

Another early ceratopsian, *Psittacosaurus* lived in eastern Asia in the Early Cretaceous. Its name means "parrot lizard." Paleontologists have uncovered and studied hundreds of *Psittacosaurus* fossils, and have identified at least 14 different species.

Differences and Similarities

Psittacosaurus varied in size—the smallest species was a third smaller than the largest—but they were all roughly the same shape. They had a distinctive, rounded skull that could have housed a large brain. They also had large eye sockets. Paleontologists think that *Psittacosaurus* had good senses of sight and smell.

Psittacosaurus had defensive horns sticking out from its cheeks.

It is possible that only some species had tail bristles, or even just some individuals.

Bristled Tail

In 2002, paleontologists announced the discovery of the most perfectly preserved *Psittacosaurus* fossil yet. It had very detailed skin impressions and, interestingly, 16-cm (6.3-in) bristles on its tail. Since then, more individuals with bristles have been found.

This fossil shows the bristles sticking out from the tail.

DID YOU KNOW? Early Cretaceous rocks in East Asia contain so many *Psittacosaurus* fossils that they are called the Psittacosaurus biochron.

	PALEOZOIC	TRIASSIC	JURASSIC	CRETACEOUS	AGE OF MAMMALS	
MILLIONS OF YEARS AGO	541	251	206	145	66	present

112

Name: *Psittacosaurus*
(SIT-uh-ko-SAWR-us)

Family: Psittacosauridae

Height: 60 cm (23.6 in)

Length: 2 m (6.6 ft)

Weight: 20 kg (44 lb)

DINOSAUR PROFILE

Psittacosaurus's rounded and flattened beak was strong enough to crack tough seeds and nuts.

Birdlike *Sinovenator* hunted in packs. It was a troodontid.

Zuniceratops

Sometimes called the missing link between the early ceratopsians and the later ones, *Zuniceratops* had a large frill and two brow horns, but no nose horn. It lived in what is now New Mexico about 10 million years before its nose-horned cousins appeared.

Face Features

Zuniceratops had a long snout with a bony ridge along it. It fed on cones, shrubs, and bark, which it stripped from tree trunks with its beaky mouth. Its cheek bones stuck out to the sides, and might have been tipped with tiny horns.

Zuniceratops is the earliest known ceratopsian with brow horns.

The Fringed Heads

Zuniceratops and the ceratopsians belonged to a group of dinosaurs called the marginocephalians, or "fringed heads," which had a thick, bony fringe at the back of the skull. The pachycephalosaurs were marginocephalians, too. Named after *Pachycephalosaurus* (pages 158–159), they include *Stegoceras* (pages 148–149) and *Stygimoloch* (pages 160–161).

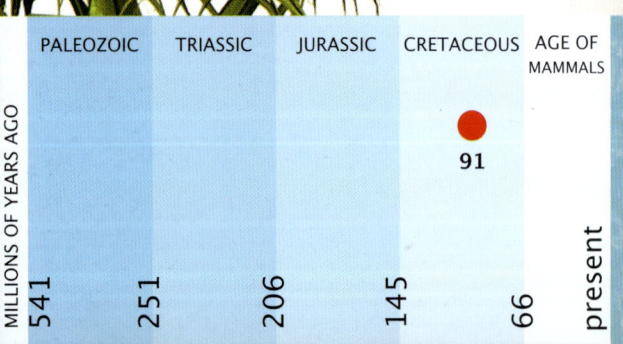

	PALEOZOIC	TRIASSIC	JURASSIC	CRETACEOUS	AGE OF MAMMALS

MILLIONS OF YEARS AGO

541 251 206 145 66 present

91

Name: *Zuniceratops* (ZOO–nee–SEH–ruh–tops)

Family: Ceratopsidae

Height: 3 m (10 ft)

Length: 3.5 m (11.5 ft)

Weight: 150 kg (350 lb)

DINOSAUR PROFILE

Zuniceratops is named after the Zuni people, a tribe of Native Americans that live in New Mexico, USA.

Zuniceratops is known from just one skull and a handful of other bones.

The brow horns continued to grow throughout the dinosaur's life.

Zuniceratops walked on all fours. It probably lived in herds to protect itself against theropods.

Holes in the frill bone kept it as light as possible. A solid frill would have made the skull too heavy for the neck to support.

DID YOU KNOW? The first *Zuniceratops* fossil was found in 1996 by an eight-year-old boy named Christopher James Wolfe!

147

Stegoceras

A small, bipedal plant-eater, *Stegoceras* (meaning "horn roof") lived in North America around 75 million years ago. As with all pachycephalosaurs (thick-headed dinosaurs), *Stegoceras*'s skull had extra-thick bone at the top.

Dome Details

Stegoceras's skull dome would have protected the brain if the dinosaur charged headfirst. Most experts no longer believe that pachycephalosaurs fought each other head-to-head, but they could have still headbutted attackers and rivals. Perhaps the dome also helped to identify *Stegoceras* males and females, or it may have been used for display.

With big eyes and complex nasal cavities, *Stegoceras* would have had good senses of sight and smell.

The face was short with a narrow snout.

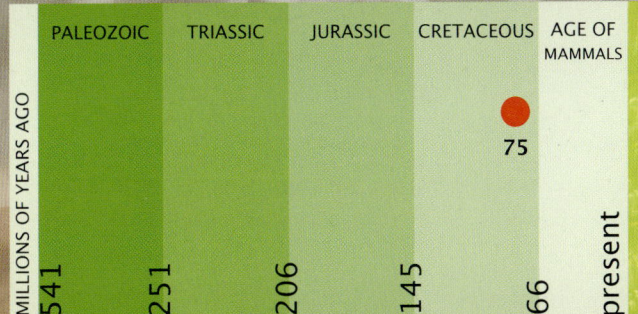

MILLIONS OF YEARS AGO	PALEOZOIC	TRIASSIC	JURASSIC	CRETACEOUS	AGE OF MAMMALS
541	251	206	145	66	present

75

Name: *Stegoceras*
(Steg–OSS–er–us)
Family: Pachycephalosauridae
Height: 65 cm (25.6 in)
Length: 2.25 m (7.4 ft)
Weight: 30 kg (66 lb)

DINOSAUR PROFILE

The skull probably started out flat and became more domed as *Stegoceras* grew.

First Fossils

Stegoceras fossils were first discovered in the Dinosaur Park Formation (page 134) by the Canadian paleontologist Lawrence Lambe. It is one of the earliest-known pachycephalosaurs. Teeth found near the first find were also thought to belong to *Stegoceras*, but were later identified as belonging to a very different dinosaur— *Troodon* (pages 82–83).

Stegoceras's back legs were about three times longer than its arms.

Early reconstructions show *Stegoceras* with a straight neck. In reality, it was curved.

DID YOU KNOW? Two species of *Stegoceras* have been discovered—one lived in the far north, in Alberta, Canada, and one was found in New Mexico, southwestern USA.

Styracosaurus

Unlike its cousin *Triceratops* (pages 156–157), *Styracosaurus* did not battle by locking horns. It did not even have brow horns. However, it did have an impressive nose horn, and a showy selection of spikes around its neck frill.

Weighty Attacker

Styracosaurus's name means "spiked lizard." The size and condition of its spikes were important for impressing would-be mates and scaring off rivals. Faced with an enemy, *Styracosaurus* probably charged at it side-on, relying on its powerful shoulders and all the force of its 3-tonne (3.3-ton) body.

Shared Environment

Herbivorous *Styracosaurus* was another dinosaur discovered in Canada's Dinosaur Park Formation (page 134). Other ceratopsians also lived in its habitat of swamps and floodplains, including *Centrosaurus* and *Chasmosaurus*. Predators included the tyrannosaurs *Albertosaurus* and *Gorgosaurus*.

Styracosaurus may have pumped blood into its fleshy frill to "blush." This could have been a signal to others of its species that it was ready to mate.

Fearsome tyrannosaur *Albertosaurus* preyed on young *Styracosaurus*.

PALEOZOIC	TRIASSIC	JURASSIC	CRETACEOUS	AGE OF MAMMALS

MILLIONS OF YEARS AGO

541 251 206 145 66 present

75

Name: *Styracosaurus* (Stih-RAK-uh-SAWR-us)

Family: Ceratopsidae

Height: 1.8 m (6 ft)

Length: 5.5 m (18 ft)

Weight: 3 tonnes (3.3 tons)

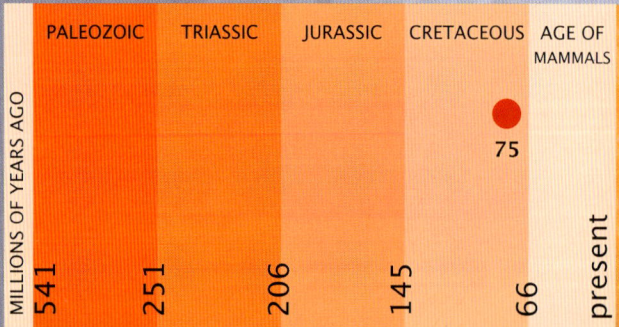

DINOSAUR PROFILE

DID YOU KNOW? No one is sure how tall *Styracosaurus*'s nose horn was. It may have been up to 60 cm (2 ft) long.

Hollow "windows" in the bone kept the neck frill light.

Styracosaurus had a tall, straight nose horn, but no brow horns.

The neck frill had at least four pairs of long spikes. There could be smaller spikes at the base of the frill, too.

Styracosaurus's short, stubby legs supported a bulky body, similar to a rhino's.

Achelousaurus

Achelousaurus was a medium-sized ceratopsian that lived in North America in the Late Cretaceous Period. It had two short cheek spikes and a pair of longer spikes at the top of its neck frill.

Wavy-Edged Frill

Achelousaurus belonged to the group of ceratopsians known as the centrosaurines, which were named after *Centrosaurus*. Their name, meaning "pointed lizards," refers to their distinguishing feature—the small hornlets dotted around the edge of their neck frill.

Achelousaurus had raised bony areas, called bosses, along its snout and above its eyes.

	PALEOZOIC	TRIASSIC	JURASSIC	CRETACEOUS	AGE OF MAMMALS	
MILLIONS OF YEARS AGO	541	251	206	145	66	present

74

Name: *Achelousaurus*
(Ah–KEL–oo–SAWR–us)

Family: Ceratopsidae

Height: 2.7 m (8.9 ft)

Length: 6 m (20 ft)

Weight: 3 tonnes (3.3 tons)

DINOSAUR PROFILE

Achelousaurus's skull was more than 1.6 m (5.2 ft) long from the tip of its spikes to the end of its beaky snout.

Horns and Lumps

Achelousaurus was closely related to another ceratopsian, *Einiosaurus*. Both had spiky frill margins and two longer spikes at the top of the frill; both had bony lumps, or bosses, instead of brow horns. *Einiosaurus* still had a nose horn—it curved downward very distinctively. *Achelousaurus* had a bony lump on its nose instead of a horn.

This *Achelousaurus* skull was dug up in Montana, USA, in 1985 by the American paleontologist Jack Horner.

Achelousaurus used its ridged, parrot-like beak to break off tough plant stems.

DID YOU KNOW? *Achelousaurus* was named after the Greek river god Achelous, whose bull-like horns were pulled off by the hero Heracles.

Protoceratops

A spectacular fossil discovered in 1971 in the Gobi Desert, Mongolia, captured two dinosaurs locked in combat. They had been buried alive. One was the plant-eating primitive ceratopsian *Protoceratops*; the other was the dromaeosaur *Velociraptor*.

Life in the Gobi

Many *Protoceratops* specimens, including fossilized nests, eggs, and babies, have been found in the red sandstone of the Gobi Desert. During the Late Cretaceous, the Gobi was not as dry as it is now. There were probably seasonal floods.

Protoceratops and *Velociraptor* had been preserved in sand mid-fight. Experts believe they were caught up in a sudden sandstorm.

Protoceratops used its wide, spade-like claws to dig nests and burrows. It laid up to 15 eggs at a time.

Like all dromaeosaurs, *Velociraptor* had a killer curved claw on the second toe of each foot. It slashed at prey to make it bleed to death.

	PALEOZOIC	TRIASSIC	JURASSIC	CRETACEOUS	AGE OF MAMMALS
MILLIONS OF YEARS AGO	541	251	206	145	73 ● 66	present

Name: *Protoceratops* (Pro-toe-SEH-ruh-tops)
Family: Ceratopsidae
Height: 70 cm (27.6 in)
Length: 1.9 m (6.2 ft)
Weight: 180 kg (397 lb)

DINOSAUR PROFILE

This fossil of a newly hatched *Protoceratops andrewsi* was discovered in 1997.

Desert Discoveries

The first *Protoceratops* specimens were discovered in the 1920s by American paleontologist Roy Chapman Andrews, so they were given the species name *andrewsi*. In 2001, a second species was identified, *Protoceratops hellenikorhinus*. Unlike *Protoceratops andrewsi*, it had two nose horns, but no front teeth.

Protoceratops had a relatively large neck frill, probably for display.

Velociraptor was about the same size as *Protoceratops*.

Protoceratops's tough, horny beak was not powerful enough to damage *Velociraptor*.

DID YOU KNOW? The theropod *Oviraptor* got its name, meaning "egg thief," because experts once thought—mistakenly—that it stole *Protoceratops* eggs.

Triceratops

Triceratops had a horned face and a bone frill that jutted over its neck. These features were probably little help in battles against large local meat-eaters such as *Tyrannosaurus*. Yet, weighing more than seven family cars, *Triceratops* could have charged at its attackers.

Three Horns

Triceratops means "three-horned face." A 1-m- (3-ft-) long horn was above each eye, while a shorter horn decorated the snout. These horns might have frightened small meat-eaters, but they were not sharp or strong enough to be very useful weapons.

Bite marks on *Triceratops* bones tell us the plant–eater lost battles against *Tyrannosaurus*.

Triceratops fossils have been found together, so it is possible this dinosaur lived in social groups, just like African elephants do today.

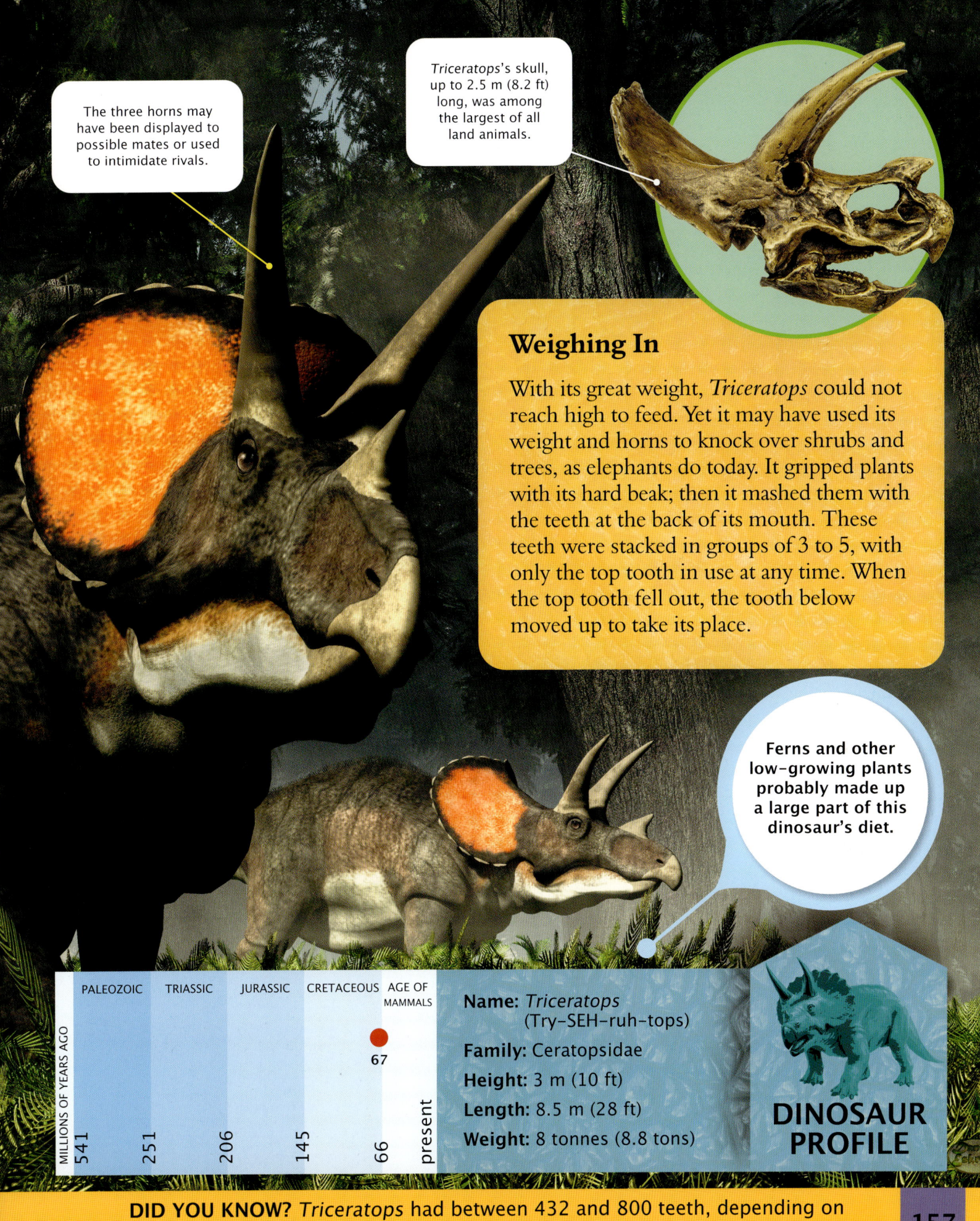

The three horns may have been displayed to possible mates or used to intimidate rivals.

Triceratops's skull, up to 2.5 m (8.2 ft) long, was among the largest of all land animals.

Weighing In

With its great weight, *Triceratops* could not reach high to feed. Yet it may have used its weight and horns to knock over shrubs and trees, as elephants do today. It gripped plants with its hard beak; then it mashed them with the teeth at the back of its mouth. These teeth were stacked in groups of 3 to 5, with only the top tooth in use at any time. When the top tooth fell out, the tooth below moved up to take its place.

Ferns and other low-growing plants probably made up a large part of this dinosaur's diet.

MILLIONS OF YEARS AGO	PALEOZOIC	TRIASSIC	JURASSIC	CRETACEOUS	AGE OF MAMMALS	
	541	251	206	145	67 66	present

Name: *Triceratops* (Try–SEH–ruh–tops)
Family: Ceratopsidae
Height: 3 m (10 ft)
Length: 8.5 m (28 ft)
Weight: 8 tonnes (8.8 tons)

DINOSAUR PROFILE

DID YOU KNOW? *Triceratops* had between 432 and 800 teeth, depending on the size of the animal, but only around 150 were in use at any one time.

Pachycephalosaurus

The pachycephalosaurs are named after *Pachycephalosaurus*, a dome-headed dinosaur from Late Cretaceous North America. Paleontologists once thought that these plant-eaters bashed their heads together like goats. However, it is unlikely that they fought each other head-to-head.

Pachycephalosaurus walked and ran on two legs, but would have foraged on all fours.

Protective Helmet

The solid bone at the top of the skull protected *Pachycephalosaurus*'s delicate brain when it charged headfirst at full speed. The bone was 25 cm (10 in) thick in places.

Pachycephalosaurus's jaw had tiny, sharp teeth for eating soft fruit, seeds, and young leaves.

MILLIONS OF YEARS AGO	PALEOZOIC	TRIASSIC	JURASSIC	CRETACEOUS	AGE OF MAMMALS	present
	541	251	206	145	● 68 / 66	

Name: *Pachycephalosaurus* (Pak–ee–SEF–uh–lo–SAWR–us)

Family: Pachycephalosauridae

Height: 1.8 m (5.9 ft)

Length: 4.5 m (15 ft)

Weight: 450 kg (992 lb)

DINOSAUR PROFILE

DID YOU KNOW? *Pachycephalosaurus* was the largest-known pachycephalosaur, while the smallest was *Foraminacephale*, just 2 m (6.6 ft) long.

Large eyes gave *Pachycephalosaurus* good binocular vision.

Pachycephalosaurus used its head to charge into rivals' thighs.

There was a circle of bony spikes around the bottom of the skull dome; there were also spikes at the end of the snout.

Pachycephalosaurus had long legs and short arms. It was not a fast runner.

Fossil Discoveries

Pachycephalosaurus was named in 1931. Not many fossils have been found—just one skull, some skull roofs, and a few other bones. In 2016, paleontologists announced that they had found skulls of two baby *Pachycephalosauruses* at the Hell Creek Formation in Montana, USA.

Stygimoloch

Discovered in the Hell Creek Formation of Montana, in the United States, *Stygimoloch* was first described in 1983. Since then, paleontologists have argued about whether this plant-eating pachycephalosaur is a species in its own right, or just a juvenile version of *Pachycephalosaurus* (pages 158–159).

Bizarre Beast

Like *Pachycephalosaurus*, *Stygimoloch* had a dome-shaped skull surrounded by bony horns. It had more horny bumps on the top of its snout. Its otherworldly appearance is reflected in its name, which combines "Styx," the river of the dead in Greek mythology, and "Moloch," a Canaanite god worshipped in the Middle East around 1500–1000 BCE.

Stygimoloch's skull was about 46 cm (18 in) long.

One of the predators at Hell Creek was the dromaeosaur *Dakotaraptor*. It was about the same size as *Utahraptor* (pages 60–61).

This portion of *Stygimoloch*'s skull shows some of its horns.

Horns and Growth

American dinosaur expert Jack Horner was one of the first to suggest that *Stygimoloch* was a young *Pachycephalosaurus*. He also thought that *Dracorex* was an earlier growth stage of the same dinosaur. *Pachycephalosaurus* had fewer horns than *Dracorex* or *Stygimoloch*. If Horner's argument is true, it must mean that the dinosaur lost horns as it aged, but that its dome grew larger.

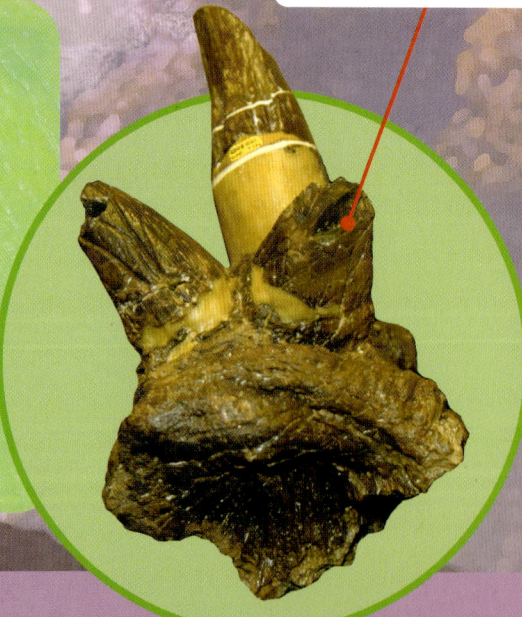

MILLIONS OF YEARS AGO	PALEOZOIC	TRIASSIC	JURASSIC	CRETACEOUS	AGE OF MAMMALS	
	541	251	206	145	66	present

66

Name: *Stygimoloch*
(Stij–ih–MOL–ock)
Family: Pachycephalosauridae
Height: 1.2 m (4 ft)
Length: 3 m (10 ft)
Weight: 78 kg (172 lb)

DINOSAUR PROFILE

Stygimoloch had a cluster of spikes at the back of the head. There was one pair of longer spikes, up to 15 cm (5.9 in) long, and a few smaller ones.

Stygimoloch had spikes on its cheeks, too—perhaps for protection.

DID YOU KNOW? There is one species of *Dracorex*—*Dracorex hogwartsia* ("dragon king of Hogwarts"). It is named after the school of magic in the Harry Potter books.

161

Chapter 5

Thyreophorans

These plant-eating dinosaurs had superb protection against fierce meat-eaters. Thyreophorans means "shield bearers" in ancient Greek. While early thyreophorans just had a covering of bony plates, their later relatives had thick plates, tall spikes, or heavy tail clubs.

Thyreophoran Groups

The earliest thyreophorans evolved in the Early Jurassic Period. They had little bony plates and were light enough to walk on their back legs. After a few more million years, better-protected thyreophorans evolved. They were larger, had bigger plates, and walked on all fours. By the middle Jurassic Period, thyreophorans had split into two subgroups: stegosaurs ("covered lizards") and ankylosaurs ("stiff lizards"). Stegosaurs had rows of spikes or plates down their backs, as well as spiked tails. Ankylosaurs were protected by almost solid plates of bone.

Around 7 m (23 ft) long and weighing 4,000 kg (8,820 lb), *Wuerhosaurus* was a stegosaur that lived in the Early Cretaceous Period.

DID YOU KNOW? *Gargoyleosaurus* was named after gargoyles, the monsters carved on medieval buildings, which had spout–like mouths to drain away rainwater.

● 154

Name: *Gargoyleosaurus* (Gahr–GOYL–ee–oh–SAWR–us)

Family: Nodosauridae

Height: 80 cm (31 in)

Length: 3.3 m (10.8 ft)

Weight: 500 kg (1,100 lb)

DINOSAUR PROFILE

With a body rather like an army tank, this ankylosaur was protected by plates of bone, known as scutes.

Gargoyleosaurus was a plant-eater with small, triangular teeth and a long, flexible tongue to help with chewing and grasping.

Heavy protection slowed ankylosaurs down, so *Gargoyleosaurus* could probably run no faster than a human can briskly walk.

Thyreophoran Legs

Apart from early thyreophorans, these dinosaurs had four thick legs and broad feet. Their front legs were usually much shorter than their back legs. Combined with the weight of their scutes, these skeletal features suggest thyreophorans were slow walkers and awkward runners. Thyreophorans were ornithischian ("bird-hipped") dinosaurs.

Having short front legs meant that the ankylosaur *Mymoorapelta* had a rounded back and held its tail above the ground.

163

Scutellosaurus

Appearing in the Early Jurassic Period, *Scutellosaurus* was an ancestor of the later shielded dinosaurs, such as *Ankylosaurus* and *Stegosaurus*. The name *Scutellosaurus* means "lizard with little shields."

Little Darter

Scutellosaurus was a plant-eater that lived in what is now Arizona, in the southern United States. Small and lightly built, it had longer back legs than front ones, so it probably moved around on two legs. Its small skull housed a small brain.

The speedy theropod *Coelophysis* would have hunted *Scutellosaurus*.

Little Shields

Scutellosaurus had small, simple scutes along its neck and back. These enabled *Scutellosaurus* to still bend and twist, but also gave some protection against the teeth and claws of small meat-eaters, such as *Kayentavenator*. Yet larger theropods were evolving in the region, including the 3-m- (10-ft-) long *Ceolophysis*. Running away was *Scutellosaurus*'s only strategy against these heftier predators.

Scutellosaurus probably went down on all fours to eat shrubby plants.

Scutellosaurus had hundreds of scutes, arranged in rows along its neck, back, and sides.

	PALEOZOIC	TRIASSIC	JURASSIC	CRETACEOUS	AGE OF MAMMALS	
MILLIONS OF YEARS AGO	541	251	206 • 196	145	66	present

Name: *Scutellosaurus*
(Scoo-tel-oh-SAWR-us)
Family: Scutellosauridae
Height: 80 cm (31.5 in)
Length: 1.2 m (3.9 ft)
Weight: 14 kg (31 lb)

DINOSAUR PROFILE

Scutellosaurus probably had fleshy cheeks, like most other ornithischians.

Scutellosaurus's long, thin tail helped it to balance. It made up more than half of its body length.

Dragonflies and other insects probably made up part of *Scutellosaurus*'s diet.

The rows of osteoderms made it hard for predators to sink their teeth or claws into the skin.

DID YOU KNOW? The *Scutellosaurus* teeth found so far by paleontologists are not worn away, which suggests that it did not chew its food before swallowing.

165

Scelidosaurus

Another of the early thyreophorans, *Scelidosaurus* was discovered in Dorset, southern England. Unlike *Scutellosaurus* (pages 164–165), it walked on all fours. Its bony plates (or scutes) were larger, too—more like those of later dinosaurs in the group.

Teeth and Jaws

Scelidosaurus had a small head, just 20 cm (7.9 in) long, and a beaky mouth. When it was first found, paleontologists thought it was a fish-eater, because of its long teeth. In reality, it ate plants. Its jaw only moved up and down, not side to side, so it had to bite through leaves rather than grinding them.

Legs and Toes

Scelidosaurus was named by Richard Owen, the same scientist who came up with the word "dinosaur." *Scelidosaurus* means "limb lizard" and refers to the dinosaur's stout back legs. The feet had four long toes with blunt claws.

Flying reptiles called *pterosaurs* lived in the Mesozoic.

The beaky mouth was used to eat ferns and conifers.

Osteoderms protected the back and tail, but not the legs or underside.

Scelidosaurus had a large stomach for breaking down plant matter.

Scelidosaurus walked on all fours. Its back legs were longer than its front ones, so its head was close to the ground.

This image shows one of the first *Scelidosaurus* finds—an incomplete skull. The snout tip is missing.

	PALEOZOIC	TRIASSIC	JURASSIC	CRETACEOUS	AGE OF MAMMALS
MILLIONS OF YEARS AGO	541	251	206	145	66 present

190

Name: *Scelidosaurus*
(Skel–ee–doe–SAWR–us)
Family: Scelidosauridae
Height: 1.5 m (5 ft)
Length: 4 m (13 ft)
Weight: 270 kg (595 lb)

DINOSAUR PROFILE

DID YOU KNOW? In 1858, a *Scelidosaurus* skeleton was found—it was the earliest complete dinosaur fossil.

167

Huayangosaurus

Huayangosaurus was an early stegosaur. It was smaller than later stegosaurs, but like its relatives, it had a spiked tail and tall plates down its back. *Huayangosaurus* walked on four legs as it searched for low-growing plants to snip off with its horn-covered beak.

Paleontologists liked the name "thagomizer" and started to use it.

Huayangosaurus pulled off leaves and twigs using its hard-edged beak.

On the Far Side

Toward the end of *Huayangosaurus*'s tail were two pairs of spikes forming a weapon known as a thagomizer. The name "thagomizer" was made up for these weapons in 1982, by Gary Larson in his funny *The Far Side* cartoons.

DID YOU KNOW? In his comic, Gary Larson joked that a stegosaur's tail spikes were named after a man named "Thag."

Being Spiky

Huayangosaurus had two rows of tall plates and spikes along its neck, back, and tail. The spiky plates above the hips were longest, perhaps to protect this fairly short dinosaur against attacks from above. *Huayangosaurus* also had two long shoulder spikes. These might have been useful during an attack, but such impressive features could also have been displayed to attract a mate.

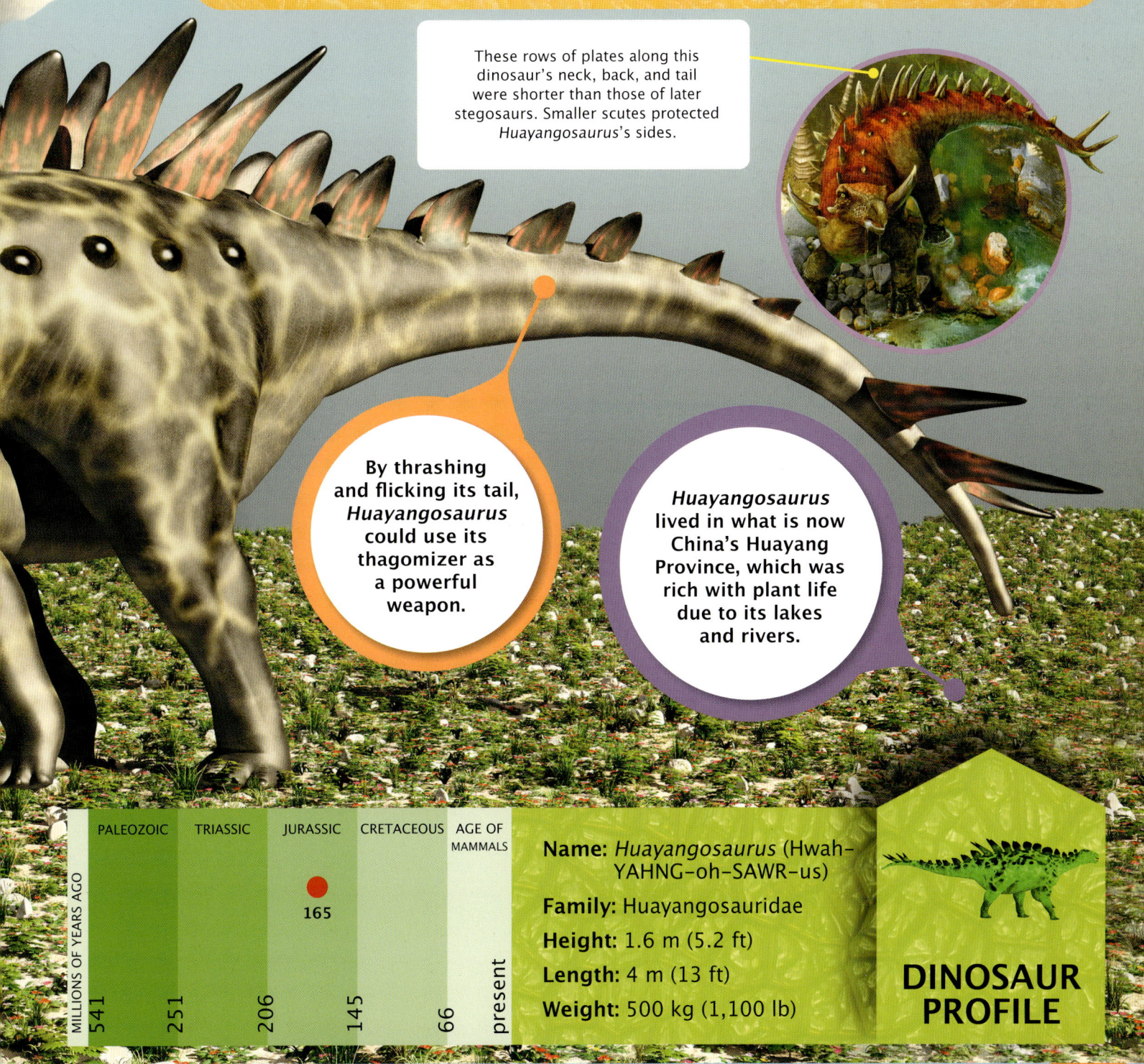

These rows of plates along this dinosaur's neck, back, and tail were shorter than those of later stegosaurs. Smaller scutes protected *Huayangosaurus*'s sides.

By thrashing and flicking its tail, *Huayangosaurus* could use its thagomizer as a powerful weapon.

Huayangosaurus lived in what is now China's Huayang Province, which was rich with plant life due to its lakes and rivers.

	PALEOZOIC	TRIASSIC	JURASSIC	CRETACEOUS	AGE OF MAMMALS
MILLIONS OF YEARS AGO	541	251	206 ● 165	145	66 present

Name: *Huayangosaurus* (Hwah-YAHNG-oh-SAWR-us)

Family: Huayangosauridae

Height: 1.6 m (5.2 ft)

Length: 4 m (13 ft)

Weight: 500 kg (1,100 lb)

DINOSAUR PROFILE

Tuojiangosaurus

Sometimes called the Asian *Stegosaurus* (pages 172–173), *Tuojiangosaurus* lived in China in the Late Jurassic. It was a typical stegosaur, with plates along the length of its back, and deadly tail spikes.

Sichuan Stegosaurs

Tuojiangosaurus means "Tuo River lizard," after the river in Sichuan Province, southwestern China, where the dinosaur was discovered. Other stegosaurs shared its habitat. Two of these—*Chungkingosaurus* and *Chialingosaurus*, both just 4 m (13 ft) long—may have been *Tuojiangosaurus* juveniles, not separate species.

Tuojiangosaurus held its tail off the ground. It could swing its sharp tail spikes at predators.

Tuojiangosaurus had a double row of horn–covered plates, just like *Kentrosaurus* (pages 174–175).

	MILLIONS OF YEARS AGO	PALEOZOIC	TRIASSIC	JURASSIC	CRETACEOUS	AGE OF MAMMALS
		541	251	206	145	66 ... present

160

Name: *Tuojiangosaurus* (Too-YANG-oh-SAWR-us)

Family: Stegosauridae

Height: 2 m (6.6 ft)

Length: 7 m (23 ft)

Weight: 1.5 tonnes (1.7 tons)

DINOSAUR PROFILE

The plates were different sizes and shapes. The largest were over the hip; they grew smaller toward the head.

Eating Habits

Tuojiangosaurus browsed on low plants. While it was eating, its head stayed slightly dipped, helped by the shorter front legs. The jaws contained at least 25 small teeth for snipping off vegetation.

The snout was long and shallow with a beaky tip.

Tuojiangosaurus ate low-growing ferns and cycads.

Early reconstructions of stegosaurs sometimes positioned the front legs sprawling out to the sides. In fact, they were held directly under the body.

DID YOU KNOW? *Tuojiangosaurus* was named in 1977, after its fossilized remains were discovered by construction workers building a dam.

171

Stegosaurus

This plant-eater had two rows of kite-shaped plates down its back. Their pattern may have helped *Stegosaurus* recognize other members of its herd from a distance. *Stegosaurus* had a small brain, suiting this dinosaur to a slow and simple life.

Terrible Thagomizer

The tip of *Stegosaurus*'s tail had four sharp spikes, known as a thagomizer. The spikes were 60 to 90 cm (2 to 3 ft) long. Injuries to *Stegosaurus* tails suggest that these dinosaurs used their thagomizers in combat. When whipped at an attacker, a thagomizer would have made deep wounds.

With a flick of its tail, a stegosaur escapes.

MILLIONS OF YEARS AGO	PALEOZOIC	TRIASSIC	JURASSIC	CRETACEOUS	AGE OF MAMMALS
	541	251	206	145	66 present

● 153

Name: *Stegosaurus* (STEG-uh-SAWR-us)

Family: Stegosauridae

Height: 2.75 m (9 ft)

Length: 9 m (30 ft)

Weight: 5 tonnes (5.5 tons)

DINOSAUR PROFILE

DID YOU KNOW? The remains of more than 80 individual *Stegosauruses* have been found, making it one of the most well-studied dinosaur species.

Unlike most stegosaurs, *Stegosaurus* had scutes that were staggered, not in pairs.

Scales Vs. Scutes

Unlike scales, which grow from the top layer of an animal's skin, *Stegosaurus*'s scutes grew from deep in its skin. Scales, like claws, are made from keratin, while scutes are made from bone. Early reconstructions of *Stegosaurus* had its scutes flat on top of its body—that is how the dinosaur got its name, which means "roofed lizard." Paleontologists now know that the plates stood upright, making the dinosaur look bigger than it was. They were almost certainly for display, but they may have also helped *Stegosaurus* to regulate its body temperature.

Stegosaurus's biggest plates were 60 cm (24 in) tall.

Stegosaurus lived in forests and on ferny plains in North America and Europe.

Stegosaurus's top speed was probably no more than around 7 km/h (4.3 mph).

173

Kentrosaurus

The small stegosaur *Kentrosaurus* lived in what is now Tanzania about 152 million years ago. It shared its wet, swampy forest habitat with one of the giants of the plant-eating dinosaurs, *Giraffatitan*.

Plenty of Plants

There was no shortage of food in Late Jurassic East Africa, so *Kentrosaurus* did not need to compete with *Giraffatitan*. Plants flourished in the wet, tropical climate. *Kentrosaurus* fed low to the ground, using its beaky mouth to snap up vegetation.

As for *Stegosaurus* (pages 172–173), the plates along its back may have helped *Kentrosaurus* lose or soak up heat.

Kentrosaurus had a narrow, pointed snout.

Kentrosaurus's tropical environment had two seasons: dry and wet.

DID YOU KNOW? Discovered in 1909, this dinosaur was named *Kentrosaurus*, which means "spiked lizard," in 1915.

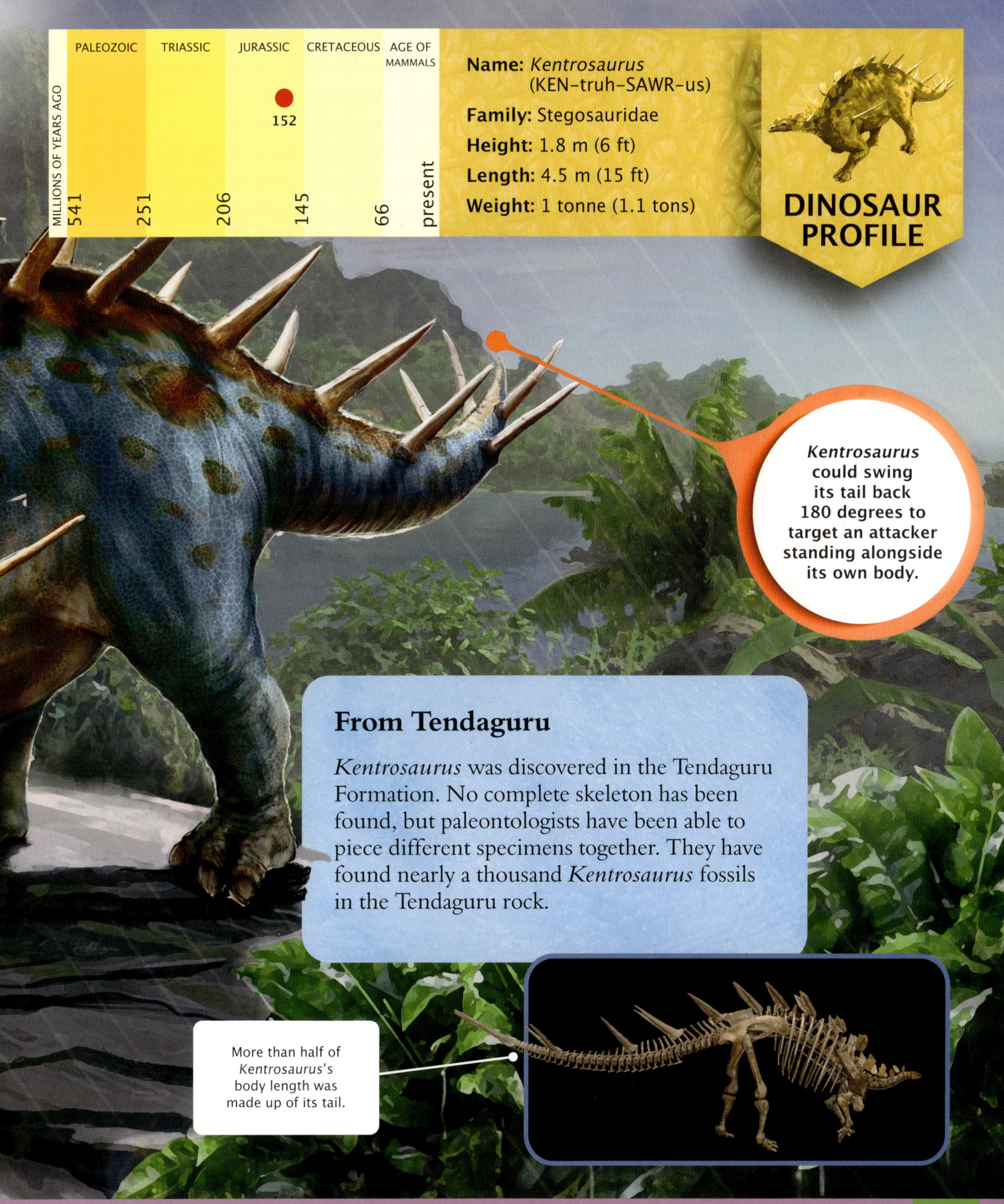

	PALEOZOIC	TRIASSIC	JURASSIC	CRETACEOUS	AGE OF MAMMALS
MILLIONS OF YEARS AGO	541	251	206	145	66	present

152

Name: *Kentrosaurus*
(KEN–truh–SAWR–us)
Family: Stegosauridae
Height: 1.8 m (6 ft)
Length: 4.5 m (15 ft)
Weight: 1 tonne (1.1 tons)

DINOSAUR PROFILE

Kentrosaurus could swing its tail back 180 degrees to target an attacker standing alongside its own body.

From Tendaguru

Kentrosaurus was discovered in the Tendaguru Formation. No complete skeleton has been found, but paleontologists have been able to piece different specimens together. They have found nearly a thousand *Kentrosaurus* fossils in the Tendaguru rock.

More than half of *Kentrosaurus*'s body length was made up of its tail.

Minmi

The small ankylosaur *Minmi* lived in what is now Queensland, Australia, around 115 million years ago. It is named after Minmi Crossing, a landmark near the place where it was first discovered in 1964.

Speed and Shields

Unlike most slow-moving ankylosaurs, *Minmi* was probably a fast runner. It had extra bones across its spine that could have anchored extra muscles. If that really is what those "paravertebrae" (across bones) were for, *Minmi* could have outrun many predators. When it encountered a speedy hunter, it relied on its protective plates to discourage them from attacking.

All-Over Protection

Most ankylosaurs had short, stubby legs. This meant that their softer-skinned bellies were held low to the ground, where they were hard to reach. *Minmi* was different. It had relatively long legs, but it also had bony plates all over its body, even on its underside.

Minmi had long legs for an ankylosaur.

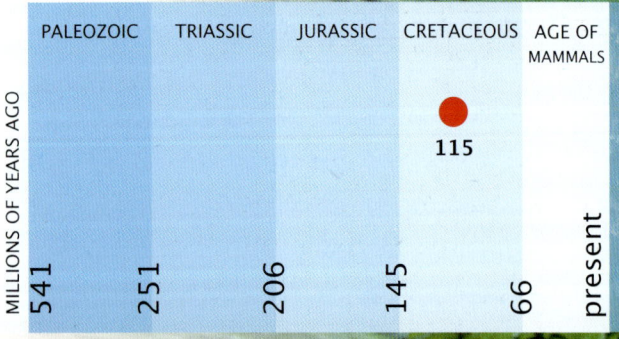

	PALEOZOIC	TRIASSIC	JURASSIC	CRETACEOUS	AGE OF MAMMALS	
MILLIONS OF YEARS AGO				🔴 115		
	541	251	206	145	66	present

Name: *Minmi* (MIN-mee)
Family: Ankylosauridae
Height: 1 m (3.3 ft)
Length: 3 m (9.8 ft)
Weight: 300 kg (661 lb)

DINOSAUR PROFILE

Early Cretaceous Queensland was an island, cut off from the rest of Australia.

Minmi lived in forests and floodplains. It ate ferns, as well as leaves, fruit, and seeds from the first flowering plants.

Protective plates covered its back and belly.

The skull was shaped like an arrowhead.

Minmi had strong back legs for sprinting through the undergrowth.

DID YOU KNOW? *Minmi* had the shortest name of any dinosaur for more than two decades. Today, *Yi* has the shortest name.

177

Sauropelta

Living across North America in the Early Cretaceous, plant-eating *Sauropelta* was a species of ankylosaur. Large, bony studs, called osteoderms, shielded its back. Two long, defensive spikes stuck out from its shoulders, and it had shorter spikes along its sides.

Well-Defended

Sauropelta means "shielded lizard." Its bones and spikes were essential protection against the predators of the day, such as *Acrocanthosaurus*, a relative of *Allosaurus* (pages 52–53), and *Deinonychus* (pages 64–65). Even with their fearsome jaws, *Sauropelta*'s studded skin was too hard to bite through.

Nodosaurs

Sauropelta is the earliest known nodosaur. Named after *Nodosaurus*, the tank-like nodosaurs were ankylosaurs that did not have tail clubs, but had certain other features, including a bony bump over each eye, another bump at the base of the skull, and spikes on the lower jaw. *Borealopelta* and *Edmontonia* were nodosaurs, too.

The 90-cm- (35-in-) long shoulder spikes helped make *Sauropelta* look bigger than it really was.

This section of fossilized *Sauropelta* skin shows the protective, bony osteoderms, or scutes.

The flattened skull was made up of plates that had fused together.

MILLIONS OF YEARS AGO	PALEOZOIC	TRIASSIC	JURASSIC	CRETACEOUS	AGE OF MAMMALS	present
	541	251	206	145	66	

108

Name: *Sauropelta*
(SAWR–oh–PEL–tah)
Family: Nodosauridae
Height: 2.4 m (8 ft)
Length: 5.2 m (17.1 ft)
Weight: 1.5 tonnes (1.65 tons)

DINOSAUR PROFILE

The long tail contained more than 40 vertebrae (spine bones) and made up half of the dinosaur's total body length.

Sauropelta's back was covered with bony bumps called osteoderms.

DID YOU KNOW? Hundreds of fossilized dinosaur footprints discovered in Alberta, Canada, were almost certainly made by herds of *Sauropelta*.

179

Borealopelta

The first fossil of *Borealopelta* was discovered in 2011. This amazing fossil shows exactly how *Borealopelta*'s plates were arranged. Most fossils show only the hard body parts, but this fossil kept the skin. The animal probably drowned, got washed out to sea, and was quickly buried by sand.

Last Meal

The 2011 discovery also shed light on *Borealopelta*'s diet. The contents of this *Borealopelta*'s stomach were preserved, showing that its last meal was almost entirely ferns. The *Borealopelta* must have died only a few hours later. The stomach contents suggest that nodosaurs were selective about the food they ate. The ferns were halfway through their growing season, indicating that they were eaten in early summer.

Borealopelta reached for its chosen leaves with its narrow, hard-edged beak.

Tests carried out on *Borealopelta*'s skin show that it was reddish brown.

DID YOU KNOW? *Borealopelta* (meaning "northern shield") was discovered in 2011 by miner Shawn Funk in a tar mine in Alberta, Canada.

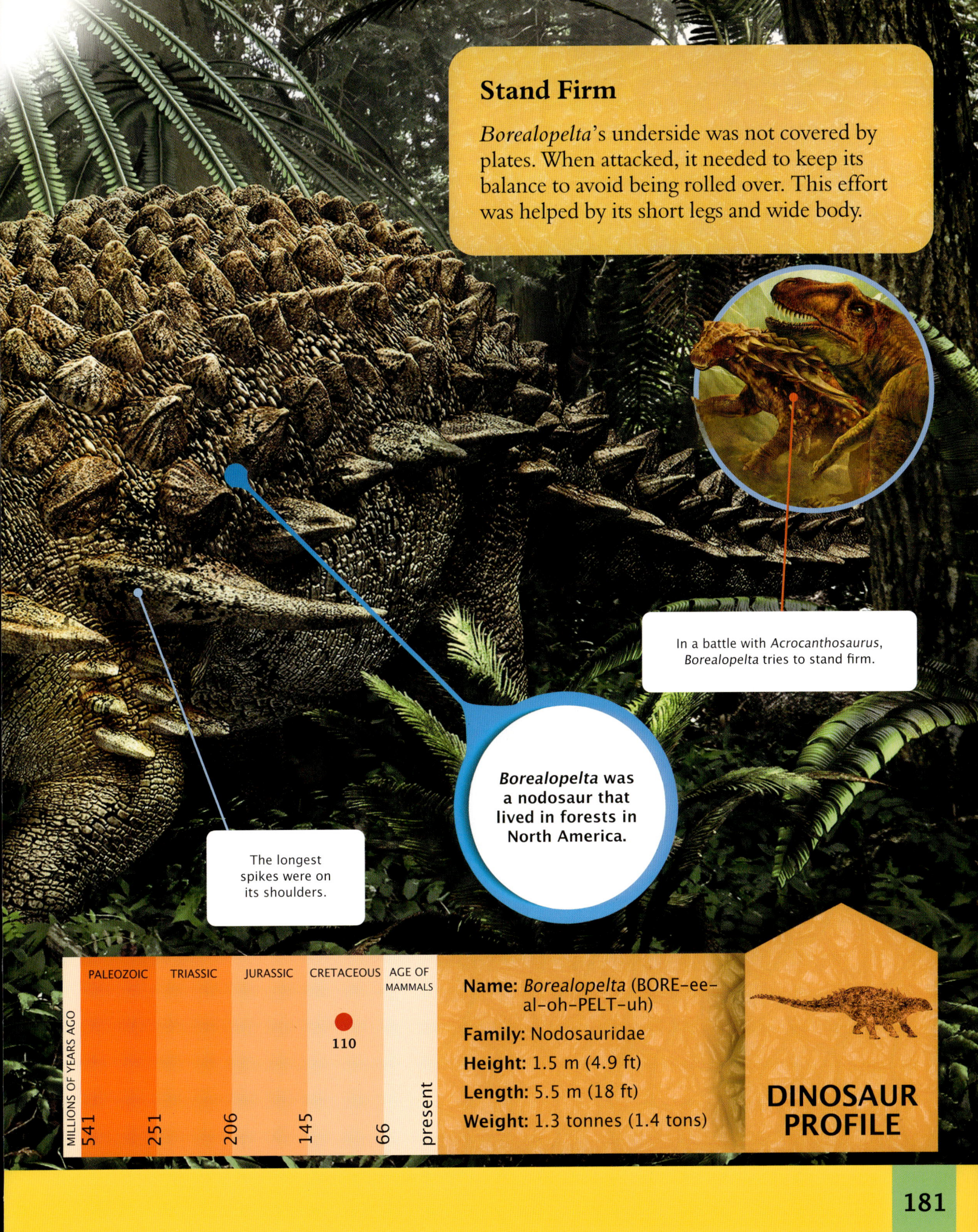

Stand Firm

Borealopelta's underside was not covered by plates. When attacked, it needed to keep its balance to avoid being rolled over. This effort was helped by its short legs and wide body.

In a battle with *Acrocanthosaurus*, *Borealopelta* tries to stand firm.

Borealopelta was a nodosaur that lived in forests in North America.

The longest spikes were on its shoulders.

PALEOZOIC	TRIASSIC	JURASSIC	CRETACEOUS	AGE OF MAMMALS	

MILLIONS OF YEARS AGO

110

541 · 251 · 206 · 145 · 66 · present

Name: *Borealopelta* (BORE-ee-al-oh-PELT-uh)
Family: Nodosauridae
Height: 1.5 m (4.9 ft)
Length: 5.5 m (18 ft)
Weight: 1.3 tonnes (1.4 tons)

DINOSAUR PROFILE

Edmontonia

One of the largest nodosaurs, herbivorous *Edmontonia* lived across North America in the Late Cretaceous. Pyramid-shaped spikes covered its back, while forward-facing shoulder spikes protected the head and neck. Sometimes, these spikes split, to create even deadlier forked tips.

Shoulder Power

Edmontonia's shoulder spikes continued growing throughout its life. They gave some protection if the dinosaur had to charge past an attacking theropod; however, their main purpose was for fighting rivals. *Edmontonia* males probably battled over territory and mates. The ones with larger shoulder spikes would have had more status.

Edmontonia has been found in Canada's Dinosaur Park Formation, along with the ankylosaur *Scolosaurus* (left) and nodosaur *Panoplosaurus* (right).

	PALEOZOIC	TRIASSIC	JURASSIC	CRETACEOUS	AGE OF MAMMALS
MILLIONS OF YEARS AGO	541	251	206	145	66 present

Name: *Edmontonia*
(Ed-mon-TOE-nee-uh)
Family: Nodosauridae
Height: 1.8 m (5.9 ft)
Length: 6.6 m (22 ft)
Weight: 3 tonnes (3.3 tons)

DINOSAUR PROFILE

DID YOU KNOW? *Edmontonia* is named after Edmonton, the capital city of the Canadian province of Alberta, in western Canada.

Stories in Rock

As *Edmontonia* was widespread, its fossils have been found in different rock formations across North America. The first identified *Edmontonia* was discovered in 1928 in Alberta's Edmonton Formation (since renamed the Horseshoe Canyon Formation).

Each shoulder spike was made from strong, dense bone.

Rival *Edmontonia* would barge at each other, shoulder to shoulder.

Edmontonia's skull was about 50 cm (19.7 in) long. It was protected by osteoderms that had fused together to form a bony helmet.

Euoplocephalus

One of the largest ankylosaurs, plant-eating *Euoplocephalus* had a spike-covered body and a wide, heavy tail club. Its short legs carried its body low to the ground, leaving its vulnerable belly almost impossible for any attacker to reach.

Solo Life

Euoplocephalus lived in what is now Canada during the Late Cretaceous. Most fossils have been found on their own, so paleontologists believe that *Euoplocephalus* was not a herd animal. They think it lived alone, like today's hippopotamus.

Horns poked out from the back of the head.

Most ankylosaurs had four toes on their back feet, but *Euoplocephalus* had just three.

PALEOZOIC	TRIASSIC	JURASSIC	CRETACEOUS	AGE OF MAMMALS
541	251	206	145	66 present

MILLIONS OF YEARS AGO

76

Name: *Euoplocephalus* (You-op-luh-SEF-uh-lus)

Family: Ankylosauridae

Height: 1.8 m (6 ft)

Length: 6 m (20 ft)

Weight: 2 tonnes (2.2 tons)

DINOSAUR PROFILE

Safe Skull

Euoplocephalus had bony "lids" over its eyes that could close to shade out the Sun. Spiky horns protected the back and sides of the head. Most importantly, the top of the skull was double-thick, because it had fused with the plates that covered it.

Bony plates protected the top of the skull.

Excluding the beaky mouth, the skull was 35 cm (13.8 in) long.

The vertebrae at the end of the tail were fused to create a stiff "handle" for the heavy tail club.

The body was very wide—about 2.4 m (7.9 ft) across.

This young *Euoplocephalus* is hitching a ride across the swamp on its mother's back.

DID YOU KNOW? *Euoplocephalus* had complicated passages in its nose, so it probably had a good sense of smell.

Ankylosaurus

Ankylosaurs all take their name from *Ankylosaurus* ("fused lizard"). It was the largest ankylosaur and one of the best-protected, with a large tail club of solid bone.

Terrifying Threats

Ankylosaurus lived in North America at the end of the Cretaceous Period. This herbivore shared its habitat with one of the most terrifying hunters of all time—*Tyrannosaurus* (pages 96–97). However, an adult *Ankylosaurus* could have swung its tail club with enough force to break *Tyrannosaurus*'s legs.

Big Head

Ankylosaurus's skull had many air passages running through it that made it bulge out at the sides. Paleontologists are still not sure what these passages were for. They may have helped with the dinosaur's sense of smell, or they may have amplified its calls (made them louder).

Four head spikes protected *Ankylosaurus*'s face.

DID YOU KNOW? *Ankylosaurus* had a very large, flexible tongue, which may have helped it pluck leaves from shrubs.

MILLIONS OF YEARS AGO	PALEOZOIC	TRIASSIC	JURASSIC	CRETACEOUS	AGE OF MAMMALS
	541	251	206	145	66 present

67

Name: *Ankylosaurus*
(Ang–KILE–uh–SAWR–us)
Family: Ankylosauridae
Height: 1.7 m (5.6 ft)
Length: 6.25 m (20.5 ft)
Weight: 6 tonnes (6.6 tons)

DINOSAUR PROFILE

Hundreds of bite–proof bony plates covered *Ankylosaurus*'s upper body.

The tail club was made of fused bones.

Ankylosaurus's jaw housed tiny teeth.

Chapter 6

Swimming Reptiles

Reptiles walked on all fours on land for around 15 million years after they first evolved. Then, 300 million years ago, some reptiles ventured into oceans and lakes. While dinosaurs reigned on land, swimming reptiles were top predators in the oceans.

Adapting to Water

Long before the dinosaurs evolved, some land-living reptiles started to adapt to life in water. Over millions of years, their legs developed into flippers and their bodies grew more smoothly shaped, or streamlined, to help with swimming. Only a few groups of swimming reptiles—including turtles and crocodile-like reptiles—survived the catastrophe of 66 million years ago, when an asteroid hit Earth. Mosasaurs and plesiosaurs, which were the top marine predators of their time, were wiped out.

Dakosaurus was a crocodile–like reptile, also known as a crocodylomorph, that lived 157 to 137 million years ago.

This plesiosaur lived in the Western Interior Seaway, a shallow sea that split North America in two during the Cretaceous Period.

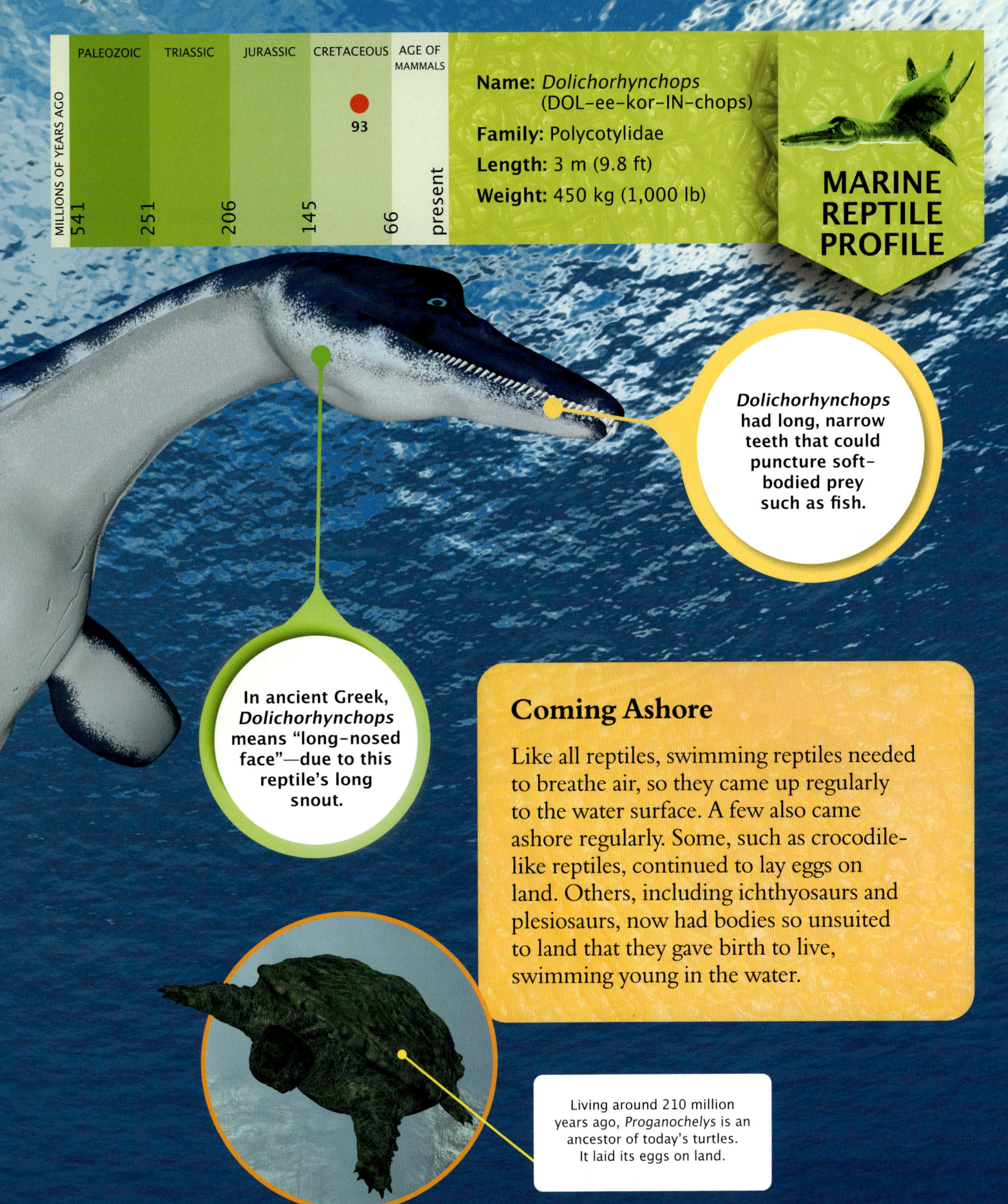

MILLIONS OF YEARS AGO	PALEOZOIC	TRIASSIC	JURASSIC	CRETACEOUS	AGE OF MAMMALS	present
	541	251	206	145	66	

93

Name: *Dolichorhynchops*
(DOL–ee–kor–IN–chops)
Family: Polycotylidae
Length: 3 m (9.8 ft)
Weight: 450 kg (1,000 lb)

MARINE REPTILE PROFILE

Dolichorhynchops had long, narrow teeth that could puncture soft-bodied prey such as fish.

In ancient Greek, *Dolichorhynchops* means "long-nosed face"—due to this reptile's long snout.

Coming Ashore

Like all reptiles, swimming reptiles needed to breathe air, so they came up regularly to the water surface. A few also came ashore regularly. Some, such as crocodile-like reptiles, continued to lay eggs on land. Others, including ichthyosaurs and plesiosaurs, now had bodies so unsuited to land that they gave birth to live, swimming young in the water.

Living around 210 million years ago, *Proganochelys* is an ancestor of today's turtles. It laid its eggs on land.

DID YOU KNOW? Today's largest swimming reptile is the saltwater crocodile, which reaches 6.3 m (21 ft) long and a weight of 1,300 kg (2,900 lb).

Psephoderma

This swimming reptile had thick rounded teeth for crushing shellfish. *Psephoderma* means "pebbly skin" in ancient Greek. Its skin was protected by small scales and larger, thicker bony plates. These plates formed a shell, called a carapace, over its body.

Its toes were webbed to help with swimming, but armed with sharp claws for protection.

Placodus was an early placodont with no bony plates.

Needing Protection

Psephoderma belonged to a group of reptiles called placodonts. Early placodonts did not have shells. As other swimming reptiles became sharper toothed, the placodonts grew more bony plates. Late placodonts looked like turtles, but the two groups are not close relatives.

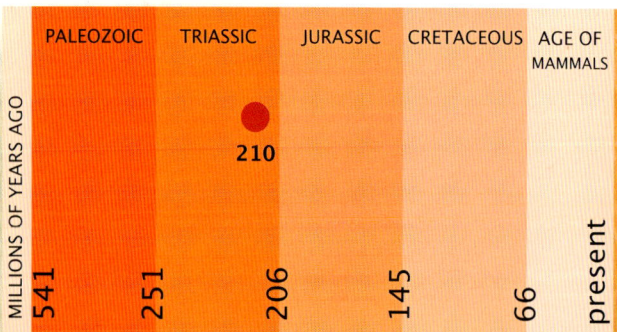

	PALEOZOIC	TRIASSIC	JURASSIC	CRETACEOUS	AGE OF MAMMALS	
MILLIONS OF YEARS AGO	541	251	210 ● 206	145	66	present

Name: *Psephoderma*
(See-foe-DERM-uh)
Family: Placochelyidae
Length: 1.8 m (6 ft)
Weight: 20 kg (44 lb)

MARINE REPTILE PROFILE

The shell was in two parts, over its rear and over its back.

Breathing Air

Like all swimming reptiles, *Psephoderma* had to go to the surface to breathe air. Weighed down by its plates, it stayed in shallow water so it could surface without getting too tired.

Like *Psephoderma*, *Henodus* was a late placodont that fed on shallow seabeds.

Using its long beak, it felt for shellfish on the seafloor.

DID YOU KNOW? Fossils of *Psephoderma* have been discovered in the rocks of the Alps, the highest mountain range lying entirely in Europe.

Plesiosaurus

Many types of reptile lived in Mesozoic oceans. The plesiosaurs were a group of long-necked swimming reptiles that first appeared in the Late Triassic, and died out at the end of the Cretaceous. They are named after *Plesiosaurus* (meaning "close lizard").

Life in the Water

Plesiosaurus lived in shallow waters, close to the coast. It is possible that it came ashore to lay its eggs, like today's turtles. It could not have moved quickly on land, because it had flippers instead of legs. Plesiosaurs evolved from nothosaurs, Triassic four-legged reptiles whose feet had adapted to swimming in the water by being webbed and paddle-like.

Kaiwhekea was one of the last plesiosaurs. A specialist squid–hunter, it grew to 7 m (23 ft) long.

Meyerasaurus lived in the Early Jurassic. It was about the same length as *Plesiosaurus*.

Short-Necked Cousins

Not all plesiosaurs had long necks. Pliosaurs, including *Pliosaurus*, *Kronosaurus* (pages 202–203) and *Meyerasaurus*, were plesiosaurs with shorter necks and bigger heads. Pliosaurs also had slightly larger back flippers than front ones (in most plesiosaurs, the front flippers were larger). All plesiosaurs shared the same feeding technique, however—snapping up fish and squid as they moved their head from side to side.

Plesiosaurus had a small head. It had small, sharp teeth for gripping slippery prey, such as squid.

The 2-m- (6.6-ft-) long shark *Hybodus* shared the seas with *Plesiosaurus*.

Plesiosaurs hunted now-extinct mollusks called ammonites.

	PALEOZOIC	TRIASSIC	JURASSIC	CRETACEOUS	AGE OF MAMMALS
MILLIONS OF YEARS AGO	541	251	206	145	66 present

185

Name: *Plesiosaurus*
(Plee-zee-oh-SAWR-us)
Family: Plesiosauridae
Length: 3.5 m (11.4 ft)
Weight: 450 kg (992 lb)

MARINE REPTILE PROFILE

DID YOU KNOW? The 19th-century fossil collector Mary Anning found the first *Plesiosaurus* in southern England in 1821. It was an almost-complete skeleton.

Temnodontosaurus

Streamlined like dolphins and usually fast-moving, ichthyosaurs were large marine reptiles that first appeared in the Middle Triassic and survived until the Late Cretaceous Period. *Temnodontosaurus* was one of the biggest ichthyosaurs, at 12 m (39 ft). Most species were around 3 m (9.8 ft) long.

Air, Land, and Sea

Ichthyosaurs had to come up for air because they could not breathe underwater—but they did not need to come ashore to lay their eggs. Like some snakes today, ichthyosaurs were viviparous. In other words, their eggs developed inside their body and then the animals gave birth to live young.

The small, sharp teeth were perfectly suited to gripping slippery fish.

Shonisaurus was massive and slow-moving. Unlike most ichthyosaurs, it did not have a dorsal (back) fin.

MILLIONS OF YEARS AGO	PALEOZOIC	TRIASSIC	JURASSIC	CRETACEOUS	AGE OF MAMMALS	present
	541	251	206 ● 182	145	66	

Name: *Temnodontosaurus* (Tem-noh-DON-tuh-SAWR-us)

Family: Temnodontosauridae

Length: 12 m (39 ft)

Weight: 4.5 tonnes (5 tons)

MARINE REPTILE PROFILE

Like most ichthyosaurs, *Temnodontosaurus* swam at high speeds. It moved its tail from side to side to propel itself through the water.

Temnodontosaurus's enormous eyes let in plenty of light, allowing the hunter to see in the ocean gloom.

Hunting Accessories

Temnodontosaurus's name means "cutting tooth lizard." Its long, narrow jaw was packed with small, sharp teeth. However, this ichthyosaur is better known for its huge eyes. In one species, *Temnodontosaurus platyodon*, these were 20 cm (8 in) across.

This is a cast of *Temnodontosaurus platyodon*'s skull.

DID YOU KNOW? The largest-known ichthyosaur was 21-m (69-ft) *Shastasaurus*, which lived approximately 235 to 205 million years ago.

Stenopterygius

This ichthyosaur had a strong, smoothly shaped body similar to a modern dolphin's. These very different animals developed the same body shape because it is perfect for fast swimming. *Stenopterygius* swam by wiggling its tail and paddling its flippers.

Dark and Light

Tests on fossilized *Stenopterygius* skin show its underside was paler than its back. This helped with camouflage. From below, the reptile looked pale against the sunlight shining down through the water. From above, it looked dark against the lightless depths.

This reptile's camouflage helped with hunting prey and hiding from predators.

Large eyes helped *Stenopterygius* see in dark, deep water.

	PALEOZOIC	TRIASSIC	JURASSIC	CRETACEOUS	AGE OF MAMMALS	
MILLIONS OF YEARS AGO	541	251	206 ● 183	145	66	present

Name: *Stenopterygius* (Sten-OP-tuh-RIDGE-ee-us)

Family: Stenopterygiidae

Length: 3 m (9.8 ft)

Weight: 160 kg (350 lb)

MARINE REPTILE PROFILE

DID YOU KNOW? Ichthyosaur babies were born tail-first, like modern whales, so they did not fill their lungs with water before they had wriggled free from their mother.

Mothers gave birth to up to 11 live babies.

The flat, half–moon–shaped tail powered this reptile through the water.

Fingers to Flippers

Over millions of years, the limbs of land-living reptiles evolved into the fins of swimming reptiles. The "fingers" in *Stenopterygius*'s front flippers had developed many extra tiny bones, making the flippers broad and strong.

The tail was made mostly of soft tissues, such as muscle, rather than bone.

Liopleurodon

Liopleurodon was among the largest flesh-eating vertebrates ever to have lived. It belonged to a group of short-necked plesiosaurs known as pliosaurs. It was an apex predator that prowled the Jurassic seas for fish and other marine life, such as ichthyosaurs and squid.

Powered by its four broad flippers, *Liopleurodon* could reach speeds of 10 km/h (6 mph), about as fast as the best human swimmers.

Top Hunter

Liopleurodon's nostrils were forward-facing, suggesting that their key use was smelling, not breathing, at the water surface. The predator probably used its sense of smell to find its next meal, perhaps picking up on the presence of flesh or blood from long distances away. Its four powerful paddles would have given it a good chance of winning a chase, and its quick acceleration would have been ideal for ambushing prey.

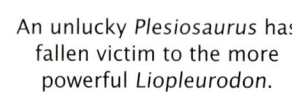

An unlucky *Plesiosaurus* has fallen victim to the more powerful *Liopleurodon*.

Strong jaw bones and muscles gave a bite powerful enough to crush scales, flesh, and bones.

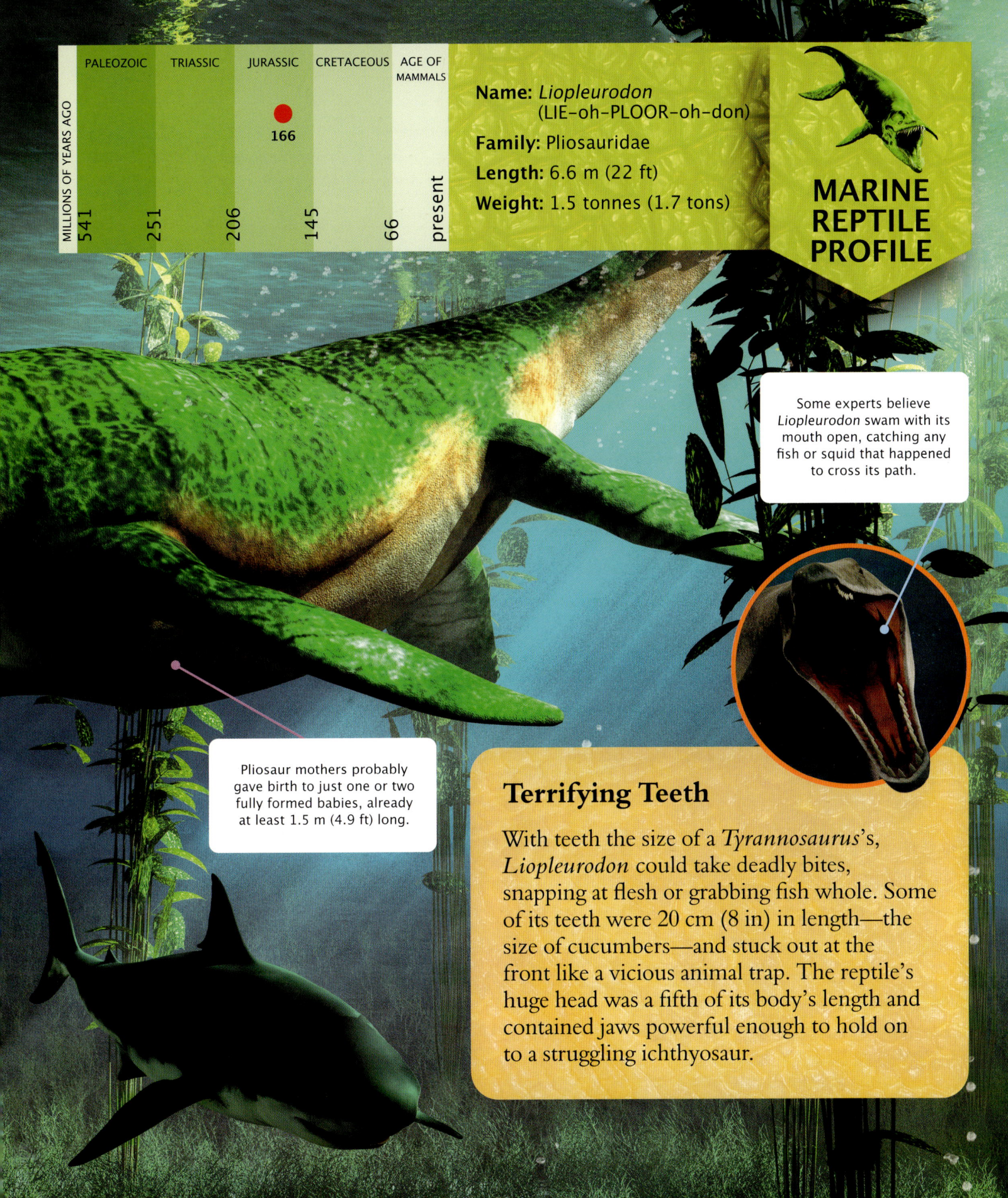

MILLIONS OF YEARS AGO	PALEOZOIC	TRIASSIC	JURASSIC	CRETACEOUS	AGE OF MAMMALS
	541	251	206	145	66	present

166

Name: *Liopleurodon*
(LIE–oh–PLOOR–oh–don)
Family: Pliosauridae
Length: 6.6 m (22 ft)
Weight: 1.5 tonnes (1.7 tons)

MARINE REPTILE PROFILE

Some experts believe *Liopleurodon* swam with its mouth open, catching any fish or squid that happened to cross its path.

Pliosaur mothers probably gave birth to just one or two fully formed babies, already at least 1.5 m (4.9 ft) long.

Terrifying Teeth

With teeth the size of a *Tyrannosaurus*'s, *Liopleurodon* could take deadly bites, snapping at flesh or grabbing fish whole. Some of its teeth were 20 cm (8 in) in length—the size of cucumbers—and stuck out at the front like a vicious animal trap. The reptile's huge head was a fifth of its body's length and contained jaws powerful enough to hold on to a struggling ichthyosaur.

DID YOU KNOW? Long before the extinctions of 66 million years ago, the pliosaurs had been driven to extinction by even larger marine predators, such as mosasaurs.

Sarcosuchus

Sarcosuchus (meaning "flesh crocodile" in ancient Greek) was a crocodylomorph, an ancient relative of today's crocodiles and alligators. Yet, at over 9 m (31 ft) long, it was much bigger than today's largest crocodile, the saltwater crocodile, which reaches over 6 m (20 ft).

River Hunter

Sarcosuchus lived in and around rivers. Like today's crocodiles, it snapped up animals in the water, as well as crawled fast onto land to grab large animals looking for a drink.

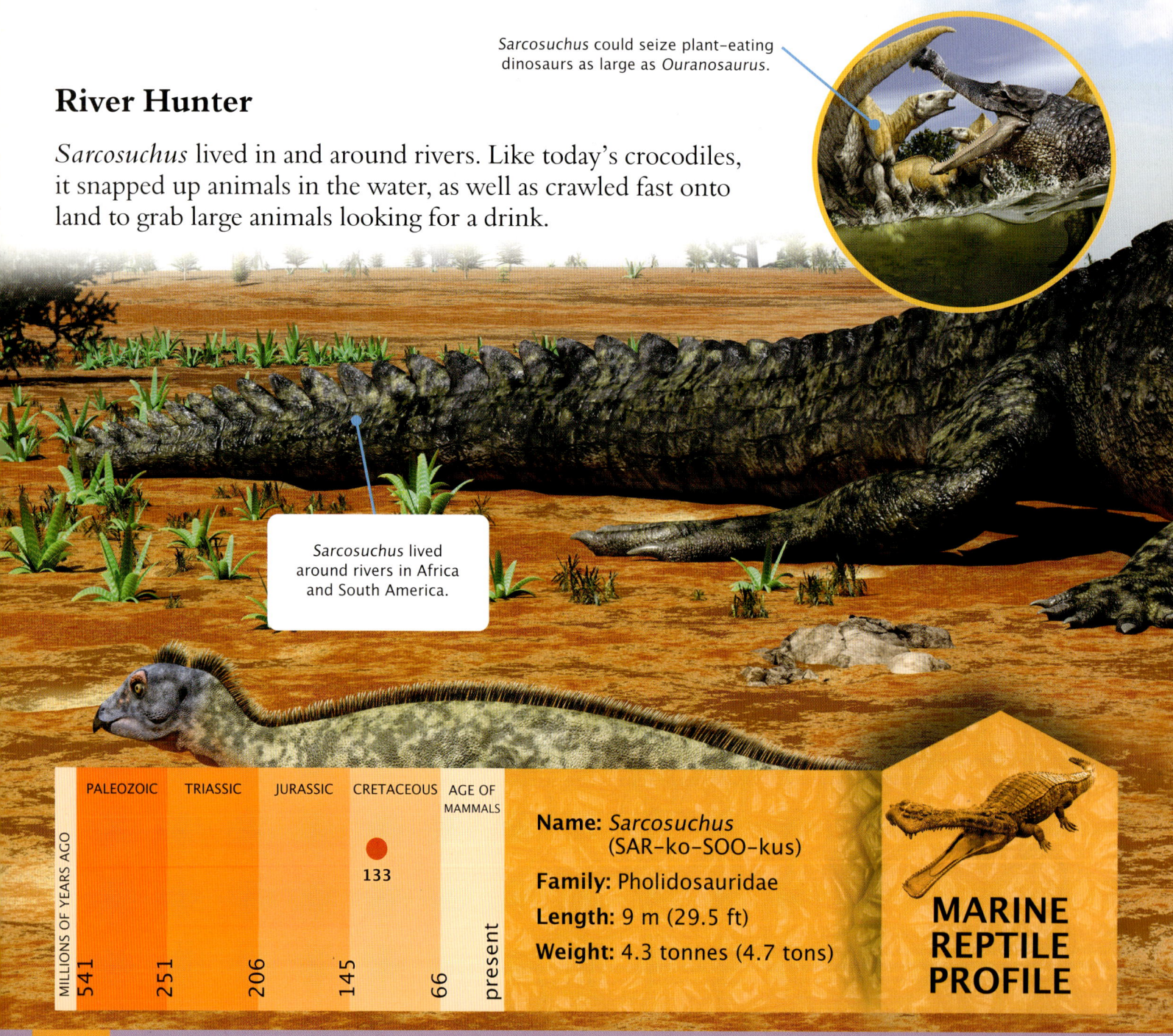

Sarcosuchus could seize plant-eating dinosaurs as large as *Ouranosaurus*.

Sarcosuchus lived around rivers in Africa and South America.

MILLIONS OF YEARS AGO	PALEOZOIC	TRIASSIC	JURASSIC	CRETACEOUS	AGE OF MAMMALS
	541	251	206	145 ● 133	66 present

Name: *Sarcosuchus* (SAR-ko-SOO-kus)
Family: Pholidosauridae
Length: 9 m (29.5 ft)
Weight: 4.3 tonnes (4.7 tons)

MARINE REPTILE PROFILE

DID YOU KNOW? Most modern crocodiles do not live to be older than 30, but studies on the bones of one *Sarcosuchus* revealed it was aged 40—and had not finished growing.

Like a Crocodile

Crocodile-like reptiles evolved at around the same time as dinosaurs, about 230 million years ago, in the Triassic Period. At first, they lived on land and were slim. Later, many grew bigger and, like today's crocodiles, had bony plates for protection. During the Jurassic Period, some crocodilomorphs became aquatic or semiaquatic.

Around 220 million years ago, *Hesperosuchus* was an early little crocodile–like reptile.

There were 132 sharp teeth in its long, strong jaws.

Sarcosuchus's skin was covered in hard, bony plates.

Kronosaurus

One of the largest pliosaurs, 10-m- (33-ft-) long *Kronosaurus* lived in the Early Cretaceous. It powered through the water after turtles and other plesiosaurs, snapping them up in its huge jaws.

Built for Speed

Pliosaurs had muscular bodies, short necks, and long heads. The short tail kept them streamlined, and they swam by moving all four flippers at once. They were fast-moving and usually outswam their prey. Once they had caught their victim, they shook it in their jaws and swallowed it whole.

Pliosaurs are named after the Late Jurassic marine reptile *Pliosaurus*.

Kronosaurus's teeth were not very sharp, but they were good at gripping and crushing prey.

DID YOU KNOW? *Kronosaurus* was named after Cronos, the leader of the Titans in Greek mythology. Cronos's son, Zeus, became king of the gods.

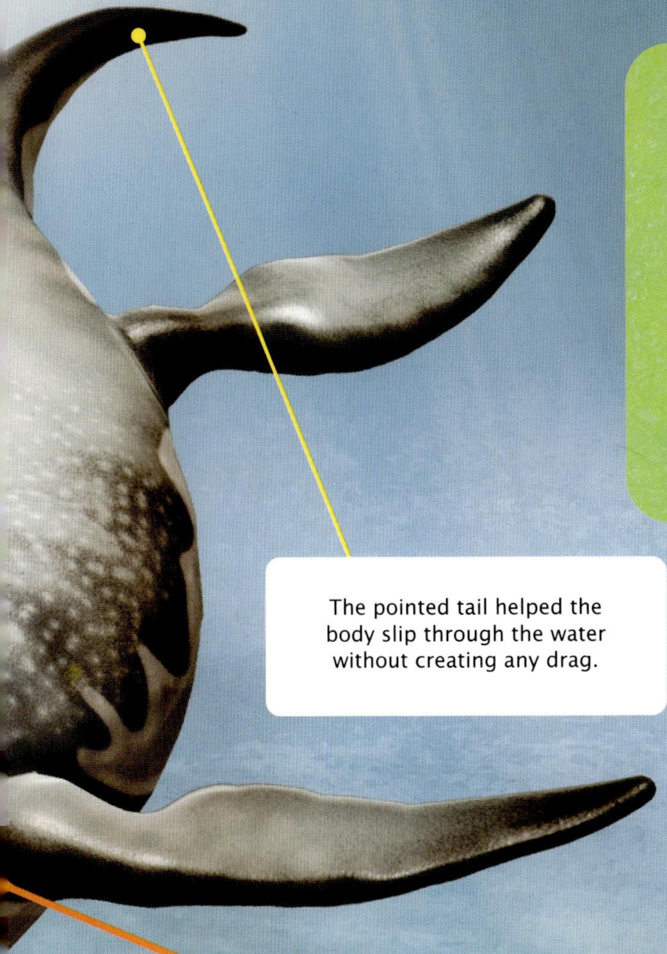

History of Discovery

The first *Kronosaurus* fossils—teeth dug up in Australia in 1899—were not identified as *Kronosaurus* until the 1920s. For decades the pliosaur was known only in Australia. In 1994, paleontologists announced that a fossil had been found in Colombia, South America. *Kronosaurus* probably lived in shallow seas worldwide.

The pointed tail helped the body slip through the water without creating any drag.

Pliosaurs "flew" through the water using their four winglike flippers.

Kronosaurus's longest teeth were around 30 cm (11.8 in) long. Even the shortest were more than 7 cm (2.8 in).

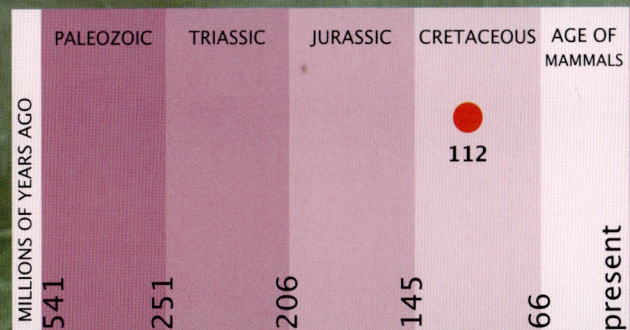

	PALEOZOIC	TRIASSIC	JURASSIC	CRETACEOUS	AGE OF MAMMALS
MILLIONS OF YEARS AGO	541	251	206	145	66 present

112

Name: *Kronosaurus*
(KROH–nuh–SAWR–us)
Family: Pliosauridae
Length: 10 m (33 ft)
Weight: 8.2 tonnes (9 tons)

MARINE REPTILE PROFILE

Albertonectes

The elasmosaurs were plesiosaurs that had incredibly long necks. *Albertonectes* ("Alberta swimmer") had the longest neck of any elasmosaur, and the greatest overall body length of any plesiosaur.

Sneaky Skills

Albertonectes was not a fast swimmer, but it had a clever hunting technique. It approached shoals of fish from below, then let its head spring up on its long neck like a jack-in-the-box. This took the fish completely by surprise, so *Albertonectes* could gulp plenty down before they swam away.

Long-Necked Family

Elasmosaurs are named after the Late Cretaceous plesiosaur *Elasmosaurus*, but may have been around from the Late Triassic. Early elasmosaurs were just 3 m (9.8 ft) long. Elasmosaur means "thin-plated lizard" and refers to the thin plates in the reptiles' pelvic girdles.

Albertonectes's neck was about 7 m (23 ft) long—half of its total body length.

Elasmosaurus had stones called gastroliths (page 72) in its stomach to help it digest its food.

Albertonectes had a flat skull and long, pointed teeth.

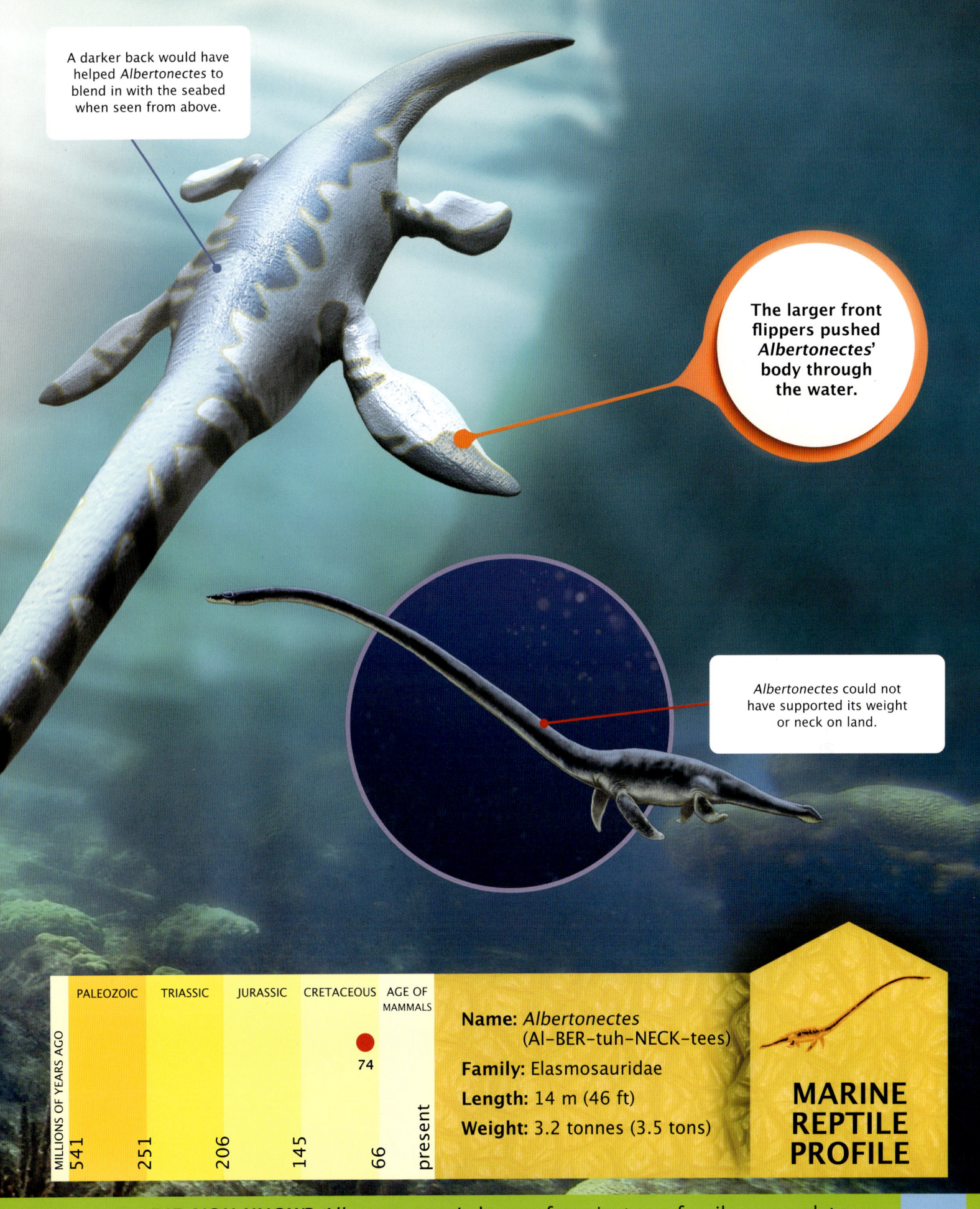

A darker back would have helped *Albertonectes* to blend in with the seabed when seen from above.

The larger front flippers pushed *Albertonectes*' body through the water.

Albertonectes could not have supported its weight or neck on land.

PALEOZOIC	TRIASSIC	JURASSIC	CRETACEOUS	AGE OF MAMMALS

MILLIONS OF YEARS AGO

74

541

251

206

145

66

present

Name: *Albertonectes*
(Al–BER–tuh–NECK–tees)
Family: Elasmosauridae
Length: 14 m (46 ft)
Weight: 3.2 tonnes (3.5 tons)

MARINE REPTILE PROFILE

DID YOU KNOW? *Albertonectes* is known from just one fossil—a complete skeleton that was found by miners. The discovery was announced in 2012.

Mosasaurus

The mosasaurs were the apex marine predators in the Late Cretaceous. They are named after *Mosasaurus*, an 18-m- (59-ft-) long hunter that went after fish, turtles, plesiosaurs, ichthyosaurs … and even smaller mosasaurs.

All in the Family

The smallest mosasaurs were less than 1 m (3.3 ft) long. Like *Mosasaurus*, they had lizard-shaped bodies and long, broad tails that helped to propel them through the water. Another family characteristic was giving birth to live young, rather than coming ashore to lay eggs.

The scales on the skin were tiny, making *Mosasaurus* smooth and streamlined.

Early Discoveries

The first known mosasaur remains were fragments of *Mosasaurus* skull found in the 1760s near Maastricht, in the Netherlands. It was mistaken for a toothed whale, and was not identified as a reptile until 1799. The animal was finally named in 1822: *Mosasaurus* means "Mass River lizard," referring to the river that flows through the city of Maastricht.

The first *Mosasaurus* fossil was found in a chalk quarry.

MILLIONS OF YEARS AGO	PALEOZOIC	TRIASSIC	JURASSIC	CRETACEOUS	AGE OF MAMMALS
	541	251	206	145	66 — present

68

Name: *Mosasaurus* (MOH–suh–SAWR–us)
Family: Mosasauridae
Length: 18 m (59 ft)
Weight: 5 tonnes (5.5 tons)

MARINE REPTILE PROFILE

The skull was 1.7 m (5.6 ft) long—about the length of a family car.

Mosasaurus had a double-hinged jaw, like a snake's, that could open wide to swallow prey whole.

Five *Mosasaurus* species have been identified. This skull belongs to *Mosasaurus lemonnieri*, discovered in 1889.

Mosasaurus's paddle-like limbs each had five digits.

DID YOU KNOW? Paleontologists cannot agree if *Mosasaurus* was more closely related to modern snakes or to monitor lizards.

Archelon

Archelon was a turtle with a shell to protect its body. The biggest fossil of *Archelon* measures 4 m (13 ft) from flipper tip to flipper tip. When alive, this turtle weighed as much as a family car. Like today's sea turtles, *Archelon* crawled onto beaches to lay its eggs.

Leathery Shell

Archelon's shell was made of curving rib bones. Unlike the shells of most of today's turtles, the ribs were not covered by bony plates. Like the shell of today's leatherback turtle, the ribs were covered in tough, leathery skin.

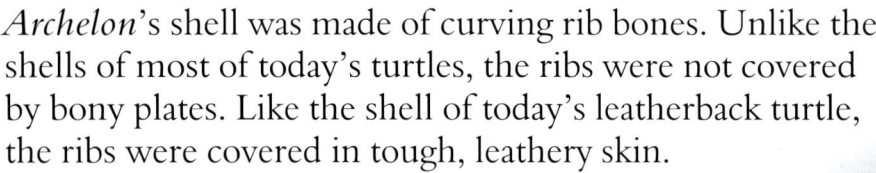

Archelon was the biggest turtle that ever lived.

Archelon's leathery shell was lighter than a bony shell.

DID YOU KNOW? Discovered in South Dakota, USA, in 1895, *Archelon* was named for the ancient Greek words for "early turtle."

MILLIONS OF YEARS AGO	PALEOZOIC	TRIASSIC	JURASSIC	CRETACEOUS	AGE OF MAMMALS	present
	541	251	206	145	66	present

80

Name: *Archelon* (ARK–ee–lon)
Family: Protostegidae
Length: 4.6 m (15 ft)
Weight: 3 tonnes (3.3 tons)

MARINE REPTILE PROFILE

Archelon lived in North America's Western Interior Seaway—and may have been driven to extinction when the sea shrank.

The hard, hooked beak was used for crushing shellfish.

Long Life

Like today's turtles, *Archelon* had a long life, reaching the age of 100 or more. Young turtles probably did not reach the safety of their full size until they were 20 or 30 years old.

Archelon had 10 "fingers" and 10 "toes," forming long flippers.

Chapter 7

Flying Reptiles

The first reptiles jumped, glided, and finally flapped into the sky around 228 million years ago, about 80 million years before bird-like dinosaurs started to fly. These flying reptiles, called pterosaurs (meaning "wing lizards" in ancient Greek), were cousins of the dinosaurs.

Adapting to the Air

Pterosaurs were the earliest backboned animals, called vertebrates, to fly. To adapt to life in the air, they developed hollow, air-filled bones to make them lightweight. Their arms and hands developed into wings. Although their skin still had patches of scales, they were largely covered in hair-like threads, softer than feathers, called pycnofibers.

Anhanguera was kept warm by its fluffy pycnofibers.

Anhanguera grasped slippery fish with its long, jutting, cone-shaped teeth.

Eudimorphodon was one of the earliest known pterosaurs. Unlike later pterosaurs, it had a very long tail.

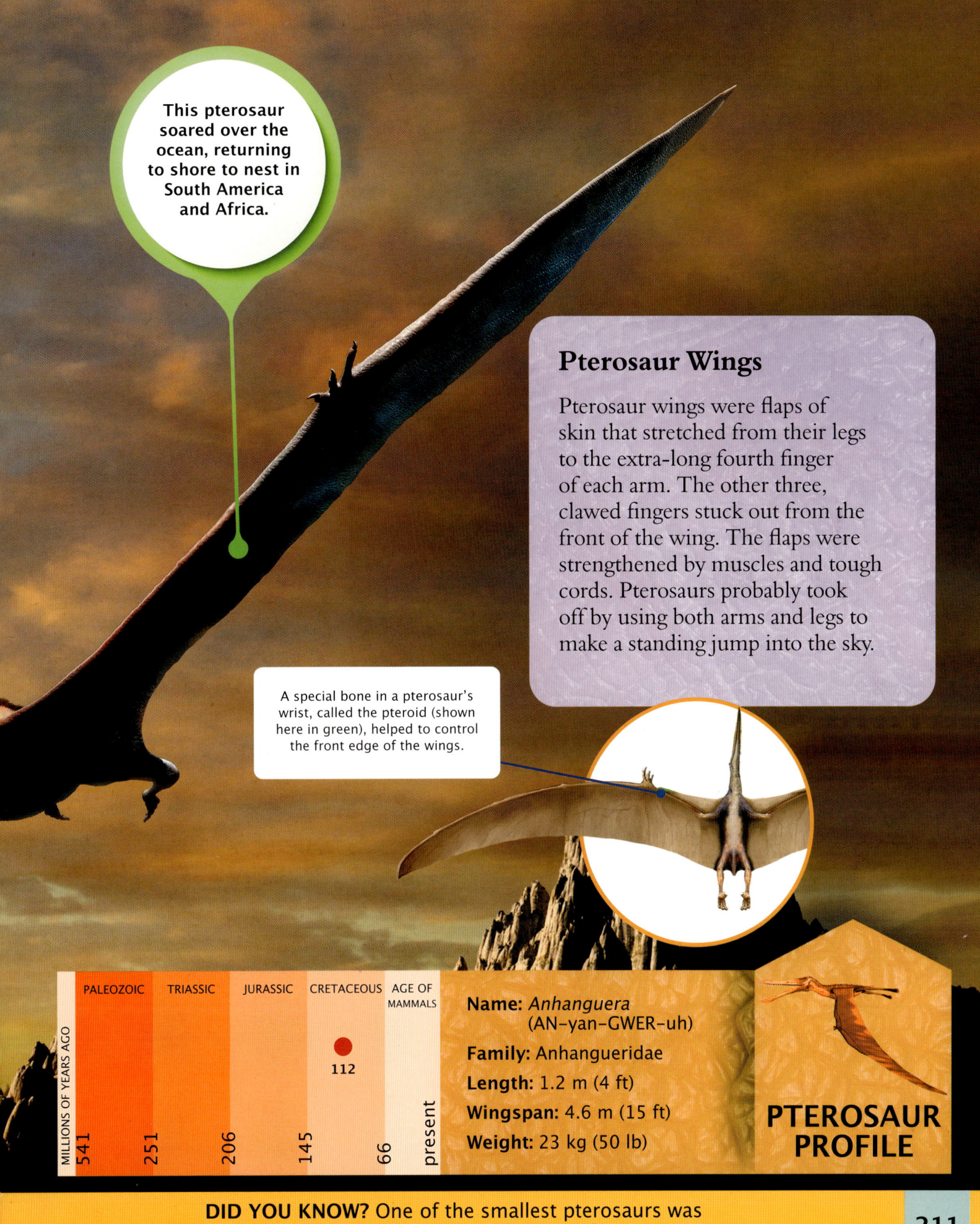

This pterosaur soared over the ocean, returning to shore to nest in South America and Africa.

Pterosaur Wings

Pterosaur wings were flaps of skin that stretched from their legs to the extra-long fourth finger of each arm. The other three, clawed fingers stuck out from the front of the wing. The flaps were strengthened by muscles and tough cords. Pterosaurs probably took off by using both arms and legs to make a standing jump into the sky.

A special bone in a pterosaur's wrist, called the pteroid (shown here in green), helped to control the front edge of the wings.

PALEOZOIC	TRIASSIC	JURASSIC	CRETACEOUS	AGE OF MAMMALS

112

MILLIONS OF YEARS AGO

541 251 206 145 66 present

Name: *Anhanguera* (AN–yan–GWER–uh)
Family: Anhangueridae
Length: 1.2 m (4 ft)
Wingspan: 4.6 m (15 ft)
Weight: 23 kg (50 lb)

PTEROSAUR PROFILE

DID YOU KNOW? One of the smallest pterosaurs was *Nemicolopterus*, which had a wingspan of around 25 cm (10 in).

Dimorphodon

Dimorphodon was an average-sized pterosaur that lived during the Early Jurassic Period. Its head looked like that of a puffin, a modern fish-eating seabird—a fact that gives us clues about this reptile's diet.

Coastal Lifestyle

Dimorphodon could fly, but not for long distances. It probably lived along coasts, climbing cliffs or moving about on all fours. It caught its main food—insects—by snapping its jaws shut very fast. It also ate fish, small animals, and carrion.

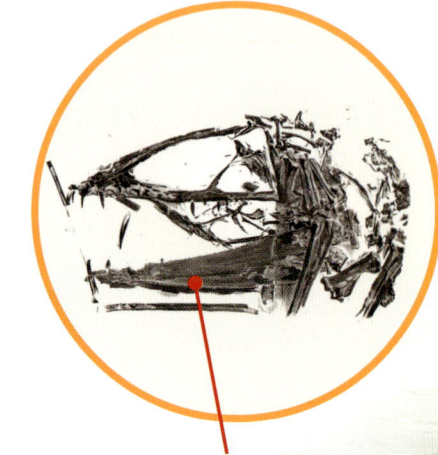

This drawing of *Dimorphodon*'s skull appeared in Richard Owen's book *A History of British Fossil Reptiles* (1849–84).

Mary's Pterosaur

The first fossil of *Dimorphodon* was found in England's Dorset by fossil collector Mary Anning in 1828. Mary was a renowned fossil collector and paleontologist who, as a woman, struggled to earn money—and be credited—for her discoveries about prehistoric life.

Dimorphodon's wingspan was about the same as a buzzard's.

The deep jaws contained up to 40 small, sharp teeth and two larger, stabbing, front teeth.

MILLIONS OF YEARS AGO	PALEOZOIC	TRIASSIC	JURASSIC	CRETACEOUS	AGE OF MAMMALS	
	541	251	206 ● 193	145	66	present

Name: *Dimorphodon*
(Dye–MAW–fuh–don)
Family: Dimorphodontidae
Length: 1 m (3.3 ft)
Wingspan: 1.4 m (4.6 ft)
Weight: 2.3 kg (5 lb)

PTEROSAUR PROFILE

A diamond–shaped flap at the end of *Dimorphodon*'s tail helped it to steer when flying.

Dimorphodon may have cared for its young as shown here, or it may have left them to fend for themselves.

DID YOU KNOW? *Dimorphodon* means "two–form tooth" in ancient Greek, as it had two distinct shapes of teeth in its robust jaws.

Rhamphorhynchus

This pterosaur had a long, stiff tail that ended in a vane—a flap of skin and body tissue that helped with steering and steadying the reptile in flight. *Rhamphorhynchus* may have been nocturnal to avoid competition with other local pterosaurs such as *Pterodactylus*.

Two Groups

Pterosaurs are divided into two main groups, called suborders: the rhamphorhynchoids and the later pterodactyloids, which had shorter tails and wider wings. The rhamphorhynchoids are named after *Rhamphorhynchus* (meaning "beak snout" in ancient Greek), which was first found and studied in Germany in 1825. The pterodactyloids include *Pterodactylus*, *Tropeognathus*, *Anhanguera*, *Tupandactylus*, *Pteranodon*, and *Quetzalcoatlus*.

Its large eyes helped *Rhamphorhynchus* to see underwater or to hunt at night.

The imprint of *Rhamphorhynchus*'s skin can be seen in this fossil: its wings (on the left) and its tail vane (on the far right).

This pterosaur's needle-like teeth interlocked when its mouth was closed, forming a trap that small fish could not escape.

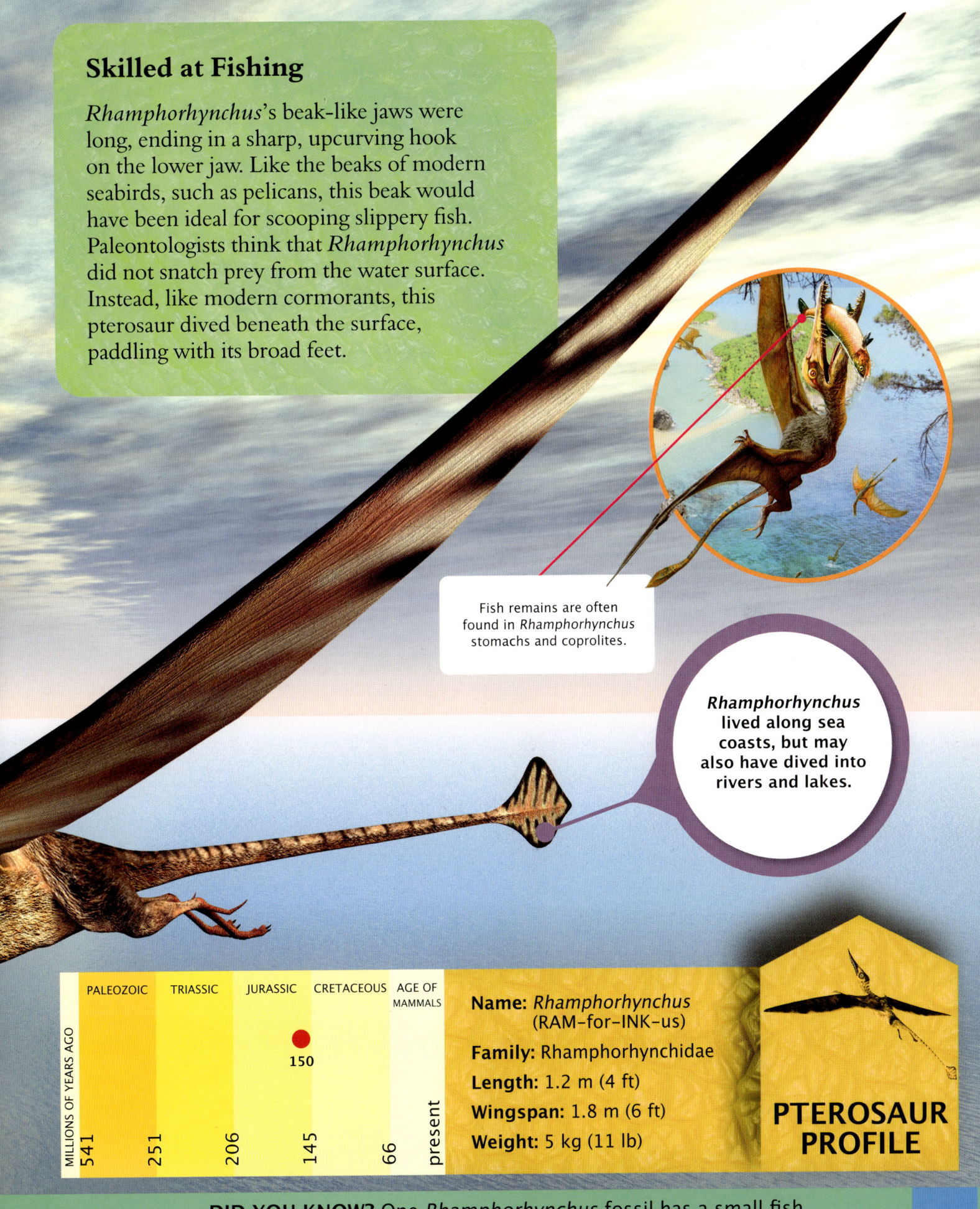

Skilled at Fishing

Rhamphorhynchus's beak-like jaws were long, ending in a sharp, upcurving hook on the lower jaw. Like the beaks of modern seabirds, such as pelicans, this beak would have been ideal for scooping slippery fish. Paleontologists think that *Rhamphorhynchus* did not snatch prey from the water surface. Instead, like modern cormorants, this pterosaur dived beneath the surface, paddling with its broad feet.

Fish remains are often found in *Rhamphorhynchus* stomachs and coprolites.

Rhamphorhynchus lived along sea coasts, but may also have dived into rivers and lakes.

MILLIONS OF YEARS AGO	PALEOZOIC	TRIASSIC	JURASSIC	CRETACEOUS	AGE OF MAMMALS
	541	251	206	145	66	present

150

Name: *Rhamphorhynchus* (RAM-for-INK-us)

Family: Rhamphorhynchidae

Length: 1.2 m (4 ft)

Wingspan: 1.8 m (6 ft)

Weight: 5 kg (11 lb)

PTEROSAUR PROFILE

DID YOU KNOW? One *Rhamphorhynchus* fossil has a small fish, *Leptolepides*, in its throat, suggesting it was killed while eating.

Pterodactylus

Non-experts often use "pterodactyl" to mean any pterosaur, probably because *Pterodactylus* was the first-known pterosaur. It was discovered in Bavaria, Germany, in limestone formed in the Late Jurassic. More than 100 specimens have been found, many of them juveniles.

Breeding Season

Paleontologists have identified *Pterodactylus* that are one, two, and three years old. Their finds show that the reptile had a set breeding season, timed so eggs hatched when the conditions were best for raising young. *Pterodactylus* probably nested in colonies, like many seabirds today.

Pterodactylus was lightly built, with long wings. It would have been a powerful flier.

Pterodactylus had a crest of soft tissue on the top of its head for display. This crest kept growing throughout the reptile's life.

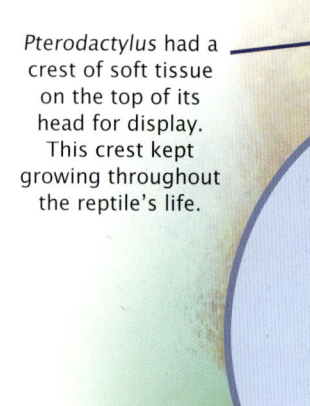

PALEOZOIC	TRIASSIC	JURASSIC	CRETACEOUS	AGE OF MAMMALS	

MILLIONS OF YEARS AGO

150

541 · 251 · 206 · 145 · 66 · present

Name: *Pterodactylus* (Ter–oh–DAK–til–us)

Family: Pterodactylidae

Length: 80 cm (31.5 in)

Wingspan: 1 m (3.3 ft)

Weight: 4.6 kg (10 lb)

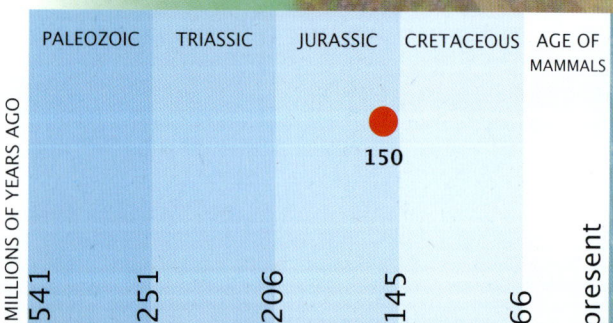

PTEROSAUR PROFILE

DID YOU KNOW? In the early 19th century, some people thought that *Pterodactylus* was a marine amphibian and that its wings were really flippers.

Early Fossil Finds

Pterodactylus was discovered in 1784, but was it not recognized as a flying reptile until 1812. Its name means "winged finger." As in all pterosaurs, *Pterodactylus*'s wing was made up of stretched skin, attached to its extra-long fourth finger.

When *Pterodactylus* dived for fish, the hair-like pycnofibers around its neck stopped it getting cold and wet.

A young *Pterodactylus* was preserved in limestone.

The jaw contained up to 90 small, sharp teeth.

The wing was made up of skin and muscle.

Tropeognathus

With a wingspan as long as a school bus, *Tropeognathus* was one of the largest known pterosaurs. It lived off the coast of what is now South America during the Early Cretaceous.

Spoon-Shaped Snout

Tropeognathus means "keel jaw." The name comes from the crests on the pterosaur's snout and lower jaw, which are shaped like keels (the steering fins on the bottom of a boat). The result is a curvy mouth that slides easily into the water to grab fish.

The rounded snout crests were probably used for display, to show off to possible mates or to rivals.

The stretchy skin of the wing was supported by the pterosaur's long wrist bone and the long bones of the fourth finger.

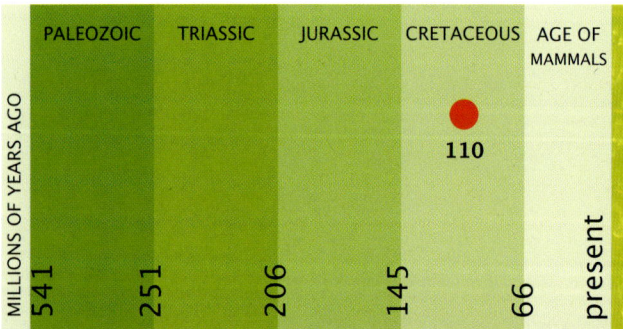

	PALEOZOIC	TRIASSIC	JURASSIC	CRETACEOUS	AGE OF MAMMALS
MILLIONS OF YEARS AGO	541	251	206	145 ● 110	66 present

Name: *Tropeognathus* (TRO-pe-oh-NA-thus)

Family: Anhangueridae

Length: 6 m (20 ft)

Wingspan: 8.2 m (27 ft)

Weight: 13 kg (27 lb)

PTEROSAUR PROFILE

Shared Skies

Maaradactylus was another large South American pterosaur, though not quite as giant as *Tropeognathus*. Its wingspan was about 6 m (19.7 ft). It lived at around the same time and had a similar lifestyle to *Tropeognathus*. It cruised close to shores, swooping down to snatch fish from the sea.

Maaradactylus had a crested snout, too.

Tropeognathus had sharp, gappy teeth for spearing fish.

The snout was shaped like the keel of a boat.

DID YOU KNOW? The crest on *Tropeognathus*'s snout was larger in males than in females, suggesting males may have used a large crest to attract a mate.

Tupandactylus

This pterosaur had a large crest on its head made of bone, horn, and skin. Its hard, sharp-edged beak was toothless. Fossils of *Tupandactylus* have been found in Brazil. It was named after the thunder god of the Tupi people, who live in Brazil's Amazon rain forest.

Crest Signals

Like today's crested birds, *Tupandactylus* probably used movements of its eye-catching crest to signal to other members of its flock. Signals could have been warnings of danger, threats to rivals, or greetings to mates.

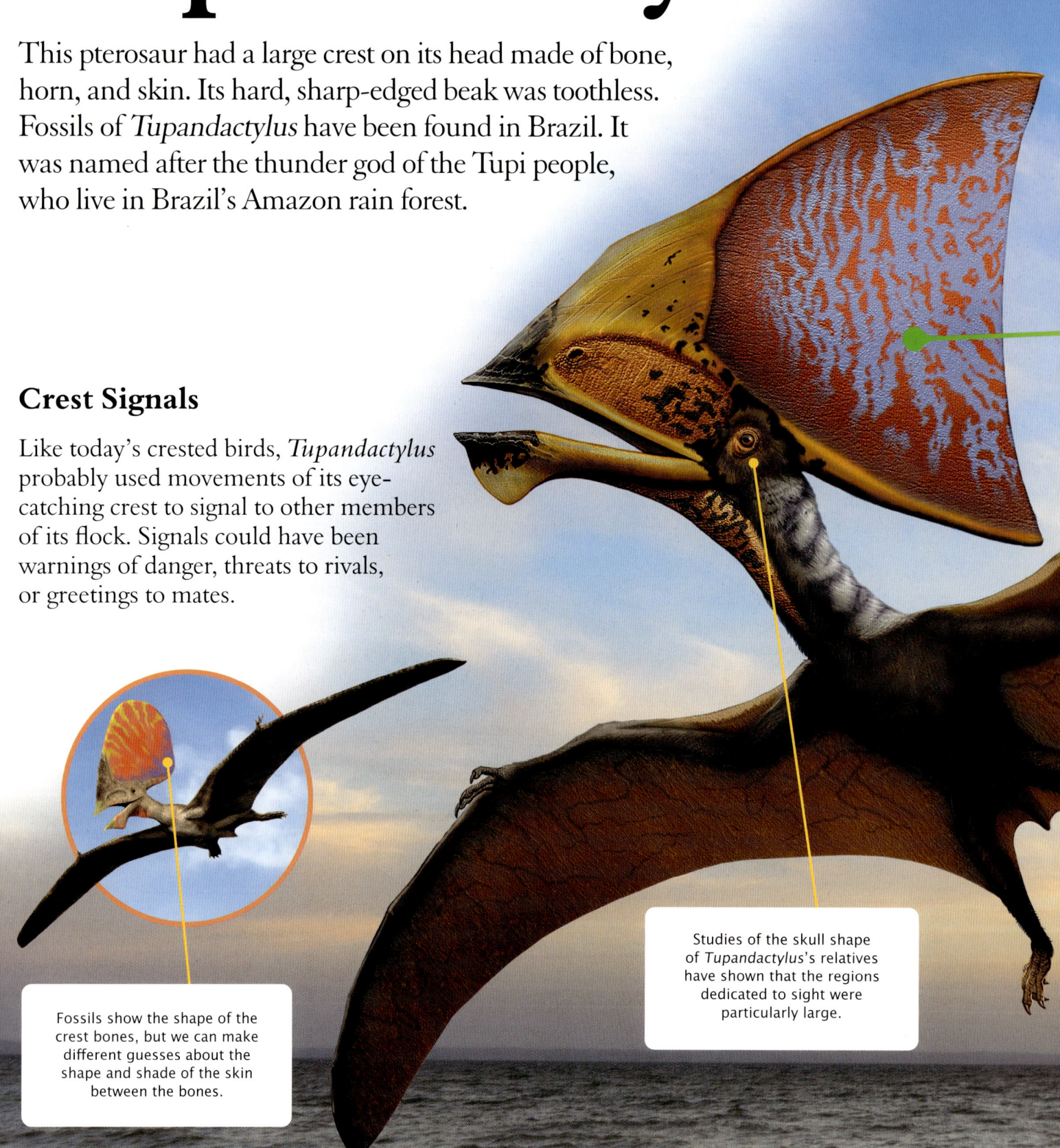

Fossils show the shape of the crest bones, but we can make different guesses about the shape and shade of the skin between the bones.

Studies of the skull shape of *Tupandactylus*'s relatives have shown that the regions dedicated to sight were particularly large.

DID YOU KNOW? Paleontologists and engineers have built a flying and walking drone based on the body shape of *Tupandactylus*, known as a pterodrone.

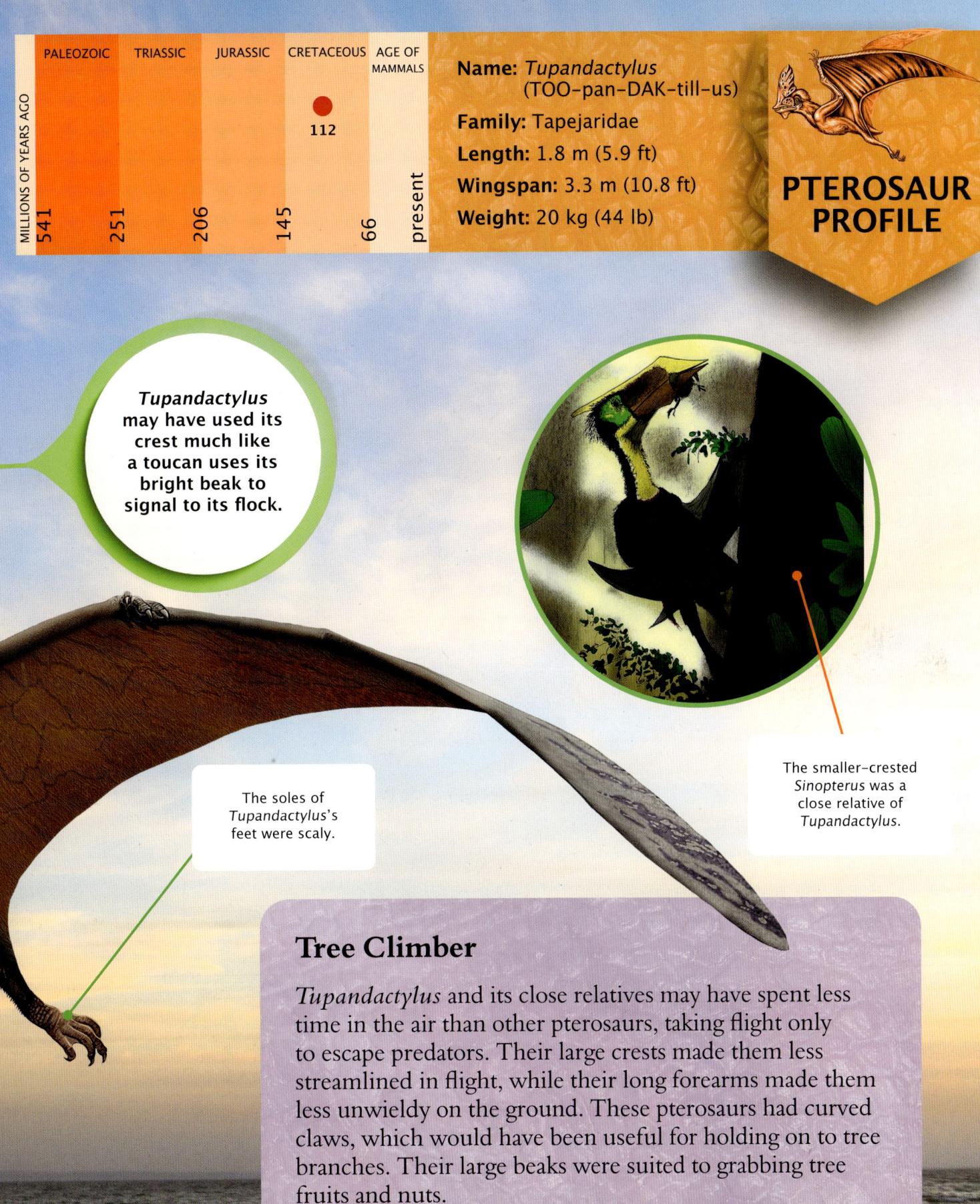

				AGE OF MAMMALS	
PALEOZOIC	TRIASSIC	JURASSIC	CRETACEOUS		

MILLIONS OF YEARS AGO

541 251 206 145 66 present

112

Name: *Tupandactylus* (TOO-pan-DAK-till-us)
Family: Tapejaridae
Length: 1.8 m (5.9 ft)
Wingspan: 3.3 m (10.8 ft)
Weight: 20 kg (44 lb)

PTEROSAUR PROFILE

Tupandactylus may have used its crest much like a toucan uses its bright beak to signal to its flock.

The soles of *Tupandactylus*'s feet were scaly.

The smaller-crested *Sinopterus* was a close relative of *Tupandactylus*.

Tree Climber

Tupandactylus and its close relatives may have spent less time in the air than other pterosaurs, taking flight only to escape predators. Their large crests made them less streamlined in flight, while their long forearms made them less unwieldy on the ground. These pterosaurs had curved claws, which would have been useful for holding on to tree branches. Their large beaks were suited to grabbing tree fruits and nuts.

Pteranodon

With its long, sharp beak and backward-pointing crest, the large pterosaur *Pteranodon* was the perfect shape for diving into the sea. It lived across what is now North America about 83 million years ago. It may also have lived in the area of Sweden, northern Europe.

Feeding Technique

Earlier pterosaurs such as *Pterodactylus* (pages 216–217) had teeth in their jaws, but *Pteranodon* had a toothless beak (its name means "wing without tooth"). A powerful flier, *Pteranodon* could have fed by diving headfirst into the water like a gannet, by dipping for food as it flew low over the sea, or by swimming and snatching fish near the surface.

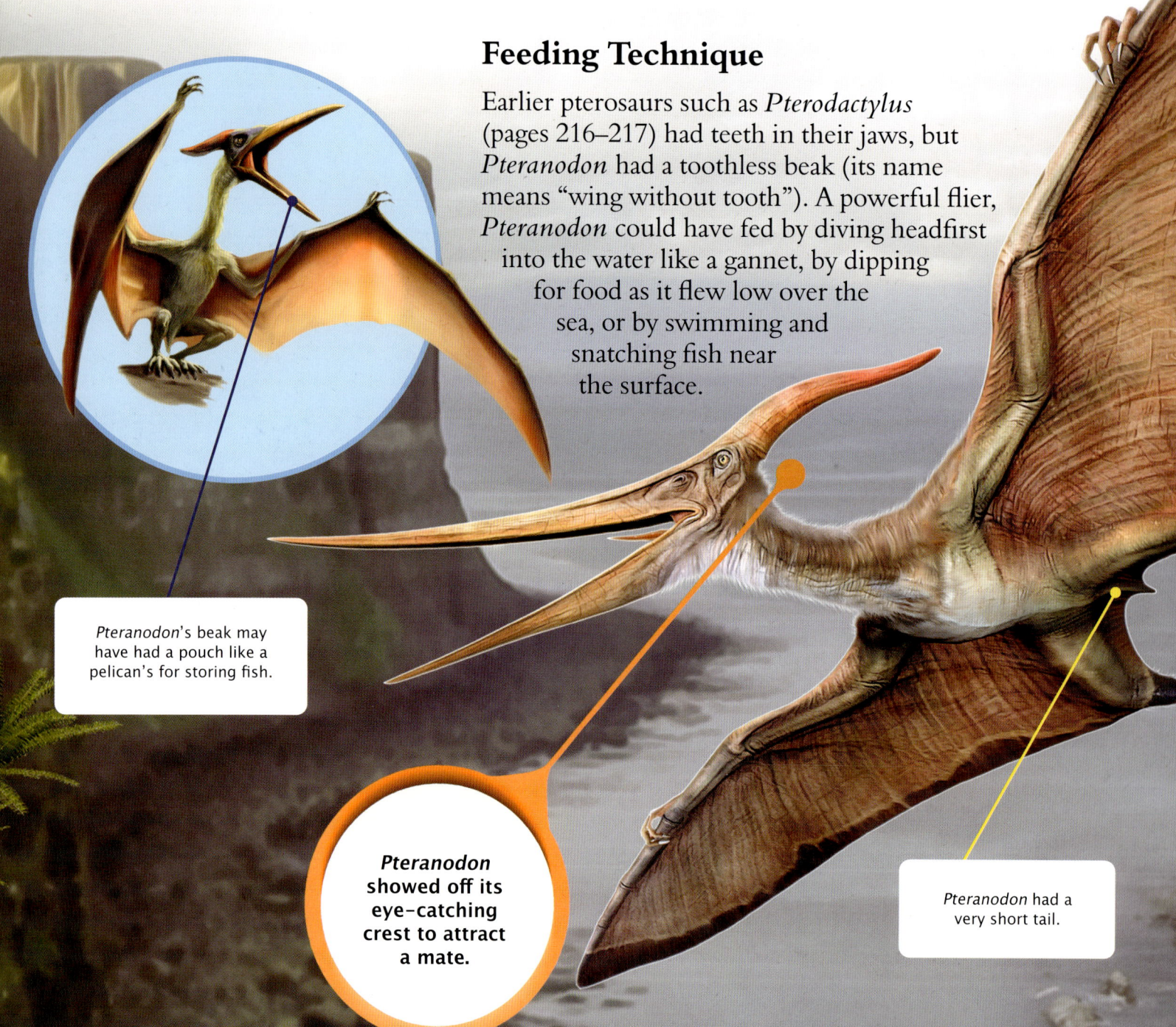

Pteranodon's beak may have had a pouch like a pelican's for storing fish.

Pteranodon showed off its eye-catching crest to attract a mate.

Pteranodon had a very short tail.

Unique Pterosaur

Pteranodon was the first pterosaur discovered outside Europe. Its wing bones were found in Kansas, USA, in 1870. Over the years, many different species were identified, but today, most paleontologists agree that there was just one species: *Pteranodon longiceps* (*longiceps* means "long-headed" and refers to the bony crest).

Pteranodon glided when it could, to save energy, but it also flapped its wings when it needed to put on a burst of speed.

Pteranodon walked quadrupedally (on all fours), rather than bipedally (upright on its back legs).

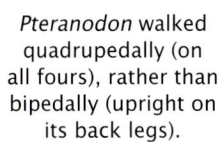

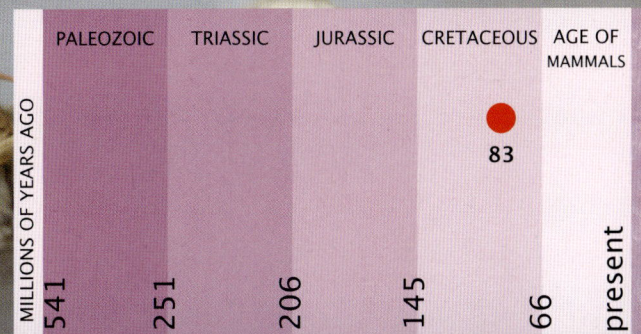

	PALEOZOIC	TRIASSIC	JURASSIC	CRETACEOUS	AGE OF MAMMALS	
MILLIONS OF YEARS AGO	541	251	206	145	66	present

83

Name: *Pteranodon* (Ter-AN-oh-don)

Family: Pteranodontidae

Length: 1.8 m (6 ft)

Wingspan: 6 m (20 ft)

Weight: 25 kg (55 lb)

PTEROSAUR PROFILE

DID YOU KNOW? More fossils have been found of *Pteranodon* than of any other pterosaur—at least 1,200 at the last count.

Quetzalcoatlus

Quetzalcoatlus was the largest pterosaur and the largest flying animal ever known to live. It was named after Quetzalcoatl, the feathered serpent god of the Aztecs: a people who lived in Central America in the 14th and 15th centuries.

Stabbing Beak

Quetzalcoatlus had a very long, sharp beak. Together with the pterosaur's long neck, this would have been useful for stabbing and grabbing small animals that tried to run or hide.

On all fours, this pterosaur was 3 m (10 ft) high at the shoulder.

The beak had no teeth, but was edged with hard horn.

Quetzalcoatlus may have spent much of its time walking on all fours, hunting for small animals in shallow water or on land.

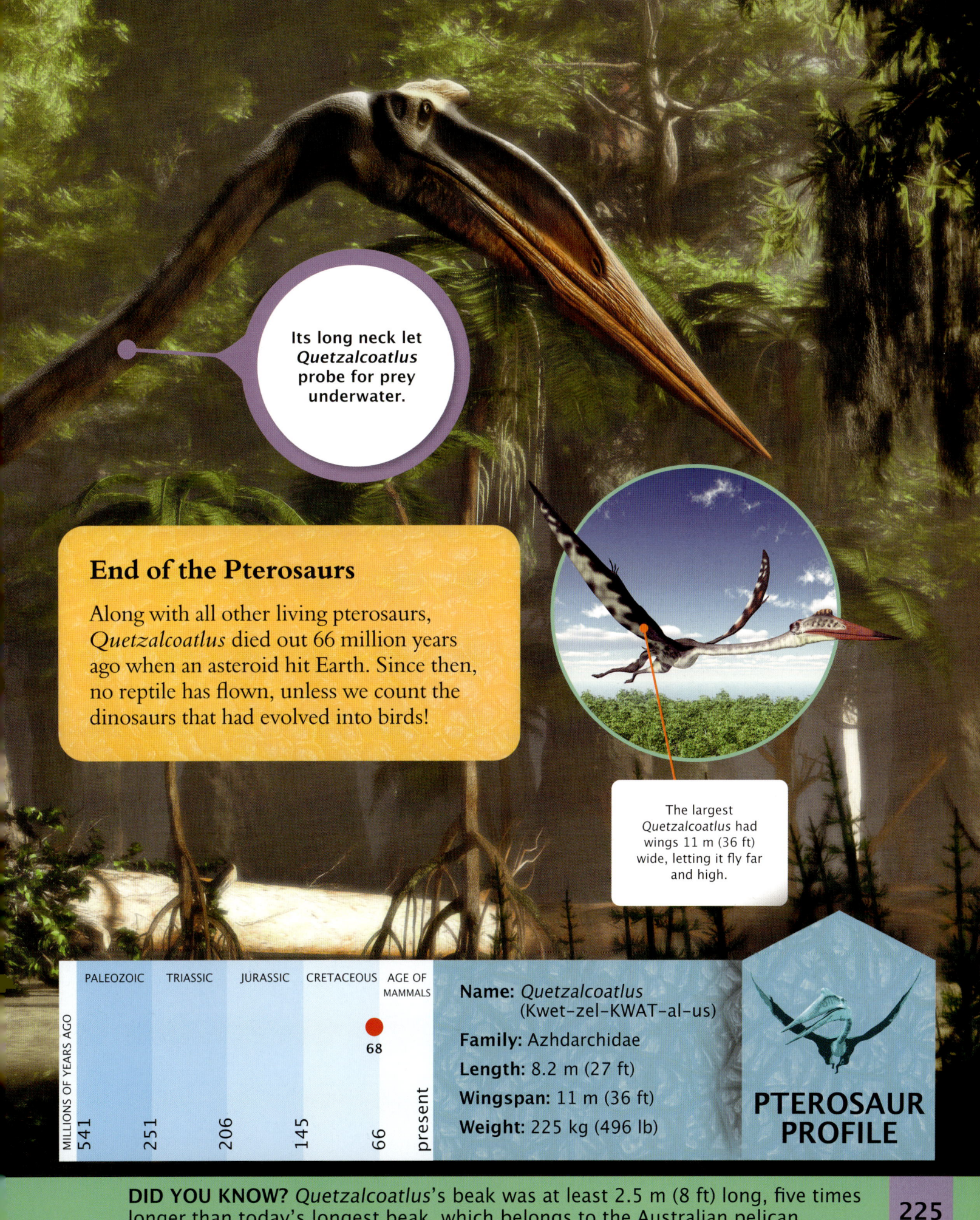

Its long neck let *Quetzalcoatlus* probe for prey underwater.

End of the Pterosaurs

Along with all other living pterosaurs, *Quetzalcoatlus* died out 66 million years ago when an asteroid hit Earth. Since then, no reptile has flown, unless we count the dinosaurs that had evolved into birds!

The largest *Quetzalcoatlus* had wings 11 m (36 ft) wide, letting it fly far and high.

MILLIONS OF YEARS AGO	PALEOZOIC	TRIASSIC	JURASSIC	CRETACEOUS	AGE OF MAMMALS
	541	251	206	145	66 present

68

Name: *Quetzalcoatlus*
(Kwet–zel–KWAT–al–us)
Family: Azhdarchidae
Length: 8.2 m (27 ft)
Wingspan: 11 m (36 ft)
Weight: 225 kg (496 lb)

PTEROSAUR PROFILE

DID YOU KNOW? *Quetzalcoatlus*'s beak was at least 2.5 m (8 ft) long, five times longer than today's longest beak, which belongs to the Australian pelican.

Questions and Answers

WHAT WERE THE DINOSAURS?

The dinosaurs were a group of land-dwelling reptiles that first appeared on Earth around 233 million years ago. There were hundreds of species of dinosaur: Some were gentle plant-eaters, while others were ferocious killers. After dominating the globe for 167 million years, the dinosaurs died out around 66 million years ago.

Utahraptor was a meat-eating dinosaur that walked the Earth 135–130 million years ago.

The story of the dinosaurs is also one of the changing landscape on Earth. When the dinosaurs evolved, Earth was made up of one joined-up supercontinent called Pangea. By 216 million years ago, early dinosaurs had spread across the globe and began to dominate. Over millions of years, Pangea gradually broke up into the smaller continents we have today. Dinosaur and other reptile remains have been found on every continent on Earth, and new species are constantly being discovered.

Allosaurus lived in forests and plains in what is now North America and Europe.

WHAT DID DINOSAURS LOOK LIKE?

Dinosaurs came in a staggering selection of different shapes, sizes, and shades. Some dinosaurs were taller than a three-floor building and weighed more than 12 elephants. Other dinosaurs were no bigger than a chicken. Certain dinosaurs had scaly, camouflaged skin and lumbered around slowly on four legs. Others were covered with bright feathers and ran around nimbly on two legs.

Ankylosaurus means "fused lizard" in ancient Greek, because some of its bones were fused (joined) together.

Living 214–204 million years ago, *Plateosaurus* grew up to 10 m (33 ft) long.

WHAT DOES "DINOSAUR" MEAN?

People have discovered dinosaur fossils for thousands of years, but until the mid-19th century, there was no agreement on what these strange finds actually were. Some people thought they were the bones of dragons or giant mammals. As the science of paleontology (study of fossils) began to get under way, the English paleontologist Sir Richard Owen proposed a new "tribe or suborder" named Dinosauria (meaning "terrible lizards" in ancient Greek) in 1842.

HOW DO WE KNOW ABOUT THE DINOSAURS?

We have learned everything we know about dinosaurs from the remains they left behind. These include fossilized bones and teeth, footprints preserved in rock, and fossilized dinosaur dung. By studying these remains, scientists are able to establish what the dinosaurs looked like, how they moved, and what they ate.

A fossil is the remains of an animal or plant that has been buried underground and preserved in rock. Fossils are mostly made up of the harder parts of an animal, such as its teeth or bones, rather than its softer body parts. Imprints such as footprints and feathers can also be fossilized.

The first *Tyrannosaurus* fossils to be discovered were teeth, found in 1874 by paleontologist Arthur Lakes in Colorado, USA.

HOW DID DINOSAURS LEAVE FOOTPRINTS?

Many dinosaurs left their footprints in soft, swampy ground that later dried in the Sun and became hard. Over time, these footprints were buried under sand, mud, and water, and became fossilized. This made the footprints as solid as stone. Dinosaur footprints tell us how much a dinosaur weighed, how it walked, and whether it was moving in a herd.

Most theropod footprints have three toes.

In 1829, English paleontologists Mary Anning and William Buckland were the first to recognize strange "stones" as poop and to name them coprolites.

WHAT'S INSIDE DINOSAUR DUNG?

Preserved dinosaur dung is called coprolite, and it reveals what dinosaurs were eating millions of years ago. Scientists have discovered pieces of bone, parts of plants, and fish scales inside dinosaur coprolite.

WERE ALL DINOSAURS RELATED?

There were hundreds of different species of dinosaur, but they all belonged to an ancient group called archosaurs, or "ruling reptiles." Modern crocodiles and birds also belong to this group. So did a range of strange and startling creatures— such as pterosaurs—that lived alongside the dinosaurs during the Mesozoic Era. Archosaurs are a group of creatures that share some common physical features. These can best be seen in their skulls. All archosaurs have an opening in front of their eye sockets called the antorbital fenestra, which helps them breathe. Another opening near the back of the lower jaw contains muscles for a strong bite.

The extra openings in an archosaur skull made it more lightweight.

WHICH WERE THE FIRST DINOSAURS?

The first true dinosaurs were small meat-eaters, such as *Eodromaeus*, that appeared in South America during the Late Triassic Period. Measuring up to 2 m (6.6 ft) tall, these predators had curved finger claws, and skulls that absorbed shock when biting prey. They ran on their back legs. Some of their descendants would evolve into the large, killer dinosaurs, such as *Tyrannosaurus*; others would evolve into peaceful plant-eaters, such as *Diplodocus*.

Herrerasaurus was one of the earliest dinosaurs, evolving in South America around 231 million years ago.

WHY DID TYRANNOSAURUS HAVE SUCH SMALL ARMS?

It is often asked why a predator as powerful as *Tyrannosaurus* had such small and skinny arms. There is a simple answer: It did not need strong arms. Instead, it used its enormous jaws and teeth to bring down prey, and then held them down with its massive clawed feet as it devoured them. *Tyrannosaurus* may have had small arms in comparison to the rest of its body, but they were not useless. Its arms were still around 1 m (3.2 ft) long and would have helped during mating. Although its arms were too short to reach its mouth, its sharp claws allowed it to grip struggling prey before taking a bite.

Tyrannosaurus had two fingers on each hand, each finger armed with a claw 10 cm (4 in) long.

WHAT WAS THE LARGEST FLYING CREATURE?

While dinosaurs dominated the land during the Mesozoic Era, a different group of reptiles ruled the air. These flying predators were called pterosaurs, or "winged lizards," and they were the terror of the skies. However, pterosaurs were not confined to the air: They hunted land and sea creatures as well. With a wingspan of 11 m (36 ft), the pterosaur *Quetzalcoatlus* is believed to have been one of the largest fliers of all time. No one is sure whether *Quetzalcoatlus* hunted mostly at sea or on land, but studies have shown it could have flown for long distances looking for food. Its top speed in the air might have been 128 km/h (80 mph).

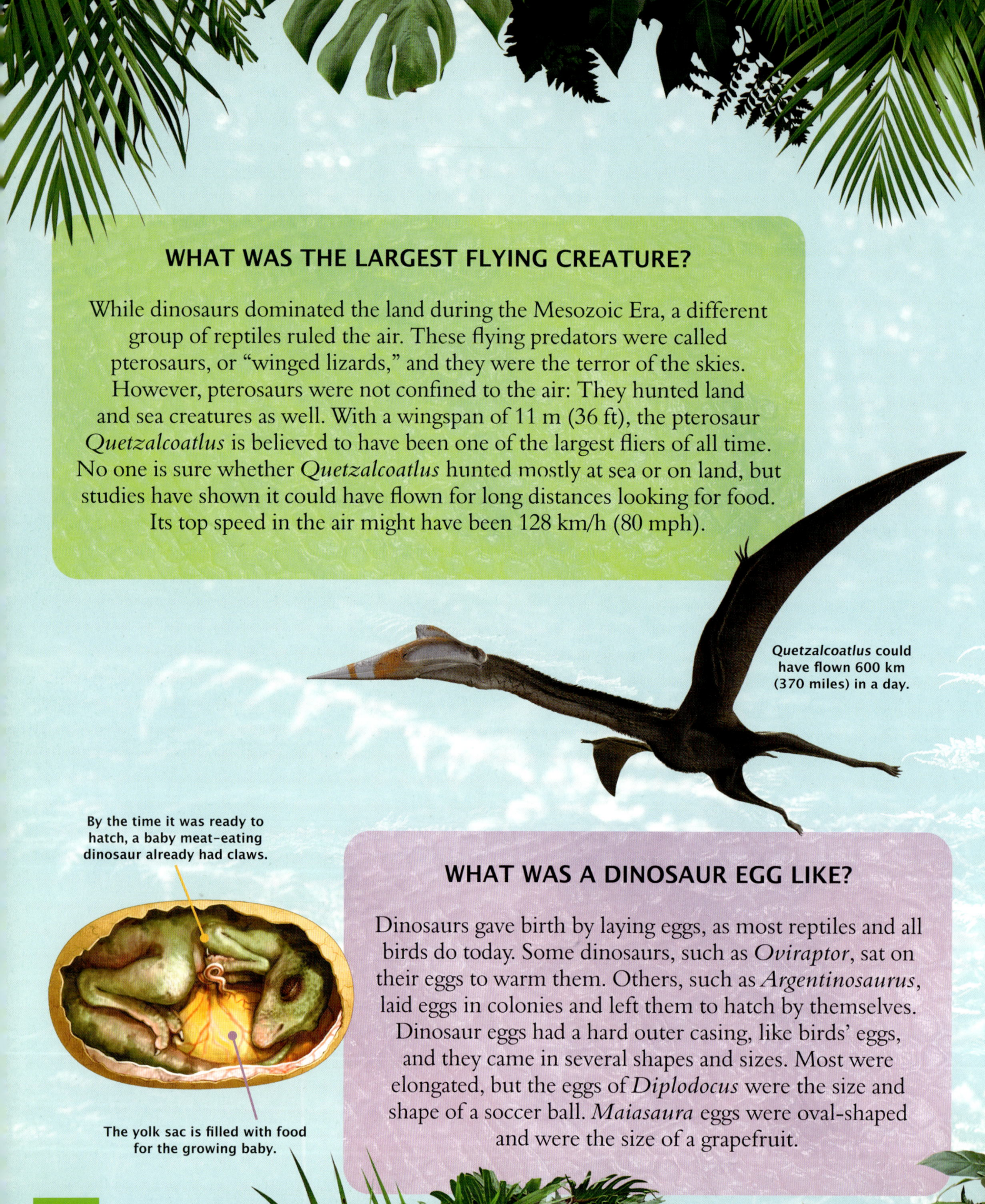

Quetzalcoatlus could have flown 600 km (370 miles) in a day.

By the time it was ready to hatch, a baby meat-eating dinosaur already had claws.

The yolk sac is filled with food for the growing baby.

WHAT WAS A DINOSAUR EGG LIKE?

Dinosaurs gave birth by laying eggs, as most reptiles and all birds do today. Some dinosaurs, such as *Oviraptor*, sat on their eggs to warm them. Others, such as *Argentinosaurus*, laid eggs in colonies and left them to hatch by themselves. Dinosaur eggs had a hard outer casing, like birds' eggs, and they came in several shapes and sizes. Most were elongated, but the eggs of *Diplodocus* were the size and shape of a soccer ball. *Maiasaura* eggs were oval-shaped and were the size of a grapefruit.

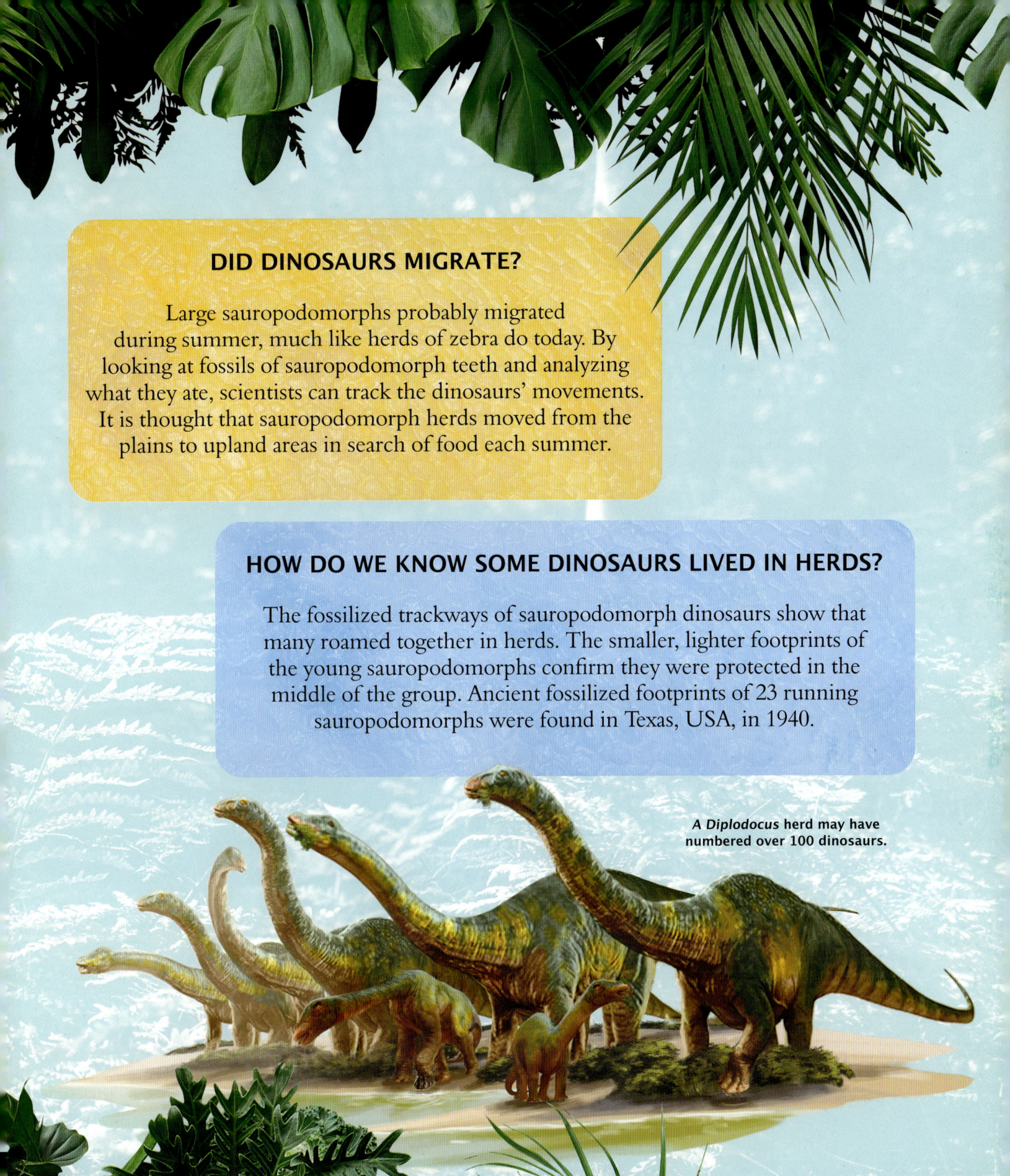

DID DINOSAURS MIGRATE?

Large sauropodomorphs probably migrated during summer, much like herds of zebra do today. By looking at fossils of sauropodomorph teeth and analyzing what they ate, scientists can track the dinosaurs' movements. It is thought that sauropodomorph herds moved from the plains to upland areas in search of food each summer.

HOW DO WE KNOW SOME DINOSAURS LIVED IN HERDS?

The fossilized trackways of sauropodomorph dinosaurs show that many roamed together in herds. The smaller, lighter footprints of the young sauropodomorphs confirm they were protected in the middle of the group. Ancient fossilized footprints of 23 running sauropodomorphs were found in Texas, USA, in 1940.

A *Diplodocus* herd may have numbered over 100 dinosaurs.

WHAT DID DINOSAUR SKIN LOOK LIKE?

Dinosaurs may have come in a broad range of shades, from dull greens and browns to bright reds, yellows, and blues. However, for years no one was sure what dinosaur skin was like. Then, in 2002, scientists discovered the skin pigmentation of a *Sinosauropteryx* under a microscope. It showed that *Sinosauropteryx* was reddish brown, covered in feathers, and had a striped tail. While some theropods like *Sinosauropteryx* had skin covered by short fluffy feathers or longer, stronger feathers, other dinosaurs had tough and scaly skin like that of modern reptiles. The skin had to be strong enough to not tear easily, but also be flexible enough for freedom of movement. It also had to be waterproof to protect against the elements. Waterproof skin prevents an animal from drying out in the Sun, as well as stopping liquid from getting in.

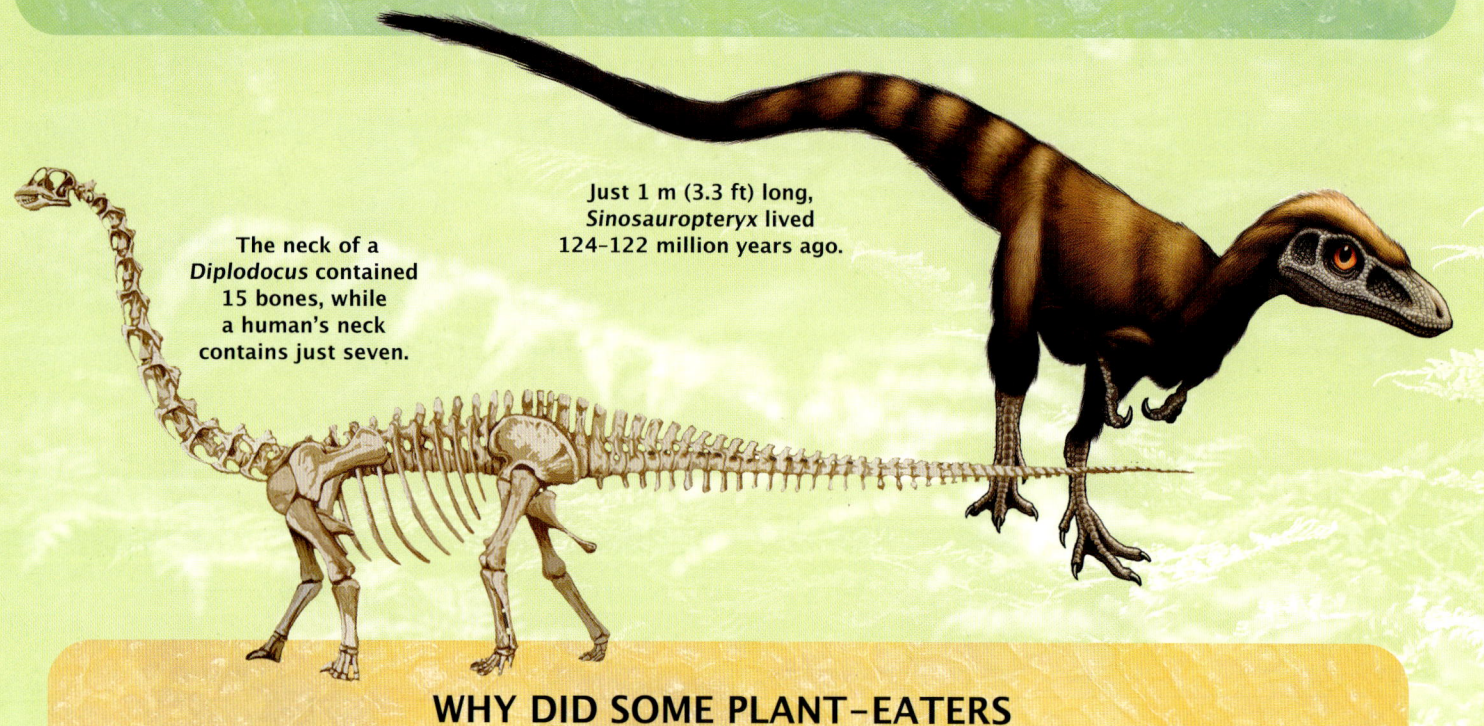

The neck of a *Diplodocus* contained 15 bones, while a human's neck contains just seven.

Just 1 m (3.3 ft) long, *Sinosauropteryx* lived 124–122 million years ago.

WHY DID SOME PLANT–EATERS HAVE LONG NECKS?

The giant sauropodomorph dinosaurs had long necks to reach the high leaves that other plant-eaters could not reach. Because they were so large, sauropodomorphs had to eat a huge amount of leaves each day to survive. By being able to reach the highest leaves, they were not competing with other, smaller herbivores for their food.

Argentinosaurus was around 7 m (23 ft) tall at the shoulder.

HOW DID SAUROPODOMORPHS DIGEST THEIR FOOD?

Because the sauropodomorphs ate so much, they did not have time to chew their food. Instead, they swallowed it whole and left their stomach to do the rest. To help with this task, sauropodomorphs swallowed stones called gastroliths, which helped grind up their food. When a gastrolith became too smooth, the dinosaur expelled it and swallowed a new one.

HOW MUCH DID THE SAUROPODOMORPHS EAT?

The sauropodomorphs became so big by making themselves the ultimate eating machines. They did this by consuming the greatest number of calories as quickly as possible. This was made possible by the blossoming of new plant and forest life that took place during the Jurassic Period. A large sauropod like *Diplodocus* had to eat around 520 kg (1,150 lb) of plant material every day just to survive. The biggest sauropod, *Argentinosaurus*, probably had to eat even more. As it grew from a 5 kg (11 lb) hatchling, *Argentinosaurus* gained up to 40 kg (90 lb) of weight every day. It took around 40 years for *Argentinosaurus* to reach its maximum weight of 75,000 kg (165,350 lb).

DID TYRANNOSAURUS HAVE A BIG BRAIN?

Tyrannosaurus had one of the largest and most developed brains of the predatory dinosaurs. The part of the brain responsible for smell was particularly acute. *Tyrannosaurus* was also armed with forward-facing eyes, which allowed its eyes to work together to sense depth. These senses combined to give *Tyrannosaurus* a formidable advantage over its prey.

The brain of an adult *Tyrannosaurus* weighed around 1 kg (2.2 lb). A human adult's brain weighs about 1.4 kg (3 lb). Yet the dinosaur was much less smart than a human—only about as smart as a modern bird.

This *Velociraptor* must have been desperately hungry to attack a sturdy *Protoceratops*.

WAS A DINOSAUR FIGHT EVER PRESERVED?

In 1971, the skeleton of a *Velociraptor* was found wrapped around the skeleton of a *Protoceratops*, preserved in a life-and-death struggle. As *Protoceratops* bit down into *Velociraptor*'s arm and *Velociraptor* slashed at *Protoceratops*'s throat, a sandstorm swept in and buried them both alive. Their fight remained frozen in time forever.

DID ALL MEAT-EATERS HAVE SHARP TEETH?

Not all meat-eaters had sharp teeth. *Gallimimus* was about the size of a turkey and, like its relatives, it had a hard-edged toothless beak. It used this beak to eat small animals, such as insects, and to crush up seeds.

Gallimimus means "chicken mimic" in Latin.

Spinosaurus grew over 14 m (46 ft) long.

WHICH WAS THE LARGEST MEAT-EATING DINOSAUR?

The largest meat-eating dinosaur—and the largest land-based predator ever seen on Earth—was *Spinosaurus*. *Spinosaurus* was a colossal killer with a list of massive measurements. It was longer than two buses, taller than a giraffe, and weighed more than 30 lions. It also had a skull measuring 2 m (6.5 ft), which is the longest of any theropod dinosaur.

WHAT DID *TYRANNOSAURUS* SOUND LIKE?

The terrible roar that *Tyrannosaurus* makes in the movies is not thought to be accurate. Based on the size of its neck and its skull bones, *Tyrannosaurus* probably made a grumbling or croaking sound, like a crocodile or a bullfrog.

Other dinosaurs had different ways of communicating. Plant-eating dinosaurs warned each other of danger by flushing their body parts with blood, flapping their feathers, or making loud noises. Some developed special ways of making themselves heard. *Parasaurolophus* used the bony crest on top of its head to make honking and hooting sounds. Inside the crest was a hollow tube that connected to *Parasaurolophus*'s nose and mouth. *Parasaurolophus* was able to blow through this natural trumpet to warn others of danger and also use the sound to attract mates.

A male *Tyrannosaurus* may have called to females at mating time.

1. Crest
2. Eye socket
3. Nostril
4. Hollow nasal passage
5. Brain
6. Mouth
7. Ear

A *Parasaurolophus* skull was about 1.6 m (5.2 ft) long, including the crest.

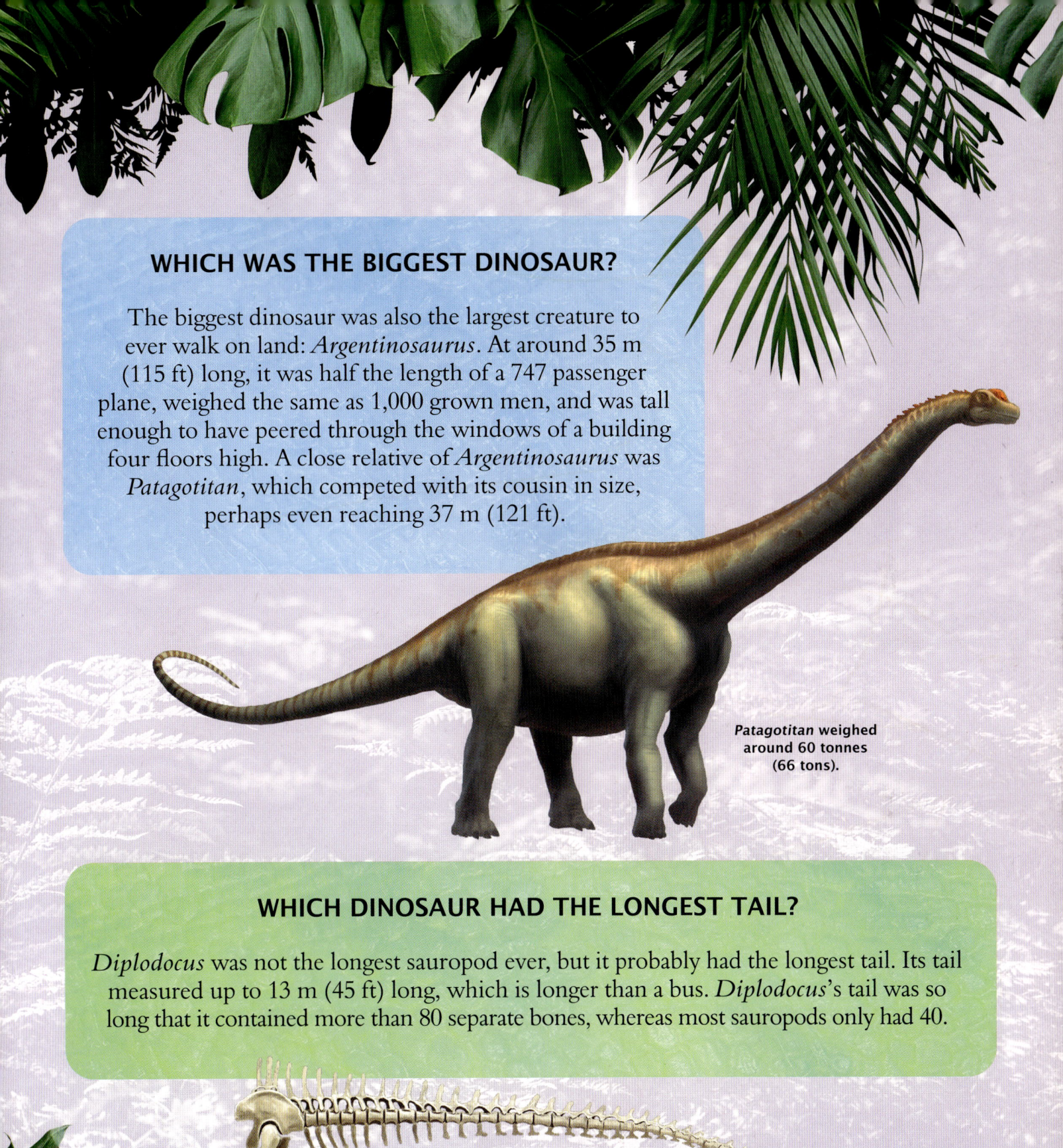

WHICH WAS THE BIGGEST DINOSAUR?

The biggest dinosaur was also the largest creature to ever walk on land: *Argentinosaurus*. At around 35 m (115 ft) long, it was half the length of a 747 passenger plane, weighed the same as 1,000 grown men, and was tall enough to have peered through the windows of a building four floors high. A close relative of *Argentinosaurus* was *Patagotitan*, which competed with its cousin in size, perhaps even reaching 37 m (121 ft).

Patagotitan weighed around 60 tonnes (66 tons).

WHICH DINOSAUR HAD THE LONGEST TAIL?

Diplodocus was not the longest sauropod ever, but it probably had the longest tail. Its tail measured up to 13 m (45 ft) long, which is longer than a bus. *Diplodocus*'s tail was so long that it contained more than 80 separate bones, whereas most sauropods only had 40.

Diplodocus could have cracked its tail like a whip to frighten away predators.

At 8 tonnes (8.8 tons) or more, *Triceratops* weighed more than *Tyrannosaurus*—and could have charged at this enemy.

DID TRICERATOPS EVER FIGHT TYRANNOSAURUS?

Triceratops and *Tyrannosaurus* were the two mightiest dinosaurs to prowl the plains and forests of Late Cretaceous North America. The image of *Tyrannosaurus*—its jaws bristling with bone-crunching teeth, battling the tank-shaped *Triceratops*, with its face full of horns—is spectacular and terrifying. But there is very little evidence of a *Tyrannosaurus* and *Triceratops* battle. Fossils have shown *Tyrannosaurus* bite marks on *Triceratops* bones, but these are thought to have occurred after death. In other words, *Tyrannosaurus* probably scavenged from a *Triceratops* carcass after it was already dead. More gruesomely, the injuries show that *Tyrannosaurus* removed *Triceratops*'s head to get at the nutrient-rich flesh in its neck.

WOULD STEGOSAURUS'S BACK PLATES HAVE PROTECTED IT?

Stegosaurus's back plates were made from bone and skin, and were used to defend and display. By flushing blood into the skin around the plates, *Stegosaurus* would have sent a warning to meat-eaters to stay away. The bone in the plates would also have offered some protection, along with a row of tough bone plates along *Stegosaurus*'s neck. However, these didn't always work, as *Allosaurus* bite marks to a *Stegosaurus* neck bone show. *Stegosaurus* would have put up a good fight though: A hole on an *Allosaurus* vertebra matches a *Stegosaurus* tail spike exactly.

Stegosaurus had between 17 and 22 plates and spines.

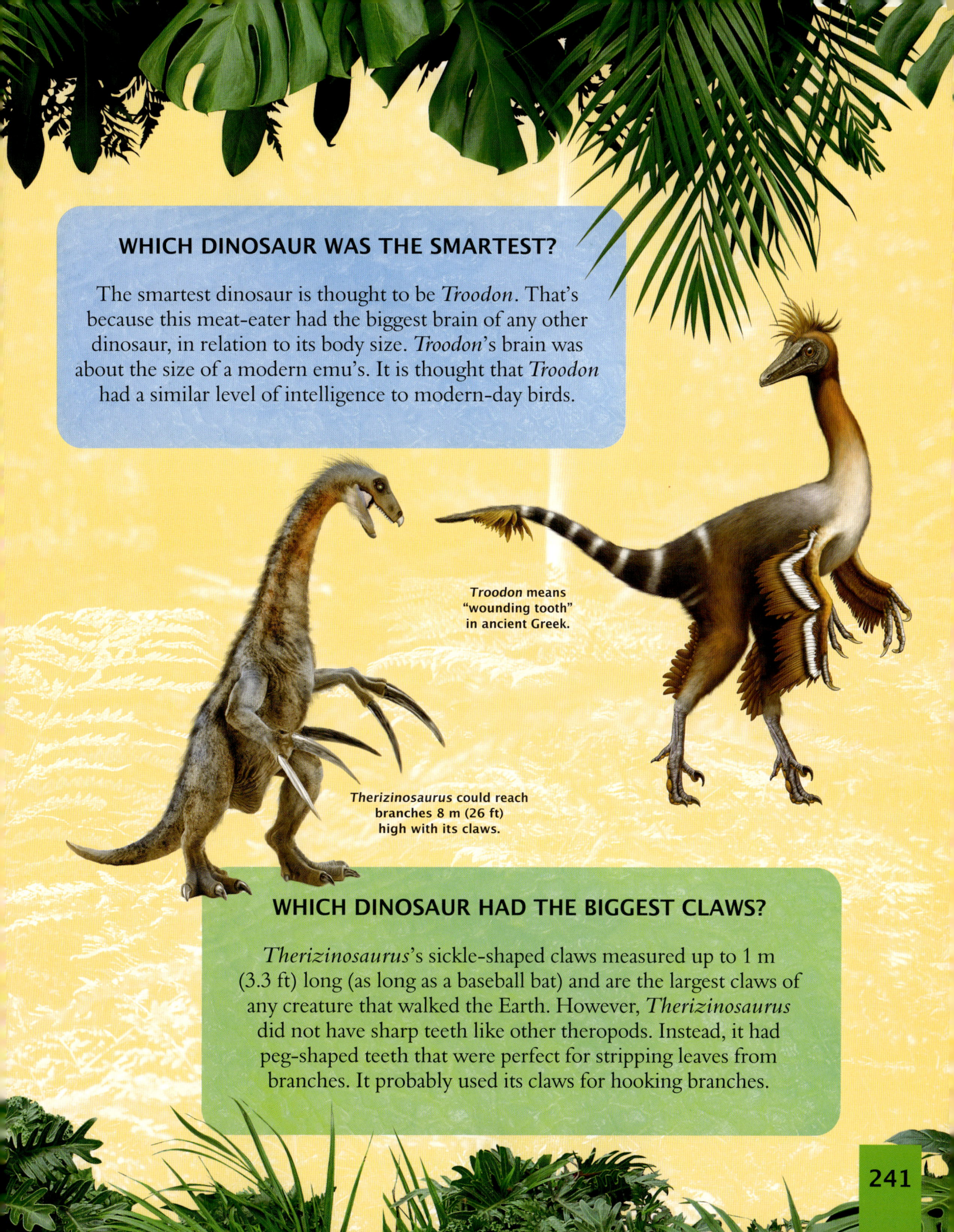

WHICH DINOSAUR WAS THE SMARTEST?

The smartest dinosaur is thought to be *Troodon*. That's because this meat-eater had the biggest brain of any other dinosaur, in relation to its body size. *Troodon*'s brain was about the size of a modern emu's. It is thought that *Troodon* had a similar level of intelligence to modern-day birds.

Troodon means "wounding tooth" in ancient Greek.

Therizinosaurus could reach branches 8 m (26 ft) high with its claws.

WHICH DINOSAUR HAD THE BIGGEST CLAWS?

Therizinosaurus's sickle-shaped claws measured up to 1 m (3.3 ft) long (as long as a baseball bat) and are the largest claws of any creature that walked the Earth. However, *Therizinosaurus* did not have sharp teeth like other theropods. Instead, it had peg-shaped teeth that were perfect for stripping leaves from branches. It probably used its claws for hooking branches.

Anchiornis had a wingspan
of up to 50 cm (20 in).

WHICH WAS THE SMALLEST DINOSAUR?

A large number of small dinosaurs came and went during the Mesozoic Era. Every time scientists think they have discovered the smallest ever dinosaur, another even tinier one is found to take its place. One of the very smallest was *Anchiornis*, a kitten-sized, feathered dinosaur that grew up to 34 cm (13 in) long. It lived in China during the Jurassic Period and, at only 110 g (3.9 oz), is the lightest dinosaur ever discovered.

WHICH DINOSAUR HAD THE BIGGEST HEAD?

The dinosaurs with the largest heads were the horned and frilled herbivores known as the ceratopsians. The heads of these giants were so big that they sometimes made up 40 percent of their overall body length. The award for biggest ever head goes jointly to two ceratopsian cousins: *Torosaurus* and *Pentaceratops*. *Torosaurus* was closely related to *Triceratops* and had a similar frill and horns. The length of *Torosaurus*'s head, which includes its frill, was 2.77 m (9.1 ft). That is as long as a small car! *Torosaurus*'s skull is thought to be the longest of any known land animal that has lived on Earth. There was little difference between the skulls of *Pentaceratops* and *Torosaurus*, but *Pentaceratops*'s was slightly smaller. It measured 2.75 m (9 ft) in length.

Torosaurus and *Pentaceratops* lived
in the Late Jurassic Period.

WHICH WAS THE BIGGEST FEATHERED DINOSAUR?

The bones of the largest feathered dinosaur were found by accident in 2005. Paleontologists were making a film in China about sauropodomorph bones when they discovered a mysterious bone buried among them. It was the leg bone of *Gigantoraptor*: the biggest feathered creature that ever walked the Earth.

At over 2,200 kg (4,850 lb), *Gigantoraptor* weighed more than 14 ostriches, which is the heaviest feathered creature alive today. *Gigantoraptor* was also 8 m (26 ft) long, which is 35 times larger than its nearest oviraptor cousin, and not much smaller than *Tyrannosaurus*.

Feathered animals are not usually as large as *Gigantoraptor* because big animals have less need of feathers or fur to keep them warm.

243

HOW DID THE DINOSAURS DIE OUT?

Around 66 million years ago, a gigantic catastrophic event killed off 75 percent of all life on Earth, including the dinosaurs. Most scientists agree that this mass extinction was caused by an asteroid. They believe a 10-km (6-mile) wide asteroid hurtled toward the Earth at twice the speed of a bullet, and struck an area near modern-day Mexico. The impact of the asteroid hitting the Earth was like a million atom bombs exploding at once. First, there was a massive shock wave, followed by tsunamis, fires, and hot dust, which filled the sky. As the dust cooled, it left a thick black cloud that lasted for months and blocked the Sun. Without sunlight, much plant and animal life died out.

The small mammal *Purgatorius* lived from 66 to 63 million years ago.

DID ALL THE DINOSAURS DIE AT ONCE?

It would have taken many months for the dinosaurs to become extinct. The first to go were the large plant-eaters, which depended on eating huge amounts of plant life to survive. This left the meat-eaters with no food, so they would have died out shortly after. However, many smaller animals, including species of amphibians, birds, fish, invertebrates, mammals (pictured above), and reptiles survived.

ARE ANY DINOSAURS ALIVE TODAY?

No dinosaur survived the mass extinction. But some creatures that are directly descended from the dinosaurs share the planet with us today. We know these creatures as birds. They are the descendants of theropod dinosaurs.

Peafowl evolved around 3 million years ago.

Glossary

ACIDIC
Able to wear away some materials.

ALLOSAUR
A large theropod with a long, narrow skull, usually with ornamental horns or crests.

AMMONITE
An extinct Mesozoic shellfish with a coiled shell.

AMPHIBIAN
An animal that is born in water and breathes underwater using gills when young. As an adult, it usually breathes air using lungs, and lives on land or in water. Today's amphibians include frogs and salamanders.

ANKYLOSAUR
A thyreophoran with defensive scutes and, sometimes, a tail club.

ARCHOSAUR
An animal whose skull has one hole between the eye socket and nostril and another at the back of the lower jaw. Dinosaurs, pterosaurs, crocodiles, and birds are all archosaurs.

ASTEROID
A rocky object that orbits the Sun in space.

AZHDARCHID
A pterosaur with long legs, a long neck, and a huge wingspan.

BIOCHRON
A layer of rock named after the fossil animal or plant that most commonly occurs in it.

BIPEDAL
Walking upright on the back legs.

BIRD
An animal with a toothless beak, wings, and feathers. Females lay hard-shelled eggs on land. Birds evolved from theropod dinosaurs.

BROWSE
To feed on shoots, leaves, and fruits of high-growing, woody plants such as shrubs and trees.

CAMOUFLAGE
The way the shade and shape of an animal make it less easy to see.

CARNIVORE
An animal that eats other animals, including invertebrates, fish, amphibians, reptiles, mammals, and birds.

CARRION
Rotting flesh from a dead animal.

CELL
The smallest working part of a living thing.

CERAPOD
An ornithischian, plant-eating dinosaur with a beak and ridged teeth.

CERATOPSIAN
A cerapod dinosaur that often had horns and neck frills.

CONTINENT
A large area of land, usually separated from other continents by ocean. Today, there are seven continents: Africa, Antarctica, Asia, Australia, Europe, North America, and South America.

CREST
A growth of bone, scales, feathers, skin, or hair on the head or back of an animal.

CRETACEOUS PERIOD
A period of Earth's history lasting from 145 to 66 million years ago.

DINOSAUR
An extinct, land-living reptile that walked with its back legs held directly beneath its body.

DIPLODOCID
A very long sauropod with relatively short legs.

DROMAEOSAUR
A small theropod with an extra-large claw on each back foot.

EVOLUTION
The process by which one species changes into another over millions of years, by passing on particular characteristics from one generation to the next.

EXTINCT
Describes an animal or plant that has disappeared forever.

FAMILY
A group of closely related genera.

FEATHER
A light, fringed growth from the skin of birds and some dinosaurs. A feather has a tough central stem, with softer threads growing from either side. Feathers are made from keratin, also called horn, the same material that is found in scales and human hair.

FLIPPER
A flat limb that has evolved to help an animal swim.

FLOODPLAIN
An area of low ground around a river that is often flooded.

FOREST
A wide area of land with many trees that are growing closely together.

FOSSIL
The remains of an animal or plant that died long ago, preserved in rock.

FRILL
A bony area around a dinosaur's neck.

GASTROLITH
A stone in the stomach that helps digestion.

GENUS (PLURAL: GENERA)
A group of closely related species.

GRASSLAND
A wide area where most plants are grasses. Grasses did not become common until toward the end of dinosaur times.

GRAZE
To feed on grass.

HABITAT
The natural home of an animal or plant.

HADROSAUR
Also known as a duckbilled dinosaur, an ornithopod with an especially beak-like mouth.

HERBIVORE
An animal that eats plants.

HOOF
Horn-covered toes.

HORN
A tough, hard material, also called keratin, that is found in scales, feathers, beaks, claws, nails, and hair. Another meaning of "horn" is a pointed, bony growth on the head.

ICHTHYOSAUR
A dolphin-like, predatory marine reptile of the Mesozoic.

IGUANODONTID
A large, plant-eating ornithopod.

INLAND SEA
A large area of water that lies within a continent.

INVERTEBRATE
An animal without a backbone, such as an insect or jellyfish.

JURASSIC PERIOD
A period of Earth's history lasting from 201 to 145 million years ago.

LENGTH
The distance from the tip of an animal's snout to the tip of its tail.

LIMB
An arm, leg, or wing.

MAMMAL
An animal that grows hair and feeds its babies on milk. Today's mammals include humans, whales, and cats.

MARGINOCEPHALIAN
An ornithischian dinosaur with thicker bone at the back of the skull.

MESOZOIC ERA
The period of geological time from 252 to 66 million years ago.

MICROORGANISM
A simple living thing that can be seen only under a microscope.

MIGRATE
To move from one area to another, usually at the same time every year.

MINERAL
A solid, natural substance that forms in the ground or in water.

MOSASAUR
A large, predatory marine reptile of the Cretaceous, which had four paddle-like limbs.

MYA
Short for "millions of years ago."

NODOSAUR
An ankylosaur with bumps and spikes on its skull, but no tail club.

NOTHOSAUR
A marine reptile of the Triassic Period, with webbed, paddle-like feet.

OMNIVORE
An animal that eats plants and animals.

ORDER
A group of closely related families.

ORNITHISCHIAN
Describes dinosaurs with hip bones arranged like a bird's. All plant-eaters, they include ornithopods, marginocephalians, and thyreophorans.

ORNITHOCHEIRID
A pterosaur with a huge wingspan and keel-shaped snout.

ORNITHOPOD
An ornithischian dinosaur with a bony, beak-like mouth.

OSTEODERM
A lumpy scale on a reptile's skin.

OXYGEN
A gas that is in the air and is also part of water. Animals need oxygen to live.

PACHYCEPHALOSAUR
A cerapod dinosaur with a thick, often domed, skull.

PALEONTOLOGIST
A scientist who studies the living things of Earth's past, as revealed by fossils.

PALEONTOLOGY
The study of fossils and extinct living things.

PALEOZOIC ERA
The period of geological time from 539 to 252 million years ago.

PLAIN
A large area of flat land.

PLATE
A protective, bony section in a reptile's skin.

PLESIOSAUR
A long-necked, predatory marine reptile that lived in the Jurassic and Cretaceous Periods.

PLIOSAUR
A kind of plesiosaur with a short neck and big head.

PREDATOR
An animal that hunts and eats other animals for food.

PREY
An animal that is hunted and eaten by other animals for food.

PROSAUROPOD
A primitive sauropod.

PTEROSAUR
A flying reptile with wings made from skin stretched over a long fourth finger. A pterosaur was a relative of dinosaurs.

PYCNOFIBER
A hairlike covering found on a pterosaur's body.

QUADRUPEDAL
Walking on all four legs.

RELATIVE
An animal that is a member of the same group of similar animals.

REPTILE
An animal with lungs that usually has scaly skin and lays eggs on land.

RHYNCHOSAUR
A small, primitive reptile.

SAURISCHIAN
Describes dinosaurs with hip bones arranged like a lizard's. They include the mostly meat-eating theropods and plant-eating sauropodomorphs.

SAUROPOD
An enormous, long-necked, plant-eating saurischian dinosaur that walked on all fours.

SAUROPODOMORPH
A long-necked, plant-eating saurischian dinosaur, including sauropods and their smaller ancestors.

SCALE
A small, hard plate that grows from the top skin layer of most reptiles. Scales are made from keratin, also called horn, the same material as in feathers and hair.

SCAVENGE
To eat carrion or leftover kills from other hunters.

SCUTE
A bony plate with a horny covering.

SERRATED
Having a notched, knife-like edge.

SHRUB
A woody plant that is smaller than a tree and usually has several stems.

SNOUT
The nose and mouth of an animal.

SPECIES
One particular type of living thing. Members of the same species look similar and can produce offspring (make babies) together.

SPINE
A long, pointed bone or body part. Another meaning of "spine" is an animal's backbone.

SPINOSAUR
A specialist theropod with a long, narrow snout for eating fish.

STEGOSAUR
A thyreophoran with rows of plates along its back and pairs of spikes at the end of its tail.

SUPERFAMILY
A group of closely related families and genera.

SWAMP
An area of low land where water collects, making it wet and soft.

SYNAPSID
A primitive, reptile-like mammal or a modern mammal.

TETRAPOD
An animal with four limbs, or with four-limbed ancestors, such as an amphibian, reptile, bird, or mammal.

THAGOMIZER
The group of defensive spikes on a stegosaur's tail.

THERIZINOSAUR
A large (probably plant-eating) theropod with huge hand claws.

THEROPOD
A saurischian dinosaur with hollow bones and, usually, three main toes.

THYREOPHORAN
An ornithischian, plant-eating dinosaur with scutes for protection.

TISSUE
A body material, such as skin, fat, or muscle.

TITANOSAUR
A huge sauropod with a relatively small head.

TRIASSIC PERIOD
A period of Earth's history lasting from 252 to 201 million years ago.

TROODONTID
A birdlike theropod with long legs and good senses.

TYRANNOSAUR
A large theropod with a huge head and relatively small arms.

VERTEBRA
(PLURAL: VERTEBRAE)
A small bone that forms the backbone.

VERTEBRATE
An animal with a backbone, such as a fish, amphibian, reptile, bird, or mammal.

WINGSPAN
The width of a flying animal's outstretched wings, from wingtip to wingtip.

WOODLAND
Land with many trees and other plants. The trees are far enough apart for sunlight to reach the ground in places.

Pronunciation

Achelousaurus Ah-KEL-oo-SAWR-us

Albertonectes Al-BER-tuh-NECK-tees

Allosaurus AL-oh-SAWR-us

Altirhinus AL-tee-RYE-nus

Amargasaurus Ah-MAR-guh-SAWR-us

Anchiornis ANK-ee-OR-nis

Anhanguera AN-yan-GWER-uh

Ankylosaurus Ang-KILE-uh-SAWR-us

Archaeopteryx ARK-ee-OPT-er-ix

Archelon ARK-ee-lon

Archosaur ARK-oh-SAWR

Argentinosaurus AH-gen-teen-uh-SAWR-us

Baryonyx Bah-ree-ON-iks

Bistahieversor Bis-tah-HEE-ay-ver-suh

Borealopelta BORE-ee-al-oh-PELT-uh

Brachiosaurus BRACK-ee-uh-SAWR-us

Camarasaurus CAM-er-uh-SAWR-us

Carcharodontosaurus CAR-car-oh-dont-oh-SAWR-us

Carnotaurus CAR-no-TAWR-us

Caudipteryx Caw-DIP-tuh-riks

Cerapod SEH-ruh-POD

Ceratosaurus Seh-RAT-oh-SAWR-us

Citipati SIT-ee-PAT-ee

Coelophysis SEE-loh-FY-sis

Compsognathus Comp-sog-NAY-thus

Daspletosaurus Das-PLEET-oh-SAWR-us

Deinocheirus Dye-NOH-KYR-us

Deinonychus Dye-NON-ik-us

Diabloceratops Dee-OB-low-SEH-ruh-tops

Dilophosaurus Dye-LOF-oh-SAWR-us

Dimetrodon Dye-MET-roh-don

Dimorphodon Dye-MAW-fuh-don

Diplocaulus Dip-loh-COWL-us

Diplodocus Dip-loh-DOK-us

Dolichorhynchops DOL-ee-kor-IN-chops

Edmontonia Ed-mon-TOE-nee-uh

Edmontosaurus Ed-MON-tuh-SAWR-us

Elasmosaurus Eh-LAZ-moh-SAWR-us

Eoraptor EE-oh-RAP-tor

Euoplocephalus You-op-luh-SEF-uh-lus

Gallimimus Gal-uh-MY-mus

Gargoyleosaurus Gahr-GOYL-ee-oh-SAWR-us

Gasparinisaurus Gas-pah-reen-ee-SAWR-uh

Giganotosaurus JIG-an-oh-tuh-SAWR-us

Gigantoraptor JIG-ant-oh-RAP-tor

Giraffatitan Ji-RAF-uh-TIE-tan

Herrerasaurus Her-RARE-uh-SAWR-us

Hesperonychus HES-per-ON-ik-us

Heterodontosaurus Het-er-uh-DON-tuh-
  SAWR-us

Huayangosaurus Hwah-YAHNG-oh-SAWR-us

Hypsilophodon Hip-sih-LO-fuh-don

Ichthyosaurus ICK-thee-oh-SAWR-us

Iguanodon Ig-WAN-oh-don

Ingentia In-JEN-tee-uh

Kentrosaurus KEN-truh-SAWR-us

Kronosaurus KROH-nuh-SAWR-us

Lambeosaurus LAM-be-uh-SAWR-us

Leaellynasaura Lee-ELL-in-ah-SAWR-ah

Liopleurodon LIE-oh-PLOOR-oh-don

Maiasaura MAI-ah-SAWR-uh

Majungasaurus Mah-JOONG-ah-SAWR-us

Mamenchisaurus Mah-MEN-chih-SAWR-us

Mapusaurus MAH-puh-SAWR-us

Melanorosaurus Mel-uh-NOR-uh-SAWR-us

Microraptor MY-kro-RAP-tor

Minmi MIN-mee

Mosasaurus MOH-suh-SAWR-us

Nigersaurus NI-juh-SAWR-us

Nodosaurus NOH-doh-SAWR-us

Ornithischian OR-nith-IS-kee-un

Ornithomimus OR-nith-OM-im-us

Oviraptor OH-vee-RAP-tor

Pachycephalosaurus Pak-ee-SEF-uh-lo-SAWR-us

Parasaurolophus Par-ah-SAWR-OL-uh-fus

Pentaceratops pen-tah-SEH-ruh-tops

Plateosaurus PLAY-tee-uh-SAWR-us

Plesiosaurus Plee-zee-oh-SAWR-us

Protoceratops Pro-toe-SEH-ruh-tops

Psephoderma See-foe-DERM-uh

Psittacosaurus SIT-uh-ko-SAWR-us

Pteranodon Ter-AN-oh-don

Pterodactylus Ter-oh-DAK-til-us

Pterosaur TEH-roh-sawr

Quetzalcoatlus Kwet-zel-KWAT-al-us

Rapetosaurus Ruh-PAY-tuh-SAWR-us

Rhamphorhynchus RAM-for-INK-us

Saltasaurus Salt-uh-SAWR-us

Sarcosuchus SAR-ko-SOO-kus

Saurischian SAWR-is-kee-un

Sauropelta SAWR-oh-PELT-uh

Sauropod SAWR-oh-POD

Sauroposeidon SAWR-oh-puh-SY-don

Scelidosaurus Skel-ee-doe-SAWR-us

Scutellosaurus Scoo-tel-oh-SAWR-us

Shantungosaurus Shan-TUNG-oh-SAWR-us

Spinosaurus SPINE-oh-SAWR-us

Stegoceras Steg-OSS-er-us

Stegosaurus STEG-uh-SAWR-us

Stenopterygius Sten-OP-tuh-RIDGE-ee-us

Stygimoloch Stij-ih-MOL-ock

Styracosaurus Stih-RAK-uh-SAWR-us

Suchomimus SOOK-oh-MIM-us

Temnodontosaurus Tem-noh-DON-tuh-SAWR-us

Therizinosaurus THAIR-uh-zeen-uh-SAWR-us

Theropod Theh-ruh-POD

Thescelosaurus Theh-SEL-uh-SAWR-us

Thyreophoran THIGH-ree-oh-FOR-un

Torosaurus TORE-oh-SAWR-us

Triceratops Try-SEH-ruh-tops

Troodon TRO-uh-don

Tropeognathus TRO-pe-oh-NA-thus

Tuojiangosaurus Too-YANG-oh-SAWR-us

Tupandactylus TOO-pan-DAK-till-us

Tyrannosaurus Ty-RAN-oh-SAWR-us

Utahraptor YOO-tah-RAP-tor

Velociraptor Veh-LOSS-ee-RAP-tor

Yinlong YIN-long

Zuniceratops ZOO-nee-SEH-ruh-tops

Index